MARKET MANIPULATION AND INSIDER TRADING

The European Union regime for fighting market manipulation and insider trading – commonly referred to as market abuse – was significantly reshuffled in the wake of the financial crisis of 2007/2008 and new legal instruments to fight market abuse were eventually adopted in 2014. In this monograph the authors identify the association between the financial crisis and market abuse, critically consider the legislative, policy and enforcement responses in the European Union, and contrast them with the approaches adopted by the United States of America and the United Kingdom respectively. The aftermath of the financial crisis, ongoing security concerns and increased legislation and policy responses to the fight against irregularities and market failures demonstrate that we need to understand, in context, the regulatory responses taken in this area. Specifically, the book investigates how the regulatory responses have changed over time since the start of the financial crisis. *Market Manipulation and Insider Trading* places the fight against market abuse in the broader framework of the fight against white collar crime and also considers some associated questions in order to better understand the contemporary market abuse regime.

Market Manipulation and Insider Trading

Regulatory Challenges in the United States of America, the European Union and the United Kingdom

Ester Herlin-Karnell
and
Nicholas Ryder

•HART•
OXFORD • LONDON • NEW YORK • NEW DELHI • SYDNEY

HART PUBLISHING

Bloomsbury Publishing Plc

Kemp House, Chawley Park, Cumnor Hill, Oxford, OX2 9PH, UK

HART PUBLISHING, the Hart/Stag logo, BLOOMSBURY and the Diana logo are trademarks of Bloomsbury Publishing Plc

First published in Great Britain 2019

A catalogue record for this book is available from the British Library.

Library of Congress Control Number: 2019944791

ISBN: HB: 978-1-50990-307-8
ePDF: 978-1-50990-308-5
ePub: 978-1-50990-309-2

Typeset by Compuscript Ltd, Shannon
Printed and bound in Great Britain by TJ International Ltd, Padstow, Cornwall

PREFACE

This is a joint project, born out of a conference at Bristol Law School, the University of Western England in June 2014, on white-collar crime and the financial crisis, organised by Nicholas. We began a series of discussions on this topic, which has resulted in this book. While much has been written about money laundering and other types of financial crime, a lot less has been said about regulatory strategies to fight market manipulation and insider trading, especially from a comparative perspective. Our joint expertise in national and EU law on financial crimes, respectively, seemed a good combination.

Whilst it is a joint project, Ester has written the chapters on the EU (chapters two and four and the EU part in chapter three) and Nicholas has written the chapters on the UK and the USA (chapters five and six as well as the UK/USA part in chapter three). Chapters one and seven have been co-authored.

Both authors would like to thank Hart Publishing for its support and for believing in this project. Finally, we would also like to thank Charlie Robson at Bristol Law School, Catherine Minahan at Hart and Claire Banyard for their excellent support with revising the manuscript.

Last but not least, we would like to thank our families for their love and support.

Ester Herlin-Karnell and Nicholas Ryder
January 2019

CONTENTS

LIST OF ABBREVIATIONS

AFSJ	Area of Freedom, Security and Justice
AIG	American Insurance Group
AIM	Alternative Investment Market
AML	Anti-Money Laundering
BoS	Bank of Scotland
CA	Court of Appeal
CFR	Charter of Fundamental Rights of the EU
CFSP	Common Foreign and Security Policy
CFTC	Commodities and Futures Trading Commission
CHF	Swiss Franc
CJA	Criminal Justice Act
CJEU	Court of Justice of the European Union
CMA	Competition and Markets Authority
CoE	Council of Europe
DoJ	Department of Justice (US)
DPA	deferred prosecution agreement
ECHR	European Convention on Human Rights
ECtHR	European Court of Human Rights
EIO	European Investigation Order
EPO	European Production Order
EPPO	European Public Prosecutor's Office
ESA	European Supervisory Authority
ESMA	European Securities and Markets Authority
ESRB	European Systemic Risk Board
EURIBOR	Euro Interbank Offered Rate
FATF	Financial Action Task Force
FBI	Federal Bureau of Investigation
FCA	Financial Conduct Authority
FOREX	Foreign Exchange Market

FSA	Financial Services Authority
FSMA	Financial Services and Markets Act
FX	Foreign Exchange
GDPR	General Data Protection Regulation (2016)
HMRC	HM Revenue and Customs
HMT	HM Treasury
ICAP	ICAP Europe Limited
IEL/ICAP	ICAP Europe Limited
ITSA	Insider Trading Sanction Act 1984
JPY	Japanese Yen
LIBOR	London Interbank Offered Rate
Lloyds	Lloyds Bank plc/Lloyds Banking Group plc/Lloyds TBC
MAD	Market Abuse Directive
MAR	Market Abuse Regulation
Martins	Martin Brokers (UK) Ltd
MiFID	Markets in Financial Instruments Directive
MiFIR	Markets in Financial Instruments Regulation
OLAF	European Anti-Fraud Office
PIF Convention	Convention on Protection of the EC's Financial Interests (1995)
PIF Directive	Directive (EU) 2017/1371
PRA	Prudential Regulation Authority
Rabobank	Coöperatieve Centrale Raiffeisen-Boerenleenbank BA
RINGA	Relevant Information Not Generally Available
SEC	Securities and Exchange Commission
SFO	Serious Fraud Office
SLS	Special Liquidity Scheme
TEU	Treaty on European Union
TFEU	Treaty on the Functioning of the European Union
UBS/UBS AG	Union Bank of Switzerland
UK	United Kingdom
UN	United Nations
US	United States
VAT	Value Added Tax

LIST OF STATUTORY PROVISIONS

UK Law

US Law

European Legislation and Treaties

EU Policy Document and Commission Documents

1

Introduction

I. Introduction

This book explores the phenomenon of market manipulation and insider trading, and how it is regulated and dealt with by the European Union (EU), the United Kingdom (UK) and the United States of America (US) respectively.

The ban on market manipulation in European law, for example, has its roots in the US, where the courts developed it based on the general common-law provisions on fraud.[1] The EU regime for fighting market manipulation and insider trading – commonly referred to as market abuse – was significantly reshuffled in the wake of the financial crisis of 2007/08, and a new Directive and Regulation were proposed in 2011 and subsequently adopted in 2014.[2] In all of the EU, US and the UK frameworks, the aftermath of the financial crisis, security concerns and increased legislation and policy responses to the fight against irregularities and market failures demonstrate that we need to understand the regulatory responses in this area in context. Specifically, the aim of this book is to investigate how the regulatory responses have changed since the start of the 2007/08 financial crisis, and to place the fight against market abuse within the broader picture of the fight against white-collar crime and the associated questions it raises in the context of the EU, US and the UK.

What, then, is market abuse? As stated, the notion of 'market abuse' is the umbrella label used to define insider trading and market manipulation. The insider trading ban, as Niamh Moloney explains, has several justifications. As she observes:

> The first rationale for insider-dealing regulation has a micro focus. It characterizes insider dealing as a breach of the fiduciary relationship of trust and confidence (a related strand characterizes insider dealing in terms of the allocation of property rights), where one can be established, between, typically, the insider and the company concerned.

[1] Eric Engle, 'Global norm convergence: capital market in US and EU law' (2010) 21 *European Business Law Review* 465.

[2] Directive 2014/57/EU of the European Parliament and of the Council of 16 April 2014 on criminal sanctions for market abuse (market abuse directive) OJ L 173, 12.6.2014, pp 179–89 (hereafter MAD), Regulation (EU) No 596/2014 of the European Parliament and of the Council of 16 April 2014 on market abuse (market abuse regulation) and repealing Directive 2003/6/EC of the European Parliament and of the Council and Commission Directives 2003/124/EC, 2003/125/EC and 2004/72/EC, OJ L 173, 12.6.2014, pp 1–61 (hereafter MAR).

> The macro focus of the second theory (which has shaped the EU regime) is on market efficiency, and on the support of efficient price formation and deep liquidity.[3]

The definition of 'market manipulation' is somewhat more vague, however. In short, market manipulation may arise in circumstances where investors have been unreasonably disadvantaged, directly or indirectly, by others who have used information that is not publicly available to trade in financial instruments to their advantage (insider dealing), have distorted the price-setting mechanism of financial instruments, or have disseminated false or misleading information.[4] In short, market manipulation can be defined as conduct that may misinform or deceive others into making ill-considered misleading investment decisions.[5] 'Market manipulation' is a term that has been used in the broader sense as including 'practices deemed harmful to the capital markets'.[6] It has also been defined as an 'unwarranted interference in the operation of ordinary market forces of supply and demand; an interference in the market's normal price-forming mechanism'.[7] For example, according to the definition provided by the UK Financial Services Authority, market manipulation encompasses three elements.[8] First, it includes financial dealings that provide fictitious indicators to obtain the price of a monetary tool at a synthetic level. Secondly, it involves a series of contracts or orders to utilise fabricated devices or products. Thirdly, it incorporates the sharing and dispersal of information that provides false or misleading signals. Examples of conduct that amounts to market manipulation include providing false statements or transactions that could result in the fluctuation of share prices.[9]

Furthermore, market manipulation can also include 'disseminating misleading information which moves the price of investments up or down', or 'improper use of market power'.[10] Other instances of market manipulation include a process called 'share romping', as illustrated during the Guinness fraud in the 1980s.[11] Wayne Carroll stated:

> Market manipulation is a general term covering a number of practices deemed harmful to the capital markets. Conduct that can lead to a violation of the market manipulation

[3] Niamh Moloney, *EU Securities and Financial Market Regulation* (Oxford, Oxford University Press, 2014) 701.

[4] See Matthias Siems and Mattijs Nelemans, 'The Reform of the Market Abuse Law: Revolution or Evolution?' (2012) 19 *Maastricht Journal of European and Comparative Law* 195.

[5] Action Fraud 'Market manipulation' (n/d), available at www.actionfraud.police.uk/a-z-of-fraud/market-manipulation.

[6] Wayne Carroll, 'Market manipulation: an international comparison' (2002) 9(4) *Journal of Financial Crime* 300.

[7] Eva Lomnicka, 'Preventing and controlling the manipulation of financial markets: towards a definition of market manipulation' (2001) 8(4) *Journal of Financial Crime* 297.

[8] Financial Services Authority 'Market Abuse Directive' (n/d), available at www.fsa.gov.uk/pages/about/what/international/pdf/mad%20(pl).pdf.

[9] ibid.

[10] See Lomnicka (n 7) 298.

[11] Rosalind Wright, 'Market abuse and market manipulation: the criminal, civil and regulatory interface' (2001) 3(1) *Journal of International Financial Markets* 19.

> provisions extends from active trading to merely spreading information about a particular security or company. Market manipulation comes in many forms, whose number is limited only by human ingenuity.[12]

The EU Market Abuse Directive (MAD) offers a slightly different version.[13] Article 5 defines market manipulation as (inter alia) someone entering into a transaction, placing an order to trade or any other behaviour which: gives false or misleading signals as to the supply of, demand for, or price of, a financial instrument or a related spot commodity contract; or secures the price of one or several financial instruments or a related spot commodity contract at an abnormal or artificial level.[14]

Moreover, in Article 8 of the Market Abuse Regulation (MAR), insider dealing (the common term in the EU context) – on the other account – is defined as arising

> where a person possesses inside information and uses that information by acquiring or disposing of, for its own account or for the account of a third party, directly or indirectly, financial instruments to which that information relates.

However, whom exactly do market manipulation and insider dealing harm? For a long time there has been a scholarly debate on what is wrong with insider dealing and who exactly is harmed by it. Scholars have asked why insider trading is banned and what the justification is.[15] The question asked is whether insider trading and market manipulation are unethical if no one is harmed by them.[16] Who exactly is harmed? The traders themselves? While the answers to these questions remain

[12] See Carroll (n 6) 300.

[13] MAD (n 2).

[14] MAD, Article 5 defines market abuse as: (a) entering into a transaction, placing an order to trade or any other behaviour which: (i) gives false or misleading signals as to the supply of, demand for, or price of, a financial instrument or a related spot commodity contract; or (ii) secures the price of one or several financial instruments or a related spot commodity contract at an abnormal or artificial level; unless the reasons for so doing of the person who entered into the transactions or issued the orders to trade are legitimate, and those transactions or orders to trade are in conformity with accepted market practices on the trading venue concerned; (b) entering into a transaction, placing an order to trade or any other activity or behaviour which affects the price of one or several financial instruments or a related spot commodity contract, which employs a fictitious device or any other form of deception or contrivance; (c) disseminating information through the media, including the internet, or by any other means, which gives false or misleading signals as to the supply of, demand for, or price of a financial instrument, or a related spot commodity contract, or secures the price of one or several financial instruments or a related spot commodity contract at an abnormal or artificial level, where the persons who made the dissemination derive for themselves or for another person an advantage or profit from the dissemination of the information in question; or (d) transmitting false or misleading information or providing false or misleading inputs or any other behaviour which manipulates the calculation of a benchmark.

[15] See, eg, Henry Manne, 'In Defense of Insider Trading' (1966) *Harvard Business Review*, November–December 113; Harry McVea, 'What is Wrong with Insider Dealing?' (1995) 15 *Legal Studies* 395; see also David Campbell, 'What is Wrong with Insider Dealing?' (1996) 16 *Legal Studies* 185; and discussion in Moloney (n 3) 699–769.

[16] See, eg, Robert McGee, 'Ethical Issues in Insider Trading: Case Studies' available at SSRN at https://ssrn.com/abstract=538682.

somewhat obscure, for the EU legislator, for example, the most important reason for banning market manipulation and insider trading is the protection of consumer confidence and investors by ensuring integrity in the market and fairness. While these matters have been debated for a long time, as a result of the global economic crisis, concerns were raised again about the effectiveness of the regime and the need to update it in light of current circumstances. Clearly, the financial crisis appeared to trigger policy reforms in this area but, as this book explains, it was not the only trigger. The development of the EU's fight against irregularities and criminal activity in the financial sector should therefore be seen in tandem with the EU's attempts to save the economy by boosting investor confidence in the EU market and securing an honest market place.

On that broader background, as a response to the financial crisis, both the EU and the US have increasingly focused on the phenomenon of white-collar crime as one of its major causes. The next section will therefore introduce the financial crisis that started over a decade ago and which is still ongoing, and explain why it is still relevant for understanding the law on market manipulation and insider trading.

II. The Financial Crisis and the Fight against Financial Crimes: Some Hardcore Data

The 2007/08 financial crisis began within the conduct of numerous US mortgage lenders,[17] who offered a variety of mortgages, including 'prime loans', 'alt-A loans' and 'subprime loans'.[18] In the lead-up to the onset of the largest financial crisis since the Great Depression, the growth of subprime loans was unparalleled, and by 2007 approximately 25 per cent of all US mortgages were subprime.[19] The growth of subprime loans was assisted by the introduction of the Fair Housing Act 1968 and the Civil Rights Act 1968,[20] which both fuelled access to convenient credit.[21] The collapse of the subprime market was accelerated by a process called securitisation,[22]

[17] The Financial Crisis Inquiry Commission, *Final Report of the National Commission on the Causes of the Financial and Economic Crisis in the United States* (Washington, DC, The Financial Crisis Inquiry Commission, 2011) 67–82.

[18] ibid.

[19] Alan White, 'The case for banning subprime mortgages' (2008) 77 *University of Cincinnati Law Review* 618. Also see Financial Crisis Inquiry Commission (n 17) 70.

[20] Pub L 90–284. The Fair Housing Act was enacted by Title VIII of the Civil Rights Act of 1968, and codified at 42 USC 3601–19.

[21] For a more detailed discussion of the problems associated with access to convenient credit, see Nicholas Ryder and Rachel Thomas, 'Convenient credit and consumer protection – a critical review of the responses of Labour and Coalition governments' (2011) 33(1) *Journal of Social Welfare and Family Law* 85.

[22] Securitisation is a financial practice that 'efficiently allows risk and capital [that] enables companies to access capital markets'. See Steven Schwarcz, 'The future of securitisation' (2008) *Duke Public Law and Legal Theory Research Paper Series* No 223.

which seeks to provide finance to financial institutions by the sale of assets.[23] The impact of the 2007/08 financial crisis on subprime lenders was catastrophic, and it claimed many corporate casualties – New Century Financial,[24] Lehman Brothers,[25] the Federal National Mortgage Association and the Federal Home Loan Mortgage Corporation, American Insurance Group (AIG)[26] and Bear Stearns.[27] It is interesting to note that prior to its takeover by the Government and JP Morgan, Bear Stearns shares were trading at $170.[28] The total losses from the collapse of the US subprime market surpassed $600 billion,[29] there was $20 trillion of lost wealth, 20 million people lost their jobs and 4 million US homeowners found their homes were repossessed.[30]

The US response was led by the Federal Reserve and the Department of Treasury, who provided emergency 'liquidity in the financial sector'.[31] The Federal Reserve reduced US interest rates, increased access to short-term liquidity, created a weekly loan service and arranged the takeover of Bear Stearns.[32] These actions were soon followed by the introduction of an over-abundance of legislative measures, including the Economic Stimulus Act 2008,[33] the Emergency Economic Stabilization Act 2008,[34] the Housing and Economic Recovery Act 2008,[35] the American Recovery and Reinvestment Act 2009,[36] the Fraud Enforcement and Recovery Act 2009[37] and the Dodd-Frank Wall Street Reform Act 2012.[38]

[23] Vincenzo Bavoso, 'Financial innovation and structured finance: the case of securitisation' (2012) 34(1) *The Company Lawyer* 4.

[24] See Julie Cresswell, 'Mortgage lender New Century Financial files for bankruptcy', 2 April 2007, available at www.nytimes.com/2007/04/02/business/worldbusiness/02iht-loans.5.5118838.html.

[25] See Graeme Wearden, David Teather and Jill Treanor, 'Banking crisis: Lehman Brothers files for bankruptcy protection', 15 September 2008, available at www.guardian.co.uk/business/2008/sep/15/lehmanbrothers.creditcrunch.

[26] The US Government was forced to intervene and agreed to lend AIG $85bn in exchange for an 80% stake of the company. Matthew Karnitschnig, Deborah Solomon, Liam Pleven and Jon Hilsenrath, 'US to Take Over AIG in $85 Billion Bailout; Central Banks Inject Cash as Credit Dries Up', 16 September 2008, available at http://online.wsj.com/article/SB122156561931242905.html.

[27] Bruno Nickolic, 'Rise and fall of regulatory state in financial markets' (2013) 28(1) *Journal of International Banking Law and Regulation* 1.

[28] Andrew Sorkin, 'JP Morgan Pays $2 a Share for Bear Stearns', 17 March 2008, available at www.nytimes.com/2008/03/17/business/17bear.html?_r=0.

[29] Laura Patterson and Cynthia Koller, 'Diffusion of fraud through subprime lending' in M Deflem (ed), *Economic Crisis and Crime* (Bingley, Emerald, 2011) 26.

[30] Gregg Barak, 'The flickering desires for white collar crime studies in the post-financial crisis will they ever shine brightly?' (2013) 13(3) *Western Criminology Review* 63.

[31] Jongmoo Choi and Michael Papaioannou, 'Financial crisis and risk management: reassessing the Asian financial crisis in light of the American financial crisis' (2010) 5 *East Asia Law Review* 455.

[32] Federal Reserve 'Press Release', 14 March 2008, available at www.federalreserve.gov/newsevents/press/monetary/20080314a.htm.

[33] Pub L 110–185.

[34] Pub L 110–343.

[35] Pub L 110–289.

[36] Pub L 111–5.

[37] Pub L 111–21.

[38] Pub L 111–203.

In the UK, the corporate casualty list included Northern Rock, Bradford & Bingley, Lloyds TSB, HBOS and the Royal Bank of Scotland (RBS), who required emergency liquidity from the Bank of England. The legislative response to the 2007/08 financial crisis in the UK included the Banking (Special Provisions) Act 2008, the Banking Act 2009, the Financial Services Act 2010 and the Financial Services Act 2012. The last of these resulted in the creation of a new system of financial regulation in the UK, managed by the Bank of England, the Financial Conduct Authority (FCA), the Prudential Regulation Authority and the Financial Policy Committee.[39]

The origins of the 2007/08 financial crisis are of course well documented, and it is not the purpose of this chapter to explore them in detail. However, it is important to provide a very brief overview of the factors leading up to it. In the UK, for example, the Financial Services Authority concluded that the causes of the financial crisis were macro-economic disparities, the multifaceted nature of securitisation, access to convenient credit, weak credit standards and the unsustainable increase in property prices.[40] The US Department of Treasury argued that the financial crisis was caused by weaknesses in the regulation of subprime mortgages, ineffective market discipline, weaknesses in the performance of credit-rating agencies and weak financial regulation.[41] Other documented factors include the subprime mortgage crisis,[42] weak banking regulation,[43] high levels of consumer debt,[44] toxic debts,[45] securitisation,[46] deregulation of banking legislation,[47] ineffective macroeconomic policies,[48]

[39] For a more detailed discussion of the UK's financial regulatory regime following these legislative reforms, see Alison Lui, *Financial stability and prudential regulation: A comparative approach to the UK, US, Canada, Australia and Germany* (Abingdon, Routledge, 2016).

[40] Financial Services Authority, *Financial Risk Outlook 2009* (London, Financial Services Authority, 2009) 7–12.

[41] Department of Treasury, 'President's Working Group on Financial Markets, Policy Statement on Financial Markets Developments', 13 March 2008, available at www.treasury.gov/resource-center/fin-mkts/Documents/pwgpolicystatemktturmoil_03122008.pdf.

[42] See, eg, European Commission *Report of the High-Level Group on Financial Supervision in the EU* (Brussels, European Commission, 2009).

[43] Shayna Hutchins, 'Flip That Prosecution Strategy: An Argument for Using RICO to Prosecute Large-Scale Mortgage Fraud' (2011) 59(1) *Buffalo Law Review* 306.

[44] See generally Mechele Dickerson, 'Over-indebtedness, the subprime mortgage crisis, and the effect on US cities' (2009) 36 *Fordham Urban Law Journal* 395.

[45] Demetra Arsalidou, 'The banking crisis: rethinking and refining the accountability of bank directors' (2010) 4 *Journal of Business Law* 292.

[46] For a critical discussion of securitisation, see Michael Nwogugu, 'Securitisation is illegal: racketeer influenced and corrupt organisations, usury, antitrust and tax issues' (2008) 23(6) *Journal of International Banking Law and Regulation* 316.

[47] The arguments on the relationship between the financial crisis and banking deregulation relate to the impact of several pieces of legislation, including the Graham-Leach-Bailey Act 1999, the Depository Institutions Deregulation and Monetary Control Act 1980 and the Garn St Germain Depository Institutions Act 1982. See Adam Levitin, 'The crisis without a face: emerging narratives of the financial crisis' (2009) 63 *University of Miami Law Review* 1004.

[48] Franklin Gevurtz, 'The role of corporate law in preventing a financial crisis: reflections on in re Citigroup Inc shareholder derivative litigation' (2010) 23 *Pacific McGeorge Global Business & Development Law Journal* 113.

weak credit regulation,[49] deregulation of consumer credit legislation[50] and the culture of banking practices.[51]

Moreover, financial crime was an important factor that contributed towards the 2007/08 financial crisis. For example, Wim Huisman stated that 'misconduct in the financial industry is widely seen as having triggered the credit crunch that has pushed the world into an economic crisis'.[52] Other commentators, such as Tomson Nguyen and Henry Pontell, asserted that prevalent mortgage fraud was associated with the financial crisis.[53] The link between the financial crisis and financial crime has been demonstrated by an increase in the related enforcement actions of the Securities and Exchange Commission (SEC), the Commodities Futures Trading Commission (CFTC), the Federal Bureau of Investigation (FBI), the Department of Justice (DoJ), the Financial Services Authority, the FCA and the Serious Fraud Office (SFO).

As will be expounded in chapter two, the financial crisis and the Euro crises have also had a considerable impact on EU law and shaped the EU responses to fight market abuse and related activity. The EU's strategy to combat irregularities in the market should be seen in the light of the history of the debate on the market abuse regime and the question as to why the suppression of financial crime is relevant in EU law. The underlying theme of the EU's involvement in the fight against financial crime is boosting investor confidence and thereby contributing to the establishment of the internal market. Against the backdrop of the financial crisis, the EU again decided to get tough on white-collar crime, and as part of this endeavour sought to remedy the alleged loopholes of the previous Market Abuse Directive by adopting a new Regulation and a Directive, as already mentioned.[54] The Directive on criminal sanctions to fight market abuse offers the first example of use of Article 83(2) of the Treaty on the Functioning of the European Union (TFEU), the 'extended' competence clause for 'harmonisation' of an area, which is essential for the effective implementation of EU law and where harmonisation measures have already been adopted. The rationale for the Directive, which is to be read in conjunction with the Regulation[55] on insider trading and market manipulation, is to ensure market integrity and enhance public confidence in securities and derivatives. The Directive creates a new framework for the purposes of fighting crime, while it regroups the previous market abuse regime into a separate

[49] Choi and Papaioannou (n 31) 443.

[50] See, eg, the impact of the decision in *Marquette National Bank of Minneapolis v First Omaha Service Corp* 439 US 299 (1978).

[51] It is not our objective to revisit these but to add to the existing literature by recognising the importance of the previously under-researched factor, market manipulation.

[52] Wim Huisman, 'White-collar crime and the economic crisis' (2012/2013) 11 *Newsletter of the European Society of Criminology* 8.

[53] Tomson Nguyen and Henry Pontell, 'Mortgage origination fraud and the global economic crisis' (2010) 9(3) *Criminology & Public Policy* 592.

[54] See the MAD and MAR respectively (n 2).

[55] ibid.

Regulation to increase the effectiveness of the system. The new Directive is a prime example of the invocation of criminal law to guarantee the effectiveness of European policies in this area.

III. Market Manipulation: The Major Crime

An emerging financial crime associated with the financial crisis is market manipulation. This is illustrated by the continual manipulation of the London Interbank Lending Rate (LIBOR), the Euro Interbank Offered Rate (EURIBOR) and the foreign exchange market (FOREX) by numerous financial institutions and traders. LIBOR is a 'benchmark that gauges the interest rate, credit premium and liquidity premium that a leading bank would expect to be offered by another similar institution'.[56] During the 2007/08 financial crisis, LIBOR was managed and regulated by the British Bankers Association, now UK Finance, the UK trade body of the banking and financial services sector. The EURIBOR rate is founded upon the interest rates at which a number of European banks borrow from each other. FOREX is the foreign exchange market on which foreign currencies are traded.[57] LIBOR and EURIBOR 'are used across the world for a range of financial products by a wide variety of financial market participants, for both hedging and speculative purposes'.[58] The integrity of LIBOR and EURIBOR rates is central to the global financial markets, and any alleged manipulation can have a significant impact on and ramifications for the global markets. The first evidence of the market manipulation of LIBOR occurred in 2005, when the Financial Services Authority determined that Barclays Bank had manipulated both the dollar LIBOR and the EURIBOR interest rates in London and New York. Subsequently, Barclays was fined £59.5 million after the Financial Services Authority determined that the bank had breached 11 of its Principles of Business and Handbook.[59] The second bank to be fined (£160 million), owing to its manipulation of LIBOR, was UBS in December 2012. The regulator concluded that between January 2005 and December 2010, UBS breached regulations 3 and 5 of the Principles of Business when it engaged in illegal behaviour regarding the calculation of LIBOR and EURIBOR.[60] The RBS became the third bank to be fined in February 2013, following revelations of LIBOR

[56] See eg www.investopedia.com/terms/l/libor.asp (last accessed March 2019).

[57] BBC News, 'How the forex scandal happened', 20 May 2015, available at www.bbc.co.uk/news/business-30003693.

[58] HM Treasury, *The Wheatley Review of LIBOR: initial discussion paper* (London, HM Treasury, 2012) 10.

[59] Financial Services Authority, 'Barclays fined £59.5m for significant failings in relation to LIBOR and EURIBOR', 27 June 2012, available at www.fca.org.uk/news/press-releases/barclays-fined-%C2%A3595-million-significant-failings-relation-libor-and-euribor.

[60] Financial Conduct Authority, 'UBS fined £160 million for significant failings in relation to LIBOR and EURIBOR', 29 March 2012, available at www.fca.org.uk/news/press-releases/ubs-fined-%C2%A3160-million-significant-failings-relation-libor-and-euribor.

rigging. The regulator fined RBS £87.5 million for its conduct between January 2006 and November 2010.[61] The overall fine would have been £125 million had it not been for a 30 per cent discount granted by the regulator. The conduct of the banks' employees was not limited to the UK; it also occurred in Japan, Singapore and the US. According to the regulator, the illegal conduct was extensive – there were over 200 inappropriate submissions, involving 21 employees and a manager.[62] The regulator imposed another financial penalty of £14 million on ICAP Europe Ltd in September 2013 for an embarrassing amount of misconduct that involved the firm's traders colluding with UBS traders to manipulate the Japanese Yen (JPY) LIBOR rates, and one trader receiving bonus or corrupt payments for assisting in the manipulation.[63] In October 2013, Rabobank was fined £105 million for 'poor internal controls that encouraged collusion between traders and LIBOR submitters and allowed systematic attempts at benchmark manipulation'.[64] In July 2014, Lloyds TSB was fined £104 million for breaches of the LIBOR and other benchmarks.[65] Additionally, Martin Brokers (UK) Ltd was fined £630,000 for significant failings in relation to LIBOR.[66]

The DoJ announced that RBS Securities Japan Limited, a wholly owned subsidiary of RBS, had pleaded guilty to wire fraud and its role in influencing the Japanese Yen London (JPY) Interbank Offered Rate. As part of a Deferred Prosecution Agreement, RBS Securities Japan Limited agreed to pay a $50 million fine. Additionally, RBS Securities Japan Limited agreed to pay a $100 million penalty.[67]

The CFTC has been heavily involved in tackling market manipulation and in particular the LIBOR scandal. In June 2012 the Commission fined Barclays $200 million for its attempted manipulation and false reporting of LIBOR and EURIBOR.[68] It also fined UBS $700 million for the same offences. David Meister stated that the enforcement action of the CFTC was a clear example of the fact

[61] Financial Services Authority, 'RBS fined £87.5m for significant failings in relation to LIBOR', 6 February 2013, available at www.fsa.gov.uk/library/communication/pr/2013/011.shtml.

[62] ibid.

[63] Financial Conduct Authority, 'ICAP Europe Limited fined £14 million for significant failings in relation to LIBOR', 25 September 2013, available at www.fca.org.uk/news/icap-europe-limited-fined.

[64] Financial Conduct Authority, 'The FCA fines Rabobank £105 million for serious LIBOR-related misconduct', 29 October 2013, available at www.fca.org.uk/news/the-fca-fines-rabobank-105-million-for-serious-libor-related-misconduct.

[65] Financial Conduct Authority, 'Lloyds Banking Group fined £105m for serious LIBOR and other benchmark failings', 28 September 2014, www.fca.org.uk/news/lloyds-banking-group-fined-105m-libor-benchmark-failings.

[66] Financial Conduct Authority, 'Martin Brokers (UK) Limited fined £630,000 for significant failings in relation to LIBOR', 15 May 2014, www.fca.org.uk/news/press-releases/martin-brokers-uk-limited-fined-630000-for-significant-failings-in-relation-to-libor.

[67] Department of Justice, 'RBS Securities Japan Limited Agrees to Plead Guilty in Connection with Long-Running Manipulation of Libor Benchmark Interest Rates', 6 February 2013, available at www.justice.gov/opa/pr/2013/February/13-crm-161.html.

[68] Commodities Futures Trading Commission, 'FTC Orders Barclays to pay $200 Million Penalty for Attempted Manipulation of and False Reporting concerning LIBOR and Euribor Benchmark Interest Rates', 27 June 2012, available at www.cftc.gov/PressRoom/PressReleases/pr6289-12.

that it will not tolerate instances of corporate misbehaviour and is prepared to utilise its extensive enforcement powers.[69] In February 2013, the CFTC fined RBS $325 million for its manipulation, attempted manipulation and false reporting of JPY and Swiss Franc LIBOR.[70] This was followed by the imposition of a financial penalty on Lloyds Banking Group plc and Lloyds Bank plc of $105 million for the attempted manipulation of LIBOR.[71] In September 2013, the CFTC fined ICAP Europe Limited $65 million in a civil monetary penalty for 'manipulation, attempted manipulation, false reporting, and aiding and abetting derivatives traders' manipulation and attempted manipulation' of LIBOR.[72] In April 2015, the CFTC imposed its largest financial penalty, $800 million, on Deutsche Bank for the attempted manipulation of the LIBOR and EURIBOR interest rate benchmarks.[73] In May 2016, Citibank paid a financial penalty of $250 million for attempted market manipulation and false reporting of the US dollar ISDAFIX benchmark.[74]

Therefore, the enforcement activities of the CFTC are identical to those adopted by the SEC – the imposition of a series of administrative penalties. It is questionable whether the financial penalties imposed by the CFTC will deter any future misconduct by financial institutions. This and other related questions will be explored in further detail throughout this book.

IV. Structure of the Chapters

In this chapter, we have sought to introduce the topic and to provide the background for our subsequent discussion. Chapter two begins by looking at the EU system for suppressing market abuse. That chapter sets out the EU framework for

[69] Commodities Futures Trading Commission, 'CFTC Orders UBS to Pay $700 Million Penalty to Settle Charges of Manipulation, Attempted Manipulation and False Reporting of LIBOR and Other Benchmark Interest Rates', 19 December 2012, available at www.cftc.gov/PressRoom/PressReleases/pr6472-12.

[70] Commodities Futures Trading Commission, 'CFTC Orders The Royal Bank of Scotland plc and RBS Securities Japan Limited to Pay $325 Million Penalty to Settle Charges of Manipulation, Attempted Manipulation, and False Reporting of Yen and Swiss Franc LIBOR', 6 February 2013, available at www.cftc.gov/PressRoom/PressReleases/pr6510-13.

[71] US Commodities Futures Trading Commission, 'CFTC Charges Lloyds Banking Group and Lloyds Bank with Manipulation, Attempted Manipulation, and False Reporting of LIBOR', 28 July 2014, available at www.cftc.gov/PressRoom/PressReleases/pr6966-14.

[72] Commodities Futures Trading Commission, 'CFTC Charges ICAP Europe Limited, a Subsidiary of ICAP plc, with Manipulation and Attempted Manipulation of Yen Libor', 25 September 2013, available at www.cftc.gov/PressRoom/PressReleases/pr6708-13.

[73] Commodities Futures Trading Commission, 'Deutsche Bank to Pay $800 Million Penalty to Settle CFTC Charges of Manipulation, Attempted Manipulation, and False Reporting of LIBOR and Euribor', 23 April 2015, available at www.cftc.gov/PressRoom/PressReleases/7159-15.

[74] Commodities Futures Trading Commission, 'CFTC Orders Citibank to Pay $250 Million for Attempted Manipulation and False Reporting of US Dollar ISDAFIX Benchmark Swap Rates', 25 May 2016, available at www.cftc.gov/PressRoom/PressReleases/7371-16.

fighting financial crime by bringing market abuse to the fore, as a threat that needs to be dealt with. The chapter explains the EU market-based preventive approach and links to the ongoing construction of the internal market. In addition, the chapter highlights the relationship between market abuse and other white-collar crimes. It surveys the evolution of the EU's suppression of market abuse by looking at the history of it, exploring how the EU strategy has changed with the measures (2014 Directive and Regulation) adopted following the general EU action for recovery of the market at large as a consequence of the global financial crisis (and links to the Markets in Financial Instruments reformation). Moreover, the chapter looks at the impact of the new criminal law powers (granted by the Lisbon Treaty) and discusses the consequences of using double measures to fight market abuse (ie, civil penalties and criminal penalties) in the specific EU context. In addition, chapter two looks at the impact of the principle of proportionality and EU fundamental rights protection, and briefly discusses the reception of the legal instruments in the Member States and possible challenges for the Court of Justice of the European Union (CJEU).

Chapter three looks more specifically at the regulatory challenges involved in tackling market abuse in the EU, UK and the US, respectively, in the context of criminal law and civil/administrative law responses, addressing the question whether market abuse should be banned at all through the use of criminal law. The chapter focuses on the use and choice of sanctions in a comparative context, and discusses the proportionality of the regime.

Subsequently, in chapter four, a detailed foray is made into the EU's approach to combatting market abuse. The chapter places the EU's fight against market abuse in the broader context of the fight against white-collar crime in the EU more generally, and addresses associated questions about data protection as well as the establishment of a European Public Prosecutor's Office (EPPO) and its possible impact on the law on market abuse. In addition, the chapter discusses fundamental rights protection and the hot issue of data protection in the EU context, examining why it is relevant to understanding the contemporary regime for combatting market abuse. In doing so, the chapter discusses the EU stance on, and the importance of, consumer confidence in the EU internal market as one of the driving motivations for the EU, and thus scans the market abuse regime in the framework of the classic Article 114 TFEU case law on the harmonisation powers of the EU and market making. The chapter links the discussion to the increased EU criminal law cooperation in EU financial crimes legislation more generally as one of the consequences of the global financial crisis, along with measures to combat terrorism and transnational criminality. Thus, the chapter also addresses the political question of to what extent the EU is a norm follower or a trendsetter in this area.

In chapter five the aim is to critically consider the UK's efforts to tackle insider dealing and market abuse. The chapter highlights how the UK criminalised insider dealing under the Criminal Justice Act 1993 and introduced the civil enforcement regime: the Market Abuse Regime. The chapter moves on to critically consider the 2007/08 financial crisis and the FSA's response to it, which included imposing a large number of financial penalties on firms and individuals. The chapter also discusses the impact of Brexit and to what extent the UK, in the event of a 'hard Brexit', will end up keeping the EU's norms.

The purpose of chapter six is to offer a detailed case study of the US approach to insider trading and market manipulation. The first part of the chapter briefly outlines the evolution of the US legislative approach towards insider trading and highlights the role of the US judiciary. The chapter then moves on to appraise the responses to market manipulation and insider trading arising from the financial crisis. This involves a detailed analysis of the responses of the SEC, the DoJ and the CFTC.

Chapter seven summarises the arguments.

V. Conclusion

The law on market manipulation and insider trading/dealing offers a fascinating picture of many interacting questions and layers in the area of financial crimes as they touch upon consumer confidence in the market, data protection, fundamental rights and – in the case of the EU – allocation of competences. This volume seeks to scan and critically examine the contemporary law and practices in the area of market manipulation and insider trading/dealing, and to explain why they are important. Why, then, the different case studies from the EU, US and the UK? The present chapter will now conclude by briefly outlining the key points explaining why we have chosen these cases.

A. Why the EU?

The EU's fight against market abuse raises many interesting regulatory questions within the EU's internal policy areas (the internal market vis-à-vis the Area of Freedom, Security and Justice (AFSJ)), as well as its external impact and cooperation with third states, most prominently the US. As will be shown, both the security concern and the financial crisis have shaped this area and illuminate a fascinating relationship between the EU internal market and the EU AFSJ, and currently shape EU integration processes. However, challenges to the EU like the Brexit negotiations also mean that the political dimension is very strong in this area, since EU law is enforced through national law. The EU is very much concerned with ensuring confidence in the market, and market abuse offers a good test of the interaction between EU internal market law, AFSJ law and broader questions about and related to the EU's fight against financial crimes.

B. Why the United States of America?

The US presents an interesting case study for this book. Since the start of the financial crisis, there have been several high-profile white-collar crimes that have either emanated from the US or been exposed by it. Consequently, US regulatory agencies have instigated numerous investigations and imposed record civil financial penalties for the illegal activities of corporations. As will be explained in this book, the decision to impose financial penalties has done little to prevent any future misconduct by US corporations.

C. Why the United Kingdom?

The UK provides a unique comparator to the US due to the impact of the financial crisis on its financial corporations, the adoption of a similar enforcement strategy to the US and the fact that the city of London is one of the largest financial centres in the world. The UK has imposed a series of substantial financial administrative penalties on corporations, which have attracted no criminal liability. The FCA has imposed a higher number of financial penalties since 2010, which have largely resulted from the LIBOR and FORX scandals. Brexit, however, presents a major challenge to the UK legislative framework, as most of the laws in this area are so intertwined with European integration. The EU Withdrawal Act (2018) is set to repeal the European Communities Act when the UK leaves the EU. The EU Withdrawal Act also seeks to convert directly applicable EU law into UK domestic law. Of relevance here are the draft Market Abuse (Amendment) (EU Exit) Regulations 2018, which would seek to address deficiencies that could arise when the UK leaves the EU. For example, this includes maintaining the scope of the regulation, transaction reporting and notification requirements, which will be retained, dealing with transfer of functions, supervisory cooperation and information sharing.[75]

[75] HM Treasury, 'Market Abuse (Amendment) (EU Exit) Regulations 2018: explanatory information', 30 November 2018, available at www.gov.uk/government/publications/draft-market-abuse-amendment-eu-exit-regulations-2018/market-abuse-amendment-eu-exit-regulations-2018-explanatory-information.

2

Market Manipulation and Insider Dealing in the EU Context

I. Introduction

The idea of this chapter is to explore the EU's regime for countering market manipulation and insider dealing (commonly referred to as 'market abuse' in the EU context).[1] It serves the purpose of critically examining EU regulatory efforts in the EU market abuse arena. The underlying objective of the EU's involvement in the fight against financial crime and market abuse is often said to be that of boosting investor confidence and thereby contributing to the functioning of the internal market – for example through harmonisation under Article 114 of the Treaty of the Functioning of the European Union (TFEU).[2]

This chapter starts by investigating the framework for understanding regulatory efforts in EU policy in the fight against financial crimes. It sets out the EU framework for fighting white-collar crime by bringing market abuse to the fore of the discussion as a threat that, according to the EU legislator, needs to be dealt with. The chapter explains the EU market-based preventive approach and links it to the ongoing construction of the internal market at the EU level, and aims to explain why the fight against market manipulation and insider dealing is a matter of high concern for the EU. The specific focus of the chapter is the competence question of the EU, as to why the EU is involved in regulating market abuse at all. In addition, the chapter looks at the question of liability for legal persons and briefly discusses why this question is still controversial in an EU perspective.

This chapter is structured as follows. The first part of the chapter sets out to discuss why countering market abuse is a central task for the EU, its legislative history and the importance of ensuring confidence in the market. In doing so it briefly explains how financial crimes became a core EU competence. Thereafter, the subsequent parts of the chapter turn to look at the development of the

[1] Directive 2014/57/EU of the European Parliament and of the Council of 16 April 2014 on criminal sanctions for market abuse (market abuse directive), OJ L 173, 12.6.2014, pp 179–89 (hereafter MAD).

[2] See Regulation (EU) No 596/2014 on market abuse (market abuse regulation) and repealing Directive 2003/6/EC of the European Parliament and of the Council and Commission Directives 2003/124/EC, 2003/125/EC and 2004/72/EC, OJ L 173, 12.6.2014, pp 1–61 (hereafter MAR).

EU's fight against market abuse, the 2014 Directive and Regulation respectively, and address the key issues raised by these measures.

Perhaps it should first be stressed that before the entry into force of the Lisbon Treaty and the increased competence to harmonise criminal law under Article 83 TFEU in particular, the EU had a very limited competence in the field of criminal law and therefore developed a unique tapestry for the enactment of sanctions through the framework of the internal market powers of Article 114 TFEU.[3] This provision grants a far-reaching competence for harmonising areas when needed for the smooth functioning of the market. In the wake of the financial crisis and the associated Eurozone crisis, the EU decided to get tougher on financial crimes with regard to, in particular, market abuse, as well as to combat the laundering of money in Europe.[4] This means that although there was a somewhat late response to the European financial crisis of 2008, as mentioned in chapter one, there is now an increased move towards regulatory strategies across different sectors in EU law, particularly with regard to EU action within the financial market sphere. Yet, the EU fight against financial crimes, together with organised crime, has for a long time formed the core of the EU's approach to anti-crime regulation and has now been intensified.[5]

One of the difficulties inherent in tackling market abuse is the difficulty of clearly distinguishing it from all other (mal-)practices.

The EU has a strong interest to counter financial crimes and fraud against the EU budget, as those crimes – so the EU legislator claims – hamper trust in the market and undermine consumer confidence in engaging in internal market transactions.[6] As is pointed out in recital 1 of the Market Abuse Directive:

> The smooth functioning of securities markets and public confidence in markets are prerequisites for economic growth and wealth. Market abuse harms the integrity of financial markets and public confidence in securities, derivatives and benchmarks.

[3] See, eg, Carlos Gómez–Jare Díez, *Federal European Criminal Law* (Cambridge, Intersentia, 2015); Jacob Öberg, *Limits to EU Powers: A Case Study of EU Regulatory Criminal Law* (Oxford, Hart Publishing, 2017); Ester Herlin-Karnell, *The Constitutional Dimension of European Criminal Law* (Oxford, Hart Publishing, 2012).

[4] See EU Commission memo, 28 March 2014, 'A comprehensive EU response to the financial crisis: substantial progress towards a strong financial framework for Europe and a banking union for the eurozone', available at http://europa.eu/rapid/press-release_MEMO-14-244_en.htm (last accessed November 2018). See further Commission Staff Working Paper, 'Impact assessment accompanying the proposals for a Regulation and a Directive on market abuse' SEC(2011) 1217 final, available at www.europarl.europa.eu/registre/docs_autres_institutions/commission_europeenne/sec/2011/1217/COM_SEC(2011)1217_EN.pdf (last accessed November 2018). See also more generally Niamh Moloney, 'EU Financial market regulation after the global financial crises: More Europe or more risks?' (2010) 47 *Common Market Law Review* 1317.

[5] On the history of EU criminal law legislation, see, eg, Steve Peers, *EU Justice and Home Affairs* (Oxford, Oxford University Press, 2011) ch 1.

[6] See, eg, Carlos Gómez-Jara Díez and Ester Herlin-Karnell, 'Prosecuting EU Financial Crimes: The European Public Prosecutor's Office in Comparison to the US Federal Regime' (2018) 19 *German Law Journal* 1191.

Moreover, as mentioned above, market manipulation and insider dealing are two forms of what the EU labels as 'market abuse'. The phenomenon is commonly defined as hindering speedy and fair disclosure of information to the public and threatening the functioning of the market.[7] Thus, insider dealing in the EU context is commonly defined as a situation where a person possesses inside information and uses that information by acquiring or disposing of, for its own account or for the account of a third party, directly or indirectly, financial instruments to which that information relates.[8] The possession of inside information has two legal consequences: a prohibition of insider transactions and a duty to disclose inside information to the market.[9]

Furthermore, inside information can be used by cancelling or amending an order concerning a financial instrument to which the information relates, where the order was placed before the person concerned possessed the inside information, which is also considered to be insider dealing (Articles 2–3 of the Market Abuse Directive 2014). Article 5 of the Market Abuse Directive, in turn, defines market manipulation as, inter alia, giving false or misleading signals as to the supply of, demand for, or price of, a financial instrument or a related spot (eg, cash) commodity contract. It can also concern disseminating information through the media, including the internet, or by any other means, which gives false or misleading signals as to the supply of, demand for, or price of a financial instrument, or a related spot commodity contract.

In addition, Article 4 of the Market Abuse Directive defines 'unlawful disclosure' as comprising a case where a person possesses inside information and discloses that information to any other person, except where the disclosure is made in the normal exercise of an employment, a profession or duties, including where the disclosure qualifies as a market sounding made in compliance with Article 11(1)–(8) of the Market Abuse Regulation.[10] 'Market sounding' refers to a communication of information, prior to the announcement of a transaction, in order to gauge the interest of one or more potential investors in that possible transaction and the conditions relating to it, such as its potential size or pricing.[11]

Generally the phenomenon of insider dealing is referred to as 'trading and tipping', meaning that an insider in possession of insider information cannot use it or tip a third party, either directly or indirectly.[12] In a comparative context,

[7] The EU agency European Security and Markets Authority is instructive: see at www.esma.europa.eu/press-news/esma-news/esma-readies-mar-guidelines-market-soundings-and-delayed-disclosure-inside (last accessed November 2018).

[8] MAD, Art 2 (n 1).

[9] See, eg Katja Langenbucher, 'Insider trading in European Law' in Stephen Bainbridge and William D Warren (eds), *Research Handbook on Insider Trading* (Cheltenham, Edward Elgar, 2013) ch 22.

[10] MAR (n 2).

[11] See, eg, the explanation given by ESMA at www.esma.europa.eu/press-news/esma-news/esma-readies-mar-guidelines-market-soundings-and-delayed-disclosure-inside (last accessed 1 November 2018).

[12] eg Langenbucher (n 9).

for example, the Canadian Securities Act prohibits persons in a 'special relationship' with an issuer from trading in the issuer's securities when they possess so-called 'material non-public information'.[13] Likewise, in the US framework certain categories of persons – like an issuer's officers, directors and advisers – are automatically captured by the insider trading and tipping prohibitions.[14] The prohibitions also capture individuals who learn about material non-public information from someone the individual knows, or 'ought reasonably to know', is in a special relationship with an issuer.[15] The regulation is similar at the EU level.

II. The EU's Fight against Financial Crimes and the Importance of 'Confidence' in the Market

The concern of the EU to ban market manipulation and abuse is part of the general EU ambition of ensuring integrity of the EU market, as already described. In 1989 the EU adopted the first Insider Dealing Directive.[16] But the scope of the regime was limited in terms of the securities and markets covered; the sanctions and enforcement regime was weak, as was the supporting structure for supervisory cooperation and, importantly it did not address market manipulation. The limited scope of it was addressed in the *Georgakis* case.[17] The case concerned members of a family who were both board members and block holders of a listed company. They engaged in transactions referred to as 'painting the tape' in order to manipulate the volume of trading. But because the 1989 Directive did not include market manipulation, the national court asked if the behaviour in question could be dealt with through an insider dealing prohibition. The court did not extend the trading prohibition of insider information to cases of market manipulation but stressed the importance of protecting investor confidence.[18]

The interesting question is then how the EU law on market abuse developed. The Market Abuse Directive is central here as the prohibition of market manipulation aims to protect market efficiency in general and hence has a very wide scope. Still, it has been argued that there are other alternatives, such as an information strategy, that might be more useful.[19] For example, does insider dealing distort

[13] See further at www.torys.com/insights/publications/2018/01/insider-trading-and-tipping-ontario-court-of-appeal-helps-set-limits (last accessed November 2018).

[14] Stephen Bainbridge, 'An Overview of Insider Trading Law and Policy: An Introduction to the Research Handbook on Insider Trading' in Bainbridge and Warren (n 9) ch 1.

[15] ibid.

[16] [1988] OJ C277/13 (the Revised Proposal); Explanatory Memorandum at COM (88) 549. Discussed in Niamh Moloney, *EU Securities and Financial Market Regulation* (Oxford, Oxford University Press, 2014) 707.

[17] Case 391/04, *Georgakis*, 2007 ECR I-3741.

[18] ibid and see Langenbucher (n 11).

[19] See eg Harry Mc Vea, 'What is Wrong with Insider Dealing?' (2995) 15 *Legal Studies* 395. See also David Campell, 'What is Wrong with Insider Dealing?' (1996) 16 *Legal Studies* 185.

the market? This is a huge question, of course.[20] Yet, in brief, what is peculiar with insider dealing is that it constitutes so called remote harm of an accumulative nature – that is; a distortion of the market would presumably occur only if others did the same thing (another issue is, then, how many it takes to distort a European market).[21]

Why then is the EU regulating this area? The first market abuse Directive was adopted in 2003.[22] In the context of the history of sanctions in EU law, the fight against market abuse and the establishing of the integrity of the market has been part of the wide ranging case law on sanctions as mentioned above.[23] As the 2014 Market Abuse Directive stipulates in its preamble, recital 7, the LIBOR scandal, which concerned a serious case of benchmark manipulation, demonstrated that relevant problems and loopholes impact gravely on market confidence and may result in significant losses to investors and distortions of the real economy.[24] The Directive also emphasised in its preamble that absence of common criminal sanction regimes across the Union creates opportunities for perpetrators of market abuse to take advantage of lighter regimes in some Member States. The imposition of criminal sanctions for market abuse would then, according to the EU legislator, have an increased deterrent effect on potential offenders.

What still remains somewhat contested as to its exact definition is that of the notion of insider information. For example, in the *Spector Photo Group* judgment, the Court of Justice of the European Union (CJEU) was asked to clarify the meaning of inside information in the context of the 2003 Market Abuse Directive.[25] Here the Court emphasised that the question is whether a primary insider in possession of inside information 'uses that information' within the meaning of Article 2(1) of Directive 2003/6 and stressed that it must be determined in light of the purpose of that Directive, which is to protect the integrity of the financial markets and to enhance investor confidence. The Court pointed out that the confidence is based, in particular, on the assurance that they will be placed on an equal footing and protected from the misuse of inside information. The Court held that usage which goes against that purpose constitutes prohibited insider dealing. Moreover, the Court stated that in order not to extend the prohibition of inside information beyond what is appropriate and necessary to attain the goals pursued by that Directive, certain situations may require a thorough examination of the factual circumstances enabling them to be ensured that the use of the inside

[20] On the ethical question see eg Kim L Scheppele, '"It's Just Not Right": The Ethics of Insider Trading' (1993) 56 *Law and Contemporary Problems* 12 and see the discussion in ch 1 above.

[21] Guido Ferrarini, 'The Market Abuse Directive' (2004) 41 *Common Market Law Review* 711.

[22] MAD 2003/6/EC, OJ L 96, 12.4.2003, pp 16–25.

[23] Case C- 68/88 *Commission v Greece* [1989] ECR 1-2965, C Harding, 'European Regimes of Crime Control: Objectives, Legal Bases and Accountability' (2000) 3 *Maastricht Journal of European and Comparative Law* 224.

[24] See eg 'The rotten heart of finance, A scandal over key interest rates is about to go global' *The Economist*, 7 July 2012.

[25] Case C-45/08, *Spector Photo Group* judgment of 23 December 2009.

information is actually unfair so as to be prohibited by the Directive in the name of the integrity of financial markets and investor confidence. The Court stressed in particular that there is a close link between the prohibition on insider dealing and the concept of inside information.[26] The Court also emphasised that capacity to have a significant effect on prices must be assessed, *a priori*, in the light of the content of the information at issue and the context in which it occurs and that it is therefore not necessary, in order to determine whether information is inside information, to examine whether its disclosure actually had a significant effect on the price of the financial instruments to which it relates.[27]

Most of the recent instruments adopted by the EU with the aim of combatting financial crimes have been enacted on the basis and with the justification that there was a need for an increased regulatory response to the 2008 financial crisis, with the concomitant goal of establishing an honest marketplace more generally.[28] Not only is there an overlap here – or hybridity in legal sources – between EU internal market policies and the growing space of the Area of Freedom, Security and Justice (AFSJ, which is the policy area that regulates, eg, criminal law), but a majority of the measures currently adopted have an external dimension as well.

In short, financial regulation in the EU setting is traditionally concerned with market efficiency, transparency and integrity, as well as with consumer protection.[29] In the EU internal market context, the importance of consumer protection and market efficiency has always been part of the EU legislator's vocabulary – particularly with regard to Article 114 TFEU.[30] Interestingly, market regulation and consumer confidence were not a focus of the EU's initial responses to the financial crisis, nor were they reflected on the international agenda.[31] Yet for a long time, as noted, the EU has had preferences for relying on the slogan 'confidence in the market' as an all-embracing justification for approximation under Article 114 TFEU, and where criminal law has been used as a tool for boosting such confidence. When discussing financial regulation it is common to refer to different generations in the financial regulation life-cycle. The first-generation instruments focused on institutional and systemic stability. The so-called 'second generation' moved to a European self-styled architecture for regulatory design where anti-fraud rules are an imperative. Criminal law, as a policy tool for this kind of regulation, forms part of this second generation, and is used to increase confidence and the enhancement of market integrity.

[26] Paragraphs 50–59 of the judgment. See also Langenbucher (n 9).

[27] Paragraph 69.

[28] See, eg, the discussion in Ester Herlin-Karnell, 'White-Collar Crime and European Financial Crises: Getting Tough on EU Market Abuse' (2012) 37 *European Law Review* 487.

[29] For an overview of what it means in the EU context, see Niamh Moloney, 'The Legacy Effects of the Financial Crises on Regulatory Design in the EU' in Ellis Ferran et al (eds), *The Regulatory Aftermath of the Global Financial Crises* (Cambridge, Cambridge University Press, 2012) 111–202.

[30] Niamh Moloney, 'Confidence and Competence: The Conundrum of EC Capital Market Law' (2004) 4 *Journal Corporate Legal Studies* 44.

[31] ibid.

The somewhat over-reliance on confidence as a justification for harmonisation has long been observed (and criticised).[32] In any case, the EU legislator has always claimed that one set of rules – a single rulebook – at the EU level is desirable and, where there are measures in place to fight irregularities, will boost investor confidence and contribute to market making. The fight against financial crimes has always been central for the EU as it has been so intimately connected to the construction of the EU market. The idea is, moreover, that investors and consumers would be discouraged if the EU budget were to be corrupted. There are, then, multiple reasons for the EU to be actively engaged in the countering of financial crimes: from the functioning of the market and increasing consumer confidence in the market, to protecting the EU's budget against fraud.[33]

The notion of market confidence at the EU level is often viewed as a matter of public interest and as essential at a macroeconomic level for the proper functioning of the market.[34] In the EU, investor protection is connected with the promotion of investor confidence. Although such protection could be driven by more paternalistic concerns, investor protection regulation seeks primarily to address market failures that hinder the attainment of investor protection.[35] Notwithstanding this, it is arguably interesting to consider the notion of paternalistic legislation in a bit more detail, as it could be questioned. In this respect, since the justification behind the EU intervention in this area seems to be that EU investors should be protected from themselves, it reveals characteristics similar to those of criminal law theory and paternalistic legislation as a justification for criminalisation.[36]

At the core of the matter in the present context is whether financial crimes such as market abuse undermine the confidence of the market at all. As Moloney has pointed out, the CJEU has already accepted a link between investor confidence and the smooth operation of securities markets – this is the ruling of *Alpine Investments*.[37] Indeed, it should be recalled that in this case the Court held:

> Financial markets play an important role in the financing of economic operators and, given the speculative nature and the complexity of commodities futures contracts, the smooth operation of financial markets is largely contingent on the confidence they inspire in investors. That confidence depends in particular on the existence of professional regulations serving to ensure the competence and trustworthiness of the financial intermediaries on whom investors are particularly reliant.[38]

The point here is that the phenomenon of market abuse is, then, tied to the risk of market failure. So the rationale for prohibiting insider dealing and market manipulation at the EU level is to achieve a unilateral system and thereby prevent

[32] eg Moloney (n 16).
[33] For more on this, see Gómez-Jara Díez and Herlin-Karnell (n 7).
[34] Moloney (n 16) at 931.
[35] ibid.
[36] See eg Lindsay Farmer, *The Making of the Modern Criminal Law: Criminalization and Civil Order* (Oxford, Oxford University Press, 2016) ch 1.
[37] Case C-384/93 *Alpine Investments* [1997] ECR I-1141.
[38] ibid, para 42.

market failure.[39] Manipulative practices are a form of market failure, which ultimately leads to an inefficient allocation of resources and damages the market place in capital allocation. Hence, the slogan 'confidence in the market' as an all-embracing justification for approximation under Article 114 TFEU has been tied to the use of criminal law which has been used as a tool for boosting such confidence in the market.

Because of the previous lack of competence in criminal law matters at the EU supranational level, the fight against financial crimes has traditionally taken place within the framework of the market creation provision of Article 114 TFEU (for the establishment of the internal market). The claim of the EU legislator has been that the rulebook needs to be changed so as to increase investor confidence in the market. For example, in the Commission's Communication on 'Driving European recovery',[40] the Commission referred to the High Level Group on Financial Supervision, which stressed the importance of confidence, which was taken for granted in well-functioning financial systems but had been lost in the present crisis.[41] But why is the fight against market abuse a question for the EU?

In order to understand why the EU regulates the suppression of market abuse and the links between the AFSJ and the EU internal market, we need to place them in the context of how EU criminal law and the regime on EU law sanctions developed. A very important axiom for the development of the EU regime to counter market abuse is that of the principle of loyal cooperation. The principle of loyalty under Article 4(3) of the Treaty on European Union (TEU), in interaction with the general principles of EU law, traditionally constituted the corollary to the classic relationship between national criminal law and the EU and the question of how the EU fights financial crimes.[42] Likewise, this principle has been the main driver for the enforcement of administrative sanctions, as it obliged Member States to ensure compliance with EU law. Thus the crucial question is whether, in practice, Member States have had a real choice in refraining from harmonising their criminal laws, while still providing for 'dissuasive and effective' sanctions.[43] However, the main significance of loyalty was always that a Member State did not have the option of choosing to do nothing about a certain situation just because its national law was ineffective. After all, the classic loyalty principle required Member States to amend any conflicting legislation in accordance with the *Greek Maize*[44] formula outlined above, taking measures 'which in any event make the penalty dissuasive, effective and proportionate'.[45]

[39] See Moloney (n 30).

[40] COM/2009/0114 final.

[41] The High Level Group on Financial Supervision in the EU available at http://ec.europa.eu/economy_finance/publications/pages/publication14527_en.pdf (last accessed November 2018) and Moloney (n 30).

[42] On EU loyalty, see, eg, Marcus Klamert, *The Principle of Loyalty in EU Law* (Oxford, Oxford University Press, 2014).

[43] eg André Klip, *European Criminal Law* (Antwerp, Intersentia, 2015).

[44] Case C-68/88 *Commission v Greece* [1989] ECR I-2965.

[45] Herlin-Karnell (n 3) ch 2.

Therefore, and as will be discussed more fully in chapter three, the administrative sanctions grid has played an important role in expanding the competences of the EU and, thereby, prior to the Lisbon Treaty, made possible a quasi-criminal law system at the expense of the due process safeguards traditionally associated with criminal law (such as the right to a fair trial under Article 6 of the European Convention on Human Rights (ECHR)). More recently, these administrative sanctions have also played a predominant role with regard to financial law regulation and the aim of ensuring increased compliance in the Member States. Interestingly, in a different context, namely in the case of economic sanctions, the UK (and if for a moment disregarding the politics of Brexit), which otherwise enjoys an opt-out with regard to criminal cooperation under Protocol No 22, has stated that it will always participate in any adoption of administrative sanctions under the framework of Article 75 TFEU to fight terrorism-related activity.[46]

Consequently, the use of sanctions in EU law, as noted, has always been shaped by the mantra of 'effectiveness, proportionality and dissuasiveness', and has dictated the EU's competence to impose restrictions on Member States and – most importantly – limited the Member States' freedom in this area.

Against this background of the complex regime for sanctions at the EU level and the development of an anti-market abuse regime at the EU level, regarding the fight against market abuse in EU law, through the Lamfalussy Process and the legislative activity that followed at the EU level is interesting here.[47] The Lamfalussy regulatory approach involved four institutional levels: the European Parliament and the Council; the Commission; committees of national supervisors; and additional power granted to the Commission to assess the responses by Member States. In the wake of the financial crisis, the EU reformed its framework for financial supervision.[48] It established a new European Systemic Risk Board (ESRB) for monitoring macro-prudential risks and transformed the level 3 Lamfalussy committees into independent authorities with enhanced powers.[49]

Most of the discussion in this context has concerned 'hardcore' financial regulation and processes, but it has now been extended to cover the area of sanctions too. The Markets in Financial Instruments Directive (MiFID I and II) has

[46] Declaration by the United Kingdom on Art 75 of the TFEU. Official Journal 115, 09/05/2008 P. 0359–0359.

[47] A specific regulatory process in financial services was first introduced in 2001, when the EU endorsed the proposals of the Lamfalussy Report. This report recommended the adoption of a new approach to improve the regulatory process in financial services in order to make it quicker and more effective. See the Commission's website, https://ec.europa.eu/info/business-economy-euro/banking-and-finance/financial-reforms-and-their-progress/regulatory-process-financial-services/regulatory-process-financial-services_en.

[48] See at https://ec.europa.eu/info/business-economy-euro/banking-and-finance/financial-reforms-and-their-progress/regulatory-process-financial-services/regulatory-process-financial-services_en (last accessed November 2018).

[49] See the discussion in eg E Grossman and P Leblond, 'European integration: finally the great leap forward' (2011) 49 *Journal of Common Market Studies* 413.

been the most important instrument here, reshaping the EU's share-trading market place and largely based on influence from various interests groups.[50] The MiFID regime applies to the provision of investment services or activities by banks and investment firms in relation to financial instruments and to the operation of regulated markets. For example, MiFID I led to clashes between the stock exchange and the brokerage sectors.[51] The system was subsequently reformed. MiFID II has introduced a market structure framework that claims to be closing loopholes and thereby ensures that trading, wherever appropriate, takes place on regulated (EU) platforms.[52]

In addition, MiFID II aims to ensure a level playing field for regulated markets and strengthens the supervisory powers of competent authorities supervised by the European Securities and Markets Authority (ESMA). The original objectives of MiFID were to improve the resilience of EU financial markets through free competition and high levels of market transparency and investor protection. But this was not enough. According to the Commission, a harmonised system of strengthened cooperation will improve the effective detection of breaches of MiFID. Moreover, according to the Commission, the Market Abuse Directive and MiFID II together guarantee the competitiveness, efficiency and integrity of EU financial markets. In order to ensure that they are fully coherent and support each other's objectives and principles, they need to be updated in tandem. Such a conjunctive approach has, however, led to some difficulties with regard to the impact of regulation in the AFSJ and its relationship to internal market policies, due to largely separate competence provisions.

Moreover, trading venues shall ensure that arrangements, systems and procedures are in place to prevent and detect market abuse or attempted market abuse in relation to such negotiated transactions in accordance with Article 16 of the Market Abuse Regulation. Interestingly, as is pointed out in the recital in MiFID II, the use of trading technology has evolved significantly throughout the past decade and is now used extensively by market participants. For example, as the EU legislator points out, risks arising from algorithmic trading should be regulated.

[50] MiFID I Directive 2004/39/EC of the European Parliament and of the Council of 21 April 2004 on markets in financial instruments amending Council Directives 85/611/EEC and 93/6/EEC and Directive 2000/12/EC of the European Parliament and of the Council and repealing Council Directive 93/22/EEC, OJ L 145, 30.4.2004, pp 1–44. MiFID II, Directive 2014/65/EU of the European Parliament and of the Council of 15 May 2014 on markets in financial instruments and amending Directive 2002/92/EC and Directive 2011/61/EU, OJ L 173, 12.6.2014.

[51] See the discussion in Guido Ferrarini and Niamh Moloney, 'Reshaping order execution in the EU and the Rule of interest groups: from MiFID I to MiFID II' (2012) 13 *European Business Organization Law Review* 557.

[52] http://europa.eu/rapid/press-release_MEMO-14-15_en.htm?locale=en. MiFID II comprises two levels of European legislation. The EU Parliament voted on MiFID II 'Level 1' in April 2014, the framework legislation consisted of two linked pieces of legislation: MiFID II and the Markets in Financial Instruments Regulation (MiFIR), Regulation (EU) No 600/2014 of the European Parliament and of the Council of 15 May 2014 on markets in financial instruments and amending Regulation (EU) No 648/2012, OJ L 173, 12.6.2014, pp 84–148.

An investment firm that engages in algorithmic trading pursuing a market-making strategy should carry out that market making continuously during a specified proportion of the trading venue's trading hours. Regulatory technical standards should clarify what constitutes a specified proportion of the trading venue's trading hours by ensuring that such specified proportion is significant in comparison to the total trading hours, taking into account the liquidity, scale and nature of the specific market and the characteristics of the financial instrument traded.

As Moloney explains, while investor confidence in the market place is notoriously difficult to assess, in the insider-dealing context it is often linked to confidence in market egalitarianism or the confidence of investors in the equality of access to information in the market place.[53] Market egalitarianism is commonly defined as meaning that 'people should be treated as equals, should treat one another as equals, should relate as equals, or enjoy an equality of social status of some sort'.[54] For Moloney the idea of market egalitarianism in the EU regime requires that in the context of impersonal markets and trading venues, investors should deal on a relatively equal basis with equal opportunities to access information, and should not be unfairly disadvantaged by dealings on the part of those with special access to non-public information. Market-efficiency-based arguments have of course been subject to extensive critique.[55] Furthermore, in relation to market integrity and transparency, Article 31 of MiFid II makes it clear that, inter alia, Member States shall require investment firms and market operators operating an multilateral trading facility COM (2010) 716 (Communication) (MFT) or an organised trading facility (OFT) to assist authorities when investigating and prosecuting market abuse occurring on or through its systems.

III. The EU Legislative Framework to Fight Market Abuse

The Market Abuse Directive is the first use of Article 83(2) TFEU.[56] Article 83(1) TFEU sets out a list of crimes in respect of which the EU shall have legislative competence such as terrorism, organised crime and money laundering. It also

[53] See Moloney (n 16) at 702.

[54] R Arneson, 'Egalitarianism' in EN Zalta (ed), *The Stanford Encyclopedia of Philosophy* (Summer 2013), available at https://plato.stanford.edu/archives/sum2013/entries/egalitarianism/.

[55] Harry Manne, 'In Defense of Insider Trading' (1966) *Harvard Business Law Review* November–December 113, discussed in Moloney (n 16) 701. Moloney points out that in a controversial and agenda-setting work, Manne argued against the prohibition of insider dealing given its beneficial effects on price formation and given its efficiency as an executive compensation device in providing entrepreneurs with stronger performance incentives and in overcoming agency costs. Manne argued that insider dealing ultimately moved prices steadily in the right direction, benefited long-term investors (including uninformed investors), harmed only speculators and increased confidence in the price-formation mechanism.

[56] MAD (n 1).

states that the Council may identify other possible areas of crime that meet the cross-border and seriousness criteria. However, interestingly, Article 83(2) establishes that the possibility exists for approximation if a measure proves essential towards ensuring the effective implementation of a Union policy in an area that has already been subject to harmonisation measures. So Article 83(2) TFEU is interesting as it provides for a more extensive competence than what one may think at first glance.

As explained above, market abuse is the umbrella label used to define insider dealing and market manipulation. In short, and to reiterate, it may arise in circumstances where investors have been unreasonably disadvantaged, directly or indirectly, by others who have used information which is not publicly available to trade in financial instruments to their advantage (insider dealing), have distorted the price-setting mechanism of financial instruments, or have disseminated false or misleading information.[57] There have been concerns raised about lack of clarification in this area.[58]

Consequently, the merits of the EU Market Abuse regime and its feasibility have been intensely debated.[59] As noted, the first Directive was adopted in 2003 and it introduced a comprehensive framework to tackle insider dealing and to boost investor confidence in the market by prohibiting those who possess inside information from trading in related financial instruments.[60] The 2003 Directive combined market manipulation and insider dealing in the same measure as market abuse related misconduct. As mentioned in chapter one, the ban on insider dealing in modern European law has its roots in the US where the courts developed it based on the general provisions on fraud.[61] The EU regime has subsequently developed into its own somewhat unique regulatory framework. The debate in connection with the 2003 Directive was centred around the question of whether the 'confidence in the market' slogan fitted Article 114 TFEU and how the fight against market abuse could be linked to it. The problem with the 2003 Directive, according to commentators, was that it was not really aimed at market making but the prohibition of the manipulation prohibition aimed to protect market efficiency in general.[62] So the burning issue here has been if

[57] Directive 2014/57/EU. See the vague definition as provided in the Proposal for a Directive on criminal sanctions for insider dealing and market manipulation, COM (2011) 654 final. See also Matthias Siems and Matthijs Nelemans, 'The Reform of the Market Abuse Law: Revolution or Evolution?' (2012) 19 *Maastricht Journal of European and Comparative Law* 195.

[58] Richard Alexander, *Insider Dealing and Money Laundering in the EU: Law and Regulation* (Aldershot, Ashgate, 2007).

[59] eg Niamh Moloney, 'Investor protection and the Treaty' in Guido Ferrarini and others (eds), *Capital markets in the age of the Euro* (The Hague, Kluwer Law, 2003) 17.

[60] Directive 2003/6/EC of the European Parliament and the Council of 28 January 2003 on insider dealing and market manipulation (market abuse), OJ L 96, 12.4.2003, p 16.

[61] Eric Engle, 'Global norm convergence: capital market in US and EU law' (2010) 21 *European Business Law Review* 465.

[62] Guido Ferrarini, 'The Market Abuse Directive' (2004) 41 *Common Market Law Review* 711.

market abuse distorts the market at all.[63] For example, Ferrarini pointed out that the Directive was not ambitious enough as the EU legislator simply stated that increased prevention could not be sufficiently achieved by the Member States and could therefore by reason of the scale and effects of it be better achieved at the EU level.[64] In short, the main source of criticism has been that there have been shortages in sophisticated arguments as presented by the EU Commission as reasons for legislation.

Despite the specific competences under Article 83(1–2) TFEU to fight financial crime, 'mainstream' internal market powers, such as Article 114 TFEU, are still of crucial importance and are particularly significant with respect to the impact in the national arena as this provision also allows for the adoption of regulations – which are directly effective without the need for implementation into national law.

The chapter will now turn to look more specifically at the Market Abuse Directive and the Market Abuse Regulation measures in the EU adopted in 2014. These instruments demonstrate the use of Article 83 TFEU and Article 114 TFEU respectively as the legal basis for the legislation. What is novel with respect to the reformation of the EU anti-market abuse regime is that the Directive creates a new framework for the purposes of fighting crime while it regroups the previous Market Abuse Directive regime into a separate Regulation to increase the effectiveness of the system.

A. The 2014 Directive

The 2014 Directive is to a great extent part of the attempts by the EU to increase confidence in the market and thereby boost trust and increase economic activity. The Directive argues that market integrity is needed for the smooth functioning of the internal market. The EU adopted it on the basis of the claim that the adoption of administrative sanctions has proved insufficient and cross-referred in its legislative proposal to the Commission's Communication on reinforcing regimes in the financial sector.[65] It appears less clear why the Directive is based on Article 83(2) TFEU at all and not Article 114 TFEU governing the internal market. In other words, you could cautiously ask yourself whether the Commission will from now on be able to pass legislation relating to the internal market more easily under Article 83(2) TFEU compared to Article 114 TFEU. In any case, the Directive claims to be boosting confidence in the market and ensuring investor protection. The 2014 Directive raises three intriguing issues. First, the

[63] See, e.g, Ester Herlin-Karnell, 'Is there more to it than the fight against Dirty Money? Article 95 and the criminal law' (2008) 19 *European Business Law Review* 558.

[64] Guido Ferrarini, 'The Market Abuse Directive' (2004) 41 *Common Market Law Review* 711.

[65] Commission, Reinforcing regimes in the financial sector COM (2010) 716 (Communication).

question arises as to the feasibility of criminal law to secure the integrity of the market at all. Secondly, the issue of the adequacy of the legal basis for the proposed instruments as well as the desirability of double measures in this area needs to be considered. And, thirdly, the issue of fundamental rights protection and the increased preventive focus as witnessed particularly with regard to the Regulation and its far-reaching requirements for the Member States to have surveillance mechanisms in place must be addressed.

The Directive is a prime example of the invocation of criminal law to guarantee effectiveness of European policies in this area. The purpose of the Directive seems to be to move closer to the objective of a single rulebook.[66] More specifically, according to the Commission the adoption of administrative sanctions in combination with the divergent approach in the Member States has proved insufficient. Thus, something needs to be done to increase the effectiveness of the regime and boost investor confidence and the question is if criminal law could offer that magic solution?

The justification for the adoption of the Directive is that it is stated that the Market Abuse Directive system has proved insufficient and that supervisory authorities must be equipped with sufficient powers and that the Member States' sanctioning regimes are regarded as, in general, weak and heterogeneous. According to the Commission, market abuse can be carried out across borders and this divergence undermines the internal market and leaves a certain scope for perpetrators of market abuse to carry such abuse in jurisdictions which do not provide for criminal sanctions for a particular offence. The Directive wants to change this by adding criminal law to the discussion and thereby fighting market abuse more effectively.

Nevertheless, the Directive argues that criminal sanctions to fight market manipulation and insider dealing are needed as a tool for the smooth functioning of the internal market and in particular to ensure market integrity. Yet, the problem is that the EU legislator does not define market integrity, though the Directive turns on it. As is stated in the recital to the preamble 'Market abuse harms the integrity of financial markets and public confidence in securities, derivatives and benchmarks.'[67] Commonly the term market integrity is however negatively defined as 'the extent to which investors engage in prohibited trading behaviour'.[68] The difficulty is however that the absence of abuse does not necessarily lead to

[66] See SEC (2011) 1217 final, Commission staff working paper, 'Impact assessment accompanying the proposals for a Regulation and a Directive on market abuse'. See also more generally, Niamh Moloney, 'EU Financial market regulation after the global financial crises: More Europe or more risks?' (2010) 47 *Common Market Law Review* 1317.

[67] Recital 1, Directive 2014/15.

[68] Michael Aitken et al, 'Trade-Based Manipulation and Market Efficiency: A Cross-Market Comparison', available at http://citeseerx.ist.psu.edu/viewdoc/download?doi=10.1.1.629.2355&rep=rep1&type=pdf (last accessed January 2019).

integrity. Still, the need to ensure integrity in the market seems inexorably linked to the question of confidence in the market.

But why then is the Directive based on Article 83(2) TFEU and not Article 114 TFEU governing the internal market one may ask?[69] Although it is true that Article 114 TFEU is residual to other specific legal basis, it could be argued that Article 114 TFEU would have been a more appropriate legal basis here. There is at least one reason for this. An interpretation of Article 83(2) TFEU, with no threshold at all in terms of market creation will become an even lower test than that of Article 114 TFEU.[70] This is arguably the case even if the post Tobacco Advertising cases[71] have similarly confirmed the European preference for 'when in doubt legislate' by not paying much tribute to the legislative limits as set by the Treaties: namely conferral, subsidiarity and proportionality. There is a further possible candidate here, namely Article 325 TFEU. This provision stipulates that the Union and the Member States shall counter fraud and any other illegal activities affecting the financial interests of the Union through measures to be taken in accordance with this Article, which shall act as a deterrent and be such as to afford effective protection in the Member States, and in all the Union's institutions, bodies, offices and agencies.

B. The 2014 Regulation

Interestingly, the Regulation[72] sets out to regulate the same area as the Directive but is in a way stricter than the Directive. The Regulation is closely associated with the so-called MiFID, Markets in Financial Instruments Directive, reform and is intended to enter into force at the same time as the current changes to MiFID review.[73] Hence the Regulation follows the same trend as the Commission's communication on 'Ensuring efficient, safe and sound derivatives markets: Future policy actions' where the Commission undertook to extend relevant provisions of the Market Abuse Directive in order to cover derivatives markets in a comprehensive fashion.[74]

As for the legal basis of the Regulation, the Commission stated in its legislative proposal for the measure that 'There is a need to establish a uniform framework in

[69] See Jacob Öberg for a different view than the one presented here, *Regulatory Competences in EU Criminal Law* (Oxford, Hart Publishing, 2017) for a recent case study of the EU market abuse regime.

[70] Herlin-Karnell (n 29).

[71] Case C-376/98 *Germany v Parliament and Council* [2000] ECR 1-8419, Case 58/08, *Vodafone*, judgment of 8 June 2010 nyr, see Stephen Weatherill, 'The limits of legislative harmonisation ten years after Tobacco Advertising: how the Court's case law has become a "drafting guide"' (2011) 12 *German Law Journal* 827.

[72] Regulation (EU) No 596/2014.

[73] Directive 2004/39/EC, markets in financial instruments, OJ L 145 21 April 2004.

[74] COM (2009) 332, 3 July 2009, European Commission, Communication on Ensuring efficient, safe and sound derivatives markets.

order to preserve market integrity and to avoid potential regulatory arbitrage as well as to provide more legal certainty and less regulatory complexity for market participants'.[75] Hence, the justification for the adoption of the Regulation is the same as for the Directive, albeit with different legal basis, namely Article 114 TFEU. It aims at contributing to the smooth functioning of the internal market. Recently the Commission has also suggested a change to the Regulation. Specifically, the proposal limits the current obligation to produce lists of persons who have access to price-sensitive information (insider list) and only have to produce lists of a more limited group of people having regular access to inside information (permanent insiders).[76] According to the Commission this alleviates the administrative burden on SMEs while ensuring that competent authorities preserve their ability to investigate cases of insider trading in order to ensure market integrity.

Why then the need for this dual approach with both a Directive and a Regulation to fight market abuse? Although it is true that it follows a similar pattern to that of anti-money laundering, where the directives[77] also based on Article 114 TFEU are complemented by a Regulation concerning the control of cash entering and leaving the Community and is aimed to supplement the Directive in question.[78] Regardless, it could be argued that this multi-level approach leads to unnecessary complexity and is therefore not in line with the 'less is more' – better and smart regulation – mantra in EU law. For example, the Council has adopted a Regulation aimed at improving controls on cash entering or leaving the Union following an agreement reached with the European Parliament.[79] As the Council points out, the existing rules require travellers entering or leaving the EU to declare cash amounting to €10,000 or more (or its equivalent) to customs authorities. The Regulation introduces administrative sanctions by stipulating that financial markets are increasingly integrated in the Union and offences can have cross-border effects in the Union. The existing divergent sanctioning regimes among Member States foster regulatory arbitrage and impair the ultimate objectives of market integrity and transparency within the Single Market for financial services.[80]

Nevertheless, it could seriously be questioned if the dual regulation with criminal law sanctions and administrative sanctions in Regulation and Directive

[75] COM (2011) 651 final, Proposal for a Regulation on insider dealing and market manipulation, adopted as MAR (n 2).

[76] Proposal for A Regulation of The European Parliament and of the Council amending Regulations (EU) No 596/2014 and (EU) 2017/1129 as regards the promotion of the use of SME growth markets, COM/2018/331 final – 2018/0165 (COD), Capital Markets Union: Making it easier for smaller businesses to get financing through capital markets, Brussels, 24 May 2018.

[77] As introduced by the third money laundering Directive, Directive 2005/60/EC OJ L309/15, 25 November 2005.

[78] Cash Controls Regulation 1889/2005.

[79] Draft Regulation of the European Parliament and of the Council on controls on cash entering or leaving the Union and repealing Regulation (EC) No 1889/200, 2016/0413 (COD).

[80] ibid.

respectively breaches the principle of *ne bis in idem* or double jeopardy and thereby Article 50 in the Charter of Fundamental Rights. Article 50 states that 'No one shall be liable to be tried or punished again in criminal proceedings for an offence for which he or she has already been finally acquitted or convicted within the Union in accordance with the law.'[81] Traditionally the notion of *ne bis in idem* only applies to criminal law. Yet it could be argued that such an approach leads to a fundamentally unfair system and that the proportionality principle has an important role to play here so as to avoid double procedures. Interestingly the Regulation claims in its preamble 39 that it respects the principles laid down in the Charter and thereby also *ne bis in idem* with regard to sanctions in the Regulation, but nothing is said as regards the relationship between the proposed Directive and the Regulation in this regard. It is to be hoped that the principle of proportionality will play a key role here in order to avoid double sanctions. The question of *ne bis in idem* will be discussed further in chapter three below.

C. Some Pertinent Questions Raised by the Directive and the Regulation[82]

While the Market Abuse Directive and the Market Abuse Regulation have been in force since 2014 they still give rise to a host of questions. From a technocratic point of view, it may still be argued that it remains unclear as to why the Directive is based on Article 83(2) TFEU and not Article 114 TFEU governing the internal market. Although it is true that Article 114 TFEU is residual to other specific legal bases, it could be argued that Article 114 TFEU would have been a more appropriate legal basis here. There is at least one reason for this, and as mentioned above: an interpretation of Article 83(2) TFEU with no threshold at all in terms of market creation will become an even lower test than that of Article 114 TFEU.

However, from a Member State perspective, there is a merit with respect to engaging Article 83(2) TFEU as compared to action taken under Article 114 TFEU, in that this provision grants the possibility for the Member States to pull an emergency brake if a proposed measure appears to be too sensitive for the national criminal law system. Moreover, use of Article 114 or Article 325 TFEU would mean that the UK (regardless of Brexit) and Ireland would not have the 'cherry-picking' possibility of opt-outs as they otherwise would regarding legislation within the AFSJ (in accordance with Protocol 21).[83] Regardless, it does not answer the question as to what extent it should be possible to use

[81] See eg, E Herlin-Karnell (n 28).

[82] This section draws partly on Herlin-Karnell (n 28).

[83] Protocol No 21 attached to the Lisbon Treaty. According to Arts 1 and 3 of this protocol, the UK and Ireland do not take part in legislation adopted within the AFSJ unless they opt to participate in such legislation by notifying the President of the Council in writing within three months after a proposal or initiative has been presented to the Council.

Article 83(2) TFEU to legislate for confidence in the market, the merits of the emergency brake notwithstanding.

In addition, it is worth asking if it would be desirable to have a dual legal basis for the adoption of the Directive or whether such an approach would lead to a conflict in legal basis. Typically, a dispute of conflicting legal basis has been resolved by recourse to the centre of gravity test.[84] As regards Article 114 TFEU, there is however no real centre of gravity test available, the question resting rather on whether the measure at issue contributes to market creation at all.[85] Consequently, it could be argued that the proposed Directive could have been based on Article 114 TFEU if a sufficiently strong market creation link could be demonstrated (which, in any event, seems largely absent under Article 83(2) TFEU).

In the proposal leading up to the Market Abuse Regulation,[86] the Commission had pointed out that the Charter of Fundamental Rights establishes some important exceptions in Article 52 to the application of the rights granted by the Charter and, as such, the right to privacy and to an effective remedy. Article 52 makes it clear that 'Any limitation on the exercise of the rights and freedoms recognized by this Charter must be provided for by law and respect the essence of those rights and freedoms. Subject to the principle of proportionality, limitations may be made only if they are necessary and genuinely meet objectives of general interest recognized by the Union or the need to protect the rights and freedoms of others.' So under the Charter, unlike the European Convention of Human Rights (ECHR), the general 'limitation clause' in Article 52 and its proportionality test applies to all rights.[87] For this reason, the Commission argued that access to data and telephone records is necessary to provide evidence and investigative leads on possible insider dealing or market manipulation, and therefore for the detection and sanctioning of market abuse.[88]

There are two dangers here. First, there is a risk that what will emerge in this area is something similar to a margin of appreciation test as developed in the ECHR case law[89] and that the proportionality test as set out in Article 52 might 'lose out' too easily unless strictly applied. Secondly, the Commission in its initial proposal for the legislation seems to forget the existence of Article 49 of the Charter, which stipulates that the severity of penalties applied must not be disproportionate to the criminal offence. It should be very difficult to derogate from the right to a proportionate penalty as stipulated in Article 49 of the Charter as it sets out a different kind of proportionality not really encompassed by Article 52. Although it is true

[84] Case C-300/89 *Commission v Council* [1991] ECR I-2867.

[85] eg Markus Ludwigs, Annotation C-380/03, (2007) 44 *Common Market Law Review* 1159.

[86] COM (2011) 651 final, Proposal for a Regulation on insider dealing and market manipulation.

[87] Sionaidh Douglas-Scott, 'The EU and Human Rights after the Treaty of Lisbon' (2011) 11 *Human Rights Law Review* 645.

[88] COM (2011) 651 final, Proposal for a Regulation on insider dealing and market manipulation.

[89] See eg Massimo Fichera and Ester Herlin-Karnell, 'The Margin of Appreciation and Balancing in the Area of Freedom Security and Justice' (2013) *European Public Law* 759.

that the Market Abuse Regulation does not deal with 'criminal law' sanctions, the effect of these sanctions comes very close to that of criminal law and should be regarded as criminal law following the classic Engel criteria.[90] According to these criteria, there should be an autonomous interpretation of sanctions and the consequences of the sanction in question should form the guiding dictum for how to conceptualise it. It could be argued that the proposed Regulation breaches proportionality requirements and that Article 49 of the Charter should apply also to the sanctions prescribed in the Regulation.[91]

In addition, the Directive and the Regulation are complemented by the Benchmark Regulation adopted in 2016.[92] This Regulation introduces a common framework to ensure the accuracy and integrity of indices used as benchmarks in financial instruments and financial contracts, or to measure the performance of investment funds in the Union. This Regulation thereby contributes to the proper functioning of the internal market while achieving a high level of consumer and investor protection. The concept of benchmark means any index by reference to which the amount is payable under a financial instrument or financial contract, or the value of a financial instrument.

In essence, the Regulation sets out to ensure that benchmark administrators are subject to prior authorisation and ongoing supervision depending on the type of benchmark (eg, commodity or interest-rate benchmarks); requiring greater transparency of how a benchmark is produced; ensuring the appropriate supervision of critical benchmarks, such as EURIBOR/LIBOR, the failure of which might create risks for many market participants and even for the functioning and integrity of markets of financial stability. It also states that the European Securities and Markets Authority (ESMA) shall develop draft regulatory technical standards to specify the procedures regarding the oversight function and the characteristics of the oversight function including its composition as well as its positioning within the organisational structure of the administrator, so as to ensure the integrity of the function and the absence of conflicts of interest.

D. Reporting Obligations and Market Abuse

Similarly to the Anti-Money Laundering Directives and their focus on risk regulation and preventive strategies in combating dirty money,[93] discussed further in

[90] ECHR *Engel and others v the Netherlands*, 8 June 1976 Series A n 22.

[91] For a strict interpretation of the 'Engel test' eg, Case C-489/10 *Bonda*, judgment of 5 June 2012 confirming previous case law, eg C-210/00 *Kaserei Champignon Hofmeister* [2002] ECR I-6453 that administrative sanctions are of a non-criminal law nature.

[92] Regulation (EU) 2016/1011 of the European Parliament and of the Council of 8 June 2016 on indices used as benchmarks in financial instruments and financial contracts or to measure the performance of investment funds and amending Directives 2008/48/EC and 2014/17/EU and Regulation (EU) No 596/2014, OJ L 171, 29.6.2016, pp 1–65.

[93] Directive (EU) 2018/843 of the European Parliament and of the Council of 30 May 2018 amending Directive (EU) 2015/849 on the prevention of the use of the financial system for the purposes of money

chapter five below, Article 17(5) of the Market Abuse Directive states that: 'the investment firm shall monitor the transactions in order to identify infringements of those rules, disorderly trading conditions or conduct that may involve market abuse and that is to be reported to the competent authority. The investment firm shall ensure that there is a binding written agreement between the investment firm and the client regarding the essential rights and obligations arising from the provision of the service and that under the agreement the investment firm retains responsibility under this Directive.'

Furthermore, the Market Abuse Regulation authorises and empowers competent authorities to access telephone and existing data traffic records held by a telecommunication operator or by an investment firm, competent authorities should be able to request existing telephone and existing data traffic records held by a telecommunication operator or by an investment firm, where a reasonable suspicion exists. Competent authorities are furthermore required to report suspicious activity. The link between money laundering and other financial crimes in the EU context will be discussed further in chapter four below.

The rationale for actively engaging the private sector in for example the anti-money laundering scheme is to make them collect the appropriate information. The reference to a risk-based approach is however absent in the Market Abuse Directive context. Nevertheless, the Market Abuse Regulation, for example, imposes a very far-reaching supervisory regime by stating that telephone and data traffic records from telecom operators constitute crucial (and sometimes the only) evidence to detect and prove the existence of market abuse. It could be questioned whether is this is in line with Article 16 TFEU and Article 8 EU Charter on the right to data protection respectively. In addition, Declaration 21 attached to the Lisbon Treaty states that specific rules on the protection of personal data and the free movement of such data in the fields of judicial cooperation in criminal matters and police cooperation based on Article 16 TFEU may prove necessary because of the specific nature of these fields.

More generally, the prevention of crime in the EU offers an example of security issues put to the test in the context of the protection of human rights and personal data.[94] Interestingly, Recital 74 of the Market Abuse Regulation states that:

> Whistleblowers may bring new information to the attention of competent authorities which assists them in detecting and imposing sanctions in cases of insider dealing and market manipulation. However, whistleblowing may be deterred for fear of retaliation, or for lack of incentives. Reporting of infringements of this Regulation is necessary to ensure that a competent authority may detect and impose sanctions for market abuse.

laundering or terrorist financing, and amending Directives 2009/138/EC and 2013/36/EU, 2018 OJ (L 156) 43–74. The risk-based approach has been highly controversial in connection with the adoption of the Third Money Laundering Directive in 2005.

[94] COM (2012) 9 final, Safeguarding Privacy in a Connected World A European Data Protection Framework for the 21st Century.

> Measures regarding whistleblowing are necessary to facilitate detection of market abuse and to ensure the protection and the respect of the rights of the whistleblower and the accused person. This Regulation should therefore ensure that adequate arrangements are in place to enable whistleblowers to alert competent authorities to possible infringements of this Regulation and to protect them from retaliation. … Member States should also ensure that whistleblowing schemes that they implement include mechanisms that provide appropriate protection of an accused person, particularly with regard to the right to the protection of his personal data and procedures to ensure the right of the accused person of defence and to be heard before the adoption of a decision concerning him as well as the right to seek effective remedy before a court against a decision concerning him.

A further matter of interest here is the issue of publication of sanctions as well as allowing competent authorities far-reaching powers similar to those of competition law raids and anti-terrorism measures. It could be argued that the Market Abuse Regulation brings us very close to the area of competition law, by imposing an (as outlined in Articles 12–15 of the Regulation) obligation for issuers of financial instruments to issue so-called listing of companies or individuals engaged in market abuse. Furthermore, as mentioned, it authorises and empowers competent authorities, required to be set up by the Member States (Article 16) for the purposes of the Regulation, to access telephone and existing data traffic records held by a telecommunications operator or by an investment firm. Accordingly, competent authorities should be able to require these records. Yet in accordance with Article 34 of the Regulation there is a possibility for a competent authority to (inter alia) consider – on a case by case basis and in the light of the principle of proportionality – if the publication of a decision to list an infringement of the Market Abuse Regulation would jeopardise an ongoing investigation or the financial market. In such cases the competent authority can decide to defer the publication of a decision to impose an administrative sanction.

Moreover, the Commission has recently suggested a new specific Directive for the protection of whistleblowers,[95] of relevance to the legislative framework for tackling market abuse at the EU level, where it is stated that the lack of whistleblower protection in a Member State can have a negative impact on the functioning of EU policies in that Member State, but also impact on other Member States. Hence, according to the Commission, by introducing new provisions on whistleblower protection it strengthens the proper functioning of the single market. Indeed, recital 18 in the proposed Directive cross refers to the Regulation by stating that certain Union acts, in particular in the area of financial services, such as market abuse, already contain detailed rules on whistleblower protection. The Commission points out that it is of particular importance to ascertain which

[95] COM (2018) 218 final on the protection of persons reporting on breaches of Union law.

legal entities in the area of financial services, the prevention of money laundering and terrorist financing are currently obliged to establish internal reporting channels. The Directive mentions that some bodies, offices and agencies of the Union, such as the European Anti-Fraud Office (OLAF) have in place external channels and procedures for receiving reports on breaches falling within the scope of this Directive, which mainly provide for confidentiality of the identity of the reporting persons. Also the European Public Prosecutor's Office (EPPO Regulation) stipulates in its recital (50) that whistleblowers may bring new information to the attention of the EPPO.[96] This confirms an interesting dynamic with regard to the accountability of EPPO and OLAF and other EU Agencies handling this kind of information, discussed further in chapter five below.

IV. Criminal Liability for Legal Persons – A Brief Overview

Both the Market Abuse Directive and the Market Abuse Regulation impose criminal liability on legal persons. The problem is that that not all Member States recognise criminal liability for legal persons, still there are a number of examples in secondary legislation already where Member States are required to impose penalties on both natural and legal persons.[97] The Directive on sanctions against employers of illegally resident third country nationals is an early post-Lisbon example of a measure that provides for the obligation to impose criminal sanctions on natural and legal employers.[98] The same holds true for, for example, the Trafficking Directive, where Member States shall take the necessary measures to ensure that legal persons can be held liable for the offences referred to in the legislative measure.[99] There are, however, well known differences between the Member States when it comes to the issue of criminal liability for legal persons. Suffice it to say in the present context that EU law usually recognises this tension and hence leaves it to the Member States to decide what sanctions to impose. The Court has previously recognised this sensitivity by stating that the Member States are free to choose whether to enforce liability on legal persons as long

[96] Council Regulation (EU) 2017/1939 of 12 October 2017 implementing enhanced cooperation for the adoption of a European Public Prosecutor's Office, L OJ 283/1, para 50. Discussed further in ch 4 below.

[97] Peers, EU Justice & Home Affairs (n 5).

[98] Directive 2009/52/EC of the European Parliament and of the Council of 18 June 2009 providing for minimum standards on sanctions and measures against employers of illegally staying third-country nationals, OJ L 168/24.

[99] Directive 2011/36/EU on preventing and combating trafficking in human beings and protecting its victims, and replacing Council Framework Decision 2002/629/JHA, OJ L/101.

as effective, proportionate and dissuasive sanctions are imposed on someone.[100] The Market Abuse Directive and the Market Abuse Regulation however ignore this sensitive question by simply requiring that there be effective criminal law sanctions against legal persons. Therefore, it is reasonable to believe that those Member States who do not recognise such liability at present will have to adapt their systems in the light of the changing EU approach.[101]

As Vanessa Franssen has recently argued, the EU's approach to corporate financial crime has not evolved all that much over the past two decades, despite the efforts to combat financial crime more effectively.[102] According to her, the EU law does still not sufficiently take into account the specific features of both criminal liability and corporate entities (as opposed to individuals), nor does it fully exploit the potential strengths of a criminal law approach, as opposed to an administrative or civil law approach. The question of criminal liability or corporate liability is a hugely sensitive matter in some Member States. Accordingly, and as indicated in the discussion on effective sanctions above, the Member States have so far been free to choose whether to impose criminal and non-criminal sanctions on legal persons as long as the relevant legal response is 'effective' from an EU law perspective.[103] However, as always there are exceptions to all rules of thumb: criminal liability of legal persons *stricto sensu* was nonetheless introduced by the third pillar Fraud Convention.[104] Therefore, EU involvement in criminal law may result in constitutional clashes between the national criminal law and EU law norms as increased involvement by the EU in these matters has an impact on the national system as it demands that it makes a choice about the content of a harmonised regime. Another good example here is the EU's current trend towards insisting on corporate criminal liability. For instance, the Commission's proposal for an amendment of the Framework Decision on the combat against terrorism stressed the importance of criminalising conduct by legal persons.[105] So although it is true that the Court has been reluctant in explicitly ruling on criminal liability for legal persons[106] it remains less certain whether the Member States in reality have much choice when asked to comply with effective sanctions. This poses potential difficulties for Member States that do not recognise criminal liability for legal persons.

[100] Case C-7/90 *Vandevenne* [1991] ECR 1-4371.

[101] See E Herlin-Karnell, *The Constitutional Dimension of European Criminal Law* (Oxford, Hart Publishing, 2012) ch 6.

[102] Vanessa Franssen, 'The EU's Fight against Corporate Financial Crime: State of Affairs and Future Potential' (2018) *German Law Journal* 1221, in special issue on EU Security Governance and Financial Crimes in (2018) *German Law Journal* issue 5.

[103] ibid.

[104] Second Protocol of the Convention on the protection of the European Communities Financial Interests [1997] OJ 221/11.

[105] Framework decision COM (2007) 650 proposal for an amending framework decision 2002/475/JHA on combating terrorism.

[106] Steve Peers *EU Justice and Home Affairs* (Oxford, Oxford University Press, 2015).

Another example is the 2017 Directive on the fight against terrorism.[107] The Directive stresses the importance of criminalising conduct by legal persons, by, inter alia (Articles 17–18) stating that Member States shall take the necessary measures to ensure that a legal person is held liable. A further recent example is the Directive on cybercrime where it is stated that Member States shall take the necessary measures to ensure that legal persons can be held liable for offences.[108] Looking more closely at this Directive, Article 11 stipulates that Member States shall take the necessary measures to ensure that legal persons can be held liable for offences committed for their benefit by any person, acting either individually or as part of an organ of the legal person, and having a leading position within the legal person. Moreover, it is held that Member States shall take the necessary measures to ensure that legal persons can be held liable where the lack of supervision or control by a person referred to in paragraph 1 has made possible the commission, by a person under its authority, of any of the offences referred to in Articles 3 to 8 for the benefit of that legal person. Although, as already mentioned above, the CJEU has been reluctant to explicitly rule on criminal liability for legal persons, as mentioned above, it remains however less certain whether the Member States in reality have much choice when asked to comply with effective sanctions.

V. Conclusion

The Market Abuse Directive and the Market Abuse Regulation should be seen in the light of the re-construction of the rest of this policy area. On the one hand, it has represented an attempt to solve the 2008 financial crises and its shadows by using the criminal law to boost investor confidence. On the other hand, it demonstrates a very experimental use of reporting obligations, to fight against market abuse: as well as a clear cut example of the relationship between AFSJ policies and the internal market. As was shown in this chapter, the EU's fight against financial crimes takes place at multiple levels in the EU regulatory machinery: both within the framework and endeavour of the establishment of an 'Area of Freedom, Security and Justice' and within the traditional playing field of the EU internal market and the need to ensure market integrity. Furthermore, the EU and the Member States are required (Article 325 TFEU) to counter fraud and any other illegal activities affecting the financial interests of the EU.

In addition, the Market Abuse Directive is one of the first examples of the use of Article 83(2) TFEU and confirms the wide-ranging scope of the provision. In addition, the chapter has highlighted having a Directive and a Regulation

[107] Directive 2017/541 on combating terrorism and replacing Council Framework Decision 2002/475/JHA and amending Council Decision 2005/671/JHA OJ L 88/6.

[108] Directive 2013/40/EU on attacks against information systems and replacing Council Framework Decision 2005/222/JHA.

regulating the same area. The fight against market abuse is about regulating market failure and the choice of legal basis remains unclear.

The next chapter will look at the specifics of a sanction in this context and explain why the definition of a sanction is important here and how it stands in comparison to the UK and the US system. The EU dimension of the fight against market abuse will be further discussed in chapter four.

3

Regulatory Strategies: On the Choice of Sanction

I. Introduction

This chapter builds on the previous chapter where the competence question of the EU strategies and agenda was discussed. This chapter will now seek to build on those findings and examine the important question as to what sanctions should properly be used when fighting market abuse. In addition, the chapter will seek to broaden the discussion and discuss not only the EU's use of sanctions but also the practices of the UK and the US. The core focus of the chapter is the EU, UK, and the US sanction system. The chapter will start with an overall discussion on the mechanism for deciding to what extent the EU has the competence to invoke sanctions and the question as to what extent the sanctions in question are 'criminal law' under the definition provided by the European Convention on Human Rights (ECHR). Thereafter, the part on the UK and the US will adopt a more practical approach. The UK is now about to leave the EU through its Brexit decision (at the time of writing the exact parameters of the possible Brexit deal are still unclear), but EU law is at present still part of the UK law. Still it represents an interesting case study in its own right in relation to the EU regime and the US framework.

While there is a wide-ranging body of literature examining the notion of a sanction,[1] it still remains a relatively open question as to what sanctions to impose the question which is considered in this chapter. The chapter is structured as follows. It starts by looking at the classical debate on sanctions and how it has shaped especially the framework of EU criminal law and where market abuse sanctions have played an important role as one of the earliest examples of administrative sanctions. In addition, the chapter will look at the type and characterisation of sanctions for fighting market abuse and insider dealing more specifically. The chapter concludes by looking at the US and UK national systems with regard to the imposition of sanctions.

As mentioned in chapter two, before the entry into force of the Lisbon Treaty, the question of what kind of sanctions the EU could impose on the Member States

[1] See eg the contributions in Lucia Zedner and Julian Roberts (eds), *Principles and Values in Criminal Law and Criminal Justice: Essays in Honour of Andrew Ashworth* (Oxford, Oxford University Press, 2012).

in order to fight financial crimes was subject to fierce debate and closely related to the development of the EU project in general with regard to the general division of competences in the EU.[2] Prior to the EU legislative competences granted in criminal law, the advantage of administrative sanctions was that they could be adopted despite the EU's lack of an explicit criminal law competence.[3] Nevertheless, administrative sanctions have been severely criticised for giving rise to a kind of 'competence creep' into the sphere of penal law and in this way creating a supranational system of sanctions through the EU legal back door and for breaching the general right of a fair trial.[4] Yet, in line with mainstream EU law influence over national law, the administrative sanctions regime has resulted in considerable harmonisation of national criminal laws, with norms either being set aside by EU law or given extended scope in pursuit of European goals. Accordingly, while there was a presumption that criminal law was a matter for the Member States, this presumption could be rebutted (as in all other areas of EU law) if its operation affected the pursuit of Union policies such as the smooth operation of the market. In this area, competence boundaries have been easily blurred and sanctions have played an important role in this process.

In short, the debate on sanctions in EU law has tended to focus on the controversial EU administrative sanctions system and on the question of whether these sanctions, contrary to their 'administrative' label, should properly be viewed as falling under the umbrella of criminal law. Such an interpretation would, in accordance with the criteria laid down by the ECtHR in the case law on Article 6 ECHR, ensure the right to a fair trial and a subjective fault element.[5] With respect to due process rights, Article 49 of the EU Charter provides for the guarantee of legality and proportionality in a more extensive way than the ECHR. Also, Article 47 of the Charter guarantees the right to an effective remedy, while Articles 48–49 stipulate the presumption of innocence and the right of defence.[6] The latter provision also makes it clear that the severity of penalties must not be disproportionate to the criminal offence. Moreover, Article 50 of the Charter guarantees the right not to be tried twice for the same (criminal) offence (*ne bis in idem*). Interestingly, criminal

[2] Estella Baker, 'Taking European Criminal Law Seriously' June (1998) *CL Rev* 361; Valsamis Mitsilegas, *EU Criminal Law* (Oxford, Hart Publishing, 2009); André Klip *EU Criminal Law* (Intersentia, 2012); Ester Herlin-Karnell, *The Constitutional Dimension of European Criminal Law* (Oxford, Hart Publishing, 2012) ch 2.

[3] Case C-137/85 *Maizena* [1987] ECR I-4587 and Case C-210/00 *KCH* [2002] ECR I-0645, discussing the use of sanctions.

[4] Chris Harding, 'Exploring the intersection of European law and national criminal law' (2000) 25 *EL Rev* 374; PA Albrecht and Stefan Braum, 'Deficiencies in the Development of European Criminal Law' (1999) 5 *European Law Journal* 293.

[5] *Engel and others v The Netherlands*, Series A no 22 [1979–1980].

[6] In her recent opinion delivered on 18 October in Radu C-396/11 (para 103), AG Sharpston, discusses the boundaries of Art 49 of the Charter by stipulating that it would be interesting to explore the boundaries of these provisions in the context of Article 3 ECHR where the ECtHR has held that a sentence that is grossly disproportionate could amount to ill-treatment contrary to Article 3 ECHR. The Court did not elaborate on this issue.

lawyers have for a long time argued that insider crime is an offence surrounded by doubts about its true effects on the market as non-criminal means of regulation could prove to be more effective.[7] Nevertheless, there seems to be a general preference for criminalising or invoking sanctions at the EU level without any real examination of the consequences of such action. In other words, the EU is often taking the 'positive' impacts for granted.[8] At present the EU relies on a complex regime combining criminal law and administrative sanctions to enforce its norms and values. Yet the use of criminal law is a method for expressing values and for indicating the wrongfulness of certain behaviour. The criminal law is a regulatory tool for influencing behaviour and its central element is its communicative function.[9] The harm principle has of course become the natural starting point for any understanding of the construction of criminal law, the 'harm to others' yardstick, that is, that the state should intervene as little as possible in people's lives.[10] According to the harm principle, as developed by JS Mill and others, the only purpose for which power can rightfully be exercised over any other member of a civilised community against his will is to prevent harm to others.[11] The assumption is that criminalisation is aimed at protecting interests from harm. Yet in the EU context it appears as if the question of the wrongfulness or harm in question has not been the central element of the debate but rather the main issue has been what sanctions to impose, and this debate on the label of the sanctions has largely shaped the development of EU sanctions law.

Accordingly the classification of a sanction may continue to play a role in the future development of EU criminal law and is interesting in the context of market abuse as the expansion of EU criminal law and the history of administrative sanctions has shaped contemporary EU market abuse law.[12] Administrative sanctions have always formed a crucial part of the EU's enforcement strategy, particularly with regard to competition fines and sanctions in the domain of EU agriculture and fisheries policies.[13] For example, in the EU context it appears as if the question of the wrongfulness or harm in question has not been the central element of the debate but rather the main issue has been what sanctions to impose, and this debate on the label of the sanctions has largely shaped the development of EU criminal law. Thus, the principle of legality is of course a general principle of

[7] Kai Hinterseer, *Criminal Finance, The political economy of money laundering in a comparative legal context* (Kluwer, The Hague, 2002) ch 2.

[8] Ester Herlin-Karnell, *The Constitutional Dimension of European Criminal Law* (Oxford, Hart Publishing, 2012) ch 2.

[9] Andrew Simester and Andreas von Hirsch, *Crimes, Harms and Wrongs* (Oxford, Hart Publishing, 2011) ch 4.

[10] See Lindsay Farmer, *Making the Modern Criminal Law* (Oxford, Oxford University Press, 2016).

[11] JS Mill, *On Liberty* (London, Routledge, 1991). For an overview see also Simester and von Hirsch (n 9) ch 2.

[12] For more on this, see E Herlin-Karnell 'Is Administrative Law still relevant? How the battle of sanctions has shaped EU Criminal law' in Valsamis Mitsilegas, Maria Bergstrom and Theodore Konstadinides (eds), *Research Handbook on EU Criminal Law* (Edward Elgar, 2015) ch 11.

[13] J Frese, *Sanctions in EU Competition Law* (Oxford, Hart Publishing, 2014).

EU law[14] and as such codified in Article 2 TEU, Article 21 TEU and in Article 49 of the Charter of Fundamental Rights. One of the first crucial cases at the EU level was *Kent Kirk*[15] concerning the retroactive application of a regulation. The Court's message in this case was clear: 'The principle that penal provisions may not have retroactive effect is one which is common to all the legal orders of the member states and is enshrined in article 7 of the European Convention for the protection of human rights and fundamental freedoms as a fundamental right; it takes its place among the general principles of law whose observance is ensured by the Court of Justice.'[16] In this way the principle of legality as a general principle of EU law and criminal law helps to control the institutions and the legislator.

As also mentioned in chapter two, the question of whether corporations should be held criminally liable is an ongoing question in EU law. Indeed, there are a number of examples in secondary legislation where Member States are required to impose penalties on both natural and legal persons.[17] There are, however, differences between the Member States when it comes to the issue of criminal liability for legal persons. Suffice it to say in the present context that EU law usually recognises this tension and hence leaves it to the Member States to decide what sanctions to impose. Furthermore, as pointed out by Peers in connection with the 2003 Market Abuse Directive, Member States 'must pierce the veil' and prohibit a natural person from using inside information even when a legal person is *de jure* the possessor of the information.[18] Yet the so-called PIF Convention, combating fraud, required the Member States to impose criminal liability on the heads of legal business. This was later transposed into the First PIF Protocol along with the Convention on national corruption law which, however, leaves it to the Member States to choose the nature of the relevant sanction.[19] In short, the Protocol stipulates that legal persons must be punished by effective, proportionate and dissuasive sanctions which shall include criminal or non-criminal fines and also other measures such as temporary or permanent disqualification. It should be observed that as regards money laundering, neither the Vienna nor the Strasbourg Convention contain any such liability (UN Narcotics Drugs Convention (1988) and Council of Europe Convention on Laundering (1990)), although the latter emphasised the advantage of such a system in cases where money laundering is pursued through them. For example, Article 6 of the Fraud Directive stipulates that each Member State should take the necessary measures to ensure that legal persons can be held liable for fraud and related activities and for the attempted commission of fraud.[20] In this respect there appears to be

[14] Takis Tridimas, *The General Principles of EU Law* (Oxford, Hart Publishing, 2006) 242.

[15] Case C-63/83, *Kent Kirk*, ECR [1984] 2689.

[16] Para 22 of the judgment.

[17] Steve Peers, *EU Justice & Home Affairs* (Oxford, Oxford University Press, 2011) ch 8.

[18] ibid at 411.

[19] Regulation No 2988/95 of 18 December 1995 on the protection of the European Communities financial interests. [1995] OJ L 312.

[20] Directive (EU) 2017/1371 of the European Parliament and of the Council of 5 July 2017 on the fight against fraud to the Union's financial interests by means of criminal law, OJ L 198, 28.7.2017, pp 29–41.

no 'excuse' regarding whether to impose criminal liability on legal persons but the focus is very much on effectiveness.[21] Moreover, for example in the related context of the EU anti-money laundering scheme, the Financial Action Task Force recommendations have emphasised the importance of criminal liability for legal persons.[22]

II. Quasi-criminal Law in the EU Context

The administrative sanctions grid played an important role in expanding the competences of the EU and, thereby, prior to the Lisbon Treaty, made possible a quasi-criminal law system at the expense of the due process safeguards traditionally associated with criminal law (such as the right to a fair trial under Article 6 ECHR, mentioned earlier). More recently, these administrative sanctions have also played a predominant role with regard to financial law regulation and the aim of ensuring increased compliance in the Member States.

Moreover, according to EU law and its well-known case law of the Greek Maize[23] judgment, Member States have to protect EU interests the same way as they protect national interests. Specifically, this case concerned fraud against the EU where the Court held that:

> … the Member States must ensure that infringements of EU law are penalised under conditions, both procedural and substantive, which are analogous to those applicable to infringements of national law of a similar nature and importance and which, in any event, make the penalty effective, proportionate and dissuasive.

In this way national criminal law was largely mainstreamed with the EU criminal law project already prior to the entry into force of the Lisbon Treaty.

The Commission's Communication on reinforcing sanctioning regimes in the financial sector is particularly intriguing when it comes to the EU competences to enact sanctions.[24] It is stated there that efficient and sufficiently convergent sanctioning regimes are the necessary corollary to the new supervisory system and that:

> Supervision cannot be effective with weak, highly variant sanctioning regimes. It is essential that within the EU and elsewhere, all supervisors are able to deploy sanctioning regimes that are sufficiently convergent, strict, resulting in deterrence.[25]

[21] Vanessa Franssen, 'The EU's Fight against Corporate Financial Crime: State of Affairs and Future Potential' (2018) 5 *German Law Journal* 1221.

[22] www.fatf-gafi.org/publications/fatfrecommendations/documents/fatf-recommendations.html (last accessed November 2018).

[23] Case C-68/88 *Commission v Greece* [1989] ECR 1-2965, paragraph 24.

[24] COM (2010) 716 final, 'Reinforcing sanctioning regimes in the financial sector'.

[25] Ibid.

Nonetheless, nothing is said about the type of sanctions to be adopted. So for example in the proposal leading up to the 2014 Market Abuse Directive, discussed above in chapter two, the Commission argued that criminal sanctions, in particular imprisonment, are generally considered to send a strong message of disapproval that could increase the dissuasiveness of sanctions, provided that they are appropriately applied by the criminal justice system.[26] However, in the aforementioned Communication on reinforcing sanctioning regimes in the financial sector, the Commission also stated that criminal sanctions may not be appropriate for all types of violations. Moreover, it stated that it would assess whether and in which areas the introduction of criminal sanctions, and the establishment of minimum rules on the definition of criminal offences and sanctions, may prove to be essential in order to ensure the effective implementation of EU financial services legislation.

Recent trends in EU legislative drafting procedure appear, in addition, to confirm a double approach in this regard, that is to increase the effectiveness of the system: on the one hand, the Commission relies on provisions within the AFSJ to adopt criminal law sanctions (Article 83 TFEU) while, on the other hand, it also legislates by using administrative sanctions located outside the AFSJ section of the Treaty and linked to the EU internal market (eg, Article 114 TFEU), in the area of market abuse, anti-money laundering for example.[27]

It can seriously be questioned whether dual regulation through criminal law sanctions and administrative sanctions, as proposed in various EU Regulations and the proposed fourth Directive, respectively, breaches the principle of *ne bis in idem* or double jeopardy and thereby the Article 50 Charter. Article 50 provides that 'No one shall be liable to be tried or punished again in criminal proceedings for an offence for which he or she has already been finally acquitted or convicted within the Union in accordance with the law'.

It is of course true that the notion of *ne bis in idem* applies only to criminal law sanctions.[28] Yet, considering the increasing use of administrative sanctions, it could be argued that such an approach leads to a fundamentally unfair system and that the proportionality principle has an important role to play here so as to avoid double procedures. A recent famous example of tensions between *ne bis in idem* and national administrative sanctions regimes was the recent case of *Åkerberg Fransson* concerning the compatibility with the *ne bis in idem* principle of a national system involving two separate sets of proceedings to penalise the

[26] COM (2011) 654 final, Proposal for a Directive on criminal sanctions for insider dealing and market manipulation, (Now Directive Directive 2014/57/EU).

[27] Regulation No 596/2014 on market abuse, Directive (EU) 2018/843 of the European Parliament and of the Council of 30 May 2018 amending Directive (EU) 2015/849 on the prevention of the use of the financial system for the purposes of money laundering or terrorist financing, and amending Directives 2009/138/EC and 2013/36/EU, 2018 OJ (L 156) 43–74.

[28] Anne Weyembergh and Ines Armada, 'The Principle of ne bis in idem in Europe's Area of Freedom, Security and Justice' in Valsamis Mitsilegas (et al), *Research Handbook on EU Criminal Law* (Edward Elgar, 2016) ch 9.

same wrongful conduct.[29] The CJEU in turn, in its ruling, did not elaborate on this aspect of proportionality as a mitigating principle.[30] Nonetheless, it is argued that the Court adopted a very broad reading of the Charter, despite the limits set by Article 51. Specifically, the Court held that although the national rules in questions did not *stricto sensu* involve any implementation of EU law as such, it was clear from Article 325 TFEU that Member States were required to fight fraud against the EU. Moreover, such an obligation could be deduced from the general obligations to punish tax fraud that stem from the VAT Directive.[31] From this it followed, in the view of the Court, that Sweden was 'implementing' EU law as it was under an established obligation to supply the same level of penalties for EU fraud and domestic fraud, respectively. In addition, the Court observed that EU law precludes a judicial practice whereby a national court's obligation to disapply any provision that is contrary to a fundamental right guaranteed by the Charter is made conditional upon the infringement being clear from the text of the Charter or the related case law. According to the Court, such an interpretation would withhold from the national court the power to assess fully whether the provision in question was compatible with the Charter.[32]

Moreover, the Charter could arguably have an impact in the context of the market abuse regime discussed above. Specifically, the proposed regime for 'blacklisting', through the publication of sanctions and the granting to competent authorities of far-reaching powers similar to those in competition law raids and anti-terrorism measures, raises some difficult questions.[33] These questions include more general issues relating to the right to a fair trial in EU law and are closely intertwined with the long-standing debate on competition fines.

III. The Eternal Debate: Criminal or Administrative Sanctions?

As mentioned above, before the entry into force of the Lisbon Treaty, the question of what kind of sanctions the EU could impose on Member States was subject to fierce debate and closely related to the development of the EU project in general with regard to the general division of competences in the EU. The debate on sanctions in EU law has tended to focus on the controversial EU administrative sanctions system and on the question of whether these sanctions, contrary

[29] Case C-617/10 *Åkerberg Fransson*, Judgment of 26 February 2013.

[30] ibid.

[31] ibid, paras 27–28. See Council Directive 2006/112/EC of 28 November 2006 on the common system of value added tax, OJ L 347, 11.12.2006, pp 1–118.

[32] ibid, para 48.

[33] See the discussion in the proposal for a Directive on criminal sanctions for insider dealing and market manipulation, COM (2011) 654 final (Now Directive Directive 2014/57/EU).

to their 'administrative' label, should properly be viewed as falling under the umbrella of criminal law.[34] The issue of whether the EU was entitled to create its own 'quasi-penal system' was raised in C-240/90 *Germany v Commission*,[35] where the CJEU held that the measures were needed to secure the internal market and were therefore within the EU's competence.[36] This approach has been frequently reiterated, for example in the *Bonda* judgment.[37] Prior to the competences granted in criminal law, the advantage of administrative sanctions was obviously that the fact these sanctions were not criminal sanctions meant that measures could be taken despite the EU's lack of an explicit criminal law competence. Nevertheless, in line with mainstream EU law influence, the administrative sanctions regime has resulted in considerable harmonisation of national criminal laws, with norms either being set aside by EU law or given extended scope in pursuit of European goals. Accordingly, while there was a presumption that criminal law was a matter for the Member States, this presumption could be rebutted (as in all other areas of EU law) if its operation affected the pursuit of Union policies such as the smooth operation of the market. Clearly, legal competence boundaries have been easily blurred in this area and sanctions have played an important role in this process.

The CJEU has stressed the political considerations behind the drafting of the Lisbon Treaty and accepted that, when choosing between legal bases, it is not only the role of the European Parliament and the increased democratic input that are the decisive factors.[38] The Court has not really defined what the critical factors are for deciding on the nature of a sanction, that is as administrative, civil or criminal law. While the *European Parliament v Council*[39] is a case which mainly concerns the dividing line between the internal and the external fight against terrorism, it is also a case which highlights the choice by the legislator to fight terrorism by means of the administrative model not the criminal law one. Therefore, this case is relevant for understanding the current practice of criminal law sanctions in the EU as the choice of sanction often seems political.[40]

[34] *Engel and others v The Netherlands*, Series A no. 22 [1979–1980].

[35] C-240/90 *Germany v Commission* [1992] ECR I-05383.

[36] AG Jacobs stated in his Opinion of 3 June 1992 that 'certainly EC law in its present state does not confer on the Commission, the CFI or the ECJ the function of a criminal tribunal. It should however be noted that that would in itself not preclude the EC from harmonizing the criminal laws of the Member States if that were necessary to attain one of the objectives of the Community'.

[37] For a strict interpretation of the 'Engel test', see C-489/10 *Criminal Proceedings against Bonda*, CJEU, Judgment of 5 June 2012, confirming previous case law, including C-210/00 *Käserei Champignon Hofmeister v Hauptzollamt Hamburg-Jonas* [2002] ECR I-6453.

[38] Case C-300/89 *Commission v Council* [1991] ECR I-2867.

[39] Case C-130/10, *European Parliament v Council*, judgment of 19 July 2012.

[40] Ester Herlin-Karnell, 'The Challenges of EU Enforcement and Elements of Criminal Law Theory: On Sanctions and Value in Contemporary "Freedom, Security and Justice" Law' (2016) *Yearbook of European Law* 1–27.

IV. Market Abuse Sanctions – The EU Context and the Question of Proportionality

While it is true that the Market Abuse Directive (MAD)[41] – as was examined above in chapter two – is based on Article 83(2) TFEU, which provides a more extensive competence than the areas listed in Article 83(1) TFEU for the effective implementation of a Union policy and so obviously involves criminal law, it also adds administrative sanctions to the picture through the Market Abuse Regulation (MAR).[42] According to the Commission, market abuse can be carried out across borders and this divergence undermines the internal market, thus creating a certain scope for perpetrators of market abuse to carry such abuse into jurisdictions that do not provide for criminal sanctions for a particular offence. The Directive[43] is seeking to change this by adding criminal law to the discussion in order to fight market abuse more effectively. For this reason, we now face two instruments: one Directive and one Regulation. Thus, it could be questioned whether dual regulation through criminal law sanctions and administrative sanctions, as proposed in various EU Regulations and the proposed fourth Directive respectively, breaches the principle of *ne bis in idem* or double jeopardy and thereby Article 50 in the Charter of Fundamental Rights. Article 50 states that 'No one shall be liable to be tried or punished again in criminal proceedings for an offence for which he or she has already been finally acquitted or convicted within the Union in accordance with the law.' Considering the increasing use of administrative sanctions, it could be argued that such an approach leads to a fundamentally unfair system and that the proportionality principle has an important role to play here so as to avoid double procedures. The tensions between *ne bis in idem* and national administrative sanctions regimes was tested in the aforementioned *Åkerberg Fransson* case concerning the compatibility with the *ne bis in idem* principle of a national system involving two separate sets of proceedings to penalise the same wrongful conduct and where the Court stipulated a general proportionality requirement.[44] But this would require a structured proportionality test, one which inserts a reasonableness check into the proportionality assessment. Here, the principle of proportionality could serve a tool for injecting quality into the legislative regime, and asks whether double systems of sanctions are strictly necessary in the area of financial crimes. In conclusion the EU relies at

[41] Directive 2014/57/EU of the European Parliament and of the Council of 16 April 2014 on criminal sanctions for market abuse (market abuse directive), OJ L 173, 12.6.2014, pp 179–89 (hereafter MAD).

[42] Regulation (EU) No 596/2014 on market abuse (market abuse regulation) and repealing Directive 2003/6/EC of the European Parliament and of the Council and Commission Directives 2003/124/EC, 2003/125/EC and 2004/72/EC, OJ L 173, 12.6.2014, pp 1–61 (hereafter MAR).

[43] ibid.

[44] C-617/10, *Åkerberg Fransson*, judgment of 26 February 2013.

present on both criminal and administrative law and focuses to a large extent on the claimed effectiveness of double sanctions at the possible expense of proportionality and fairness.

V. The United Kingdom

The UK has in place an extensive legal framework for the impositions of financial penalties. The UK's legislative efforts to tackle financial crime and market abuse originated with the introduction of the Fraud (Investments) Acts of 1939 and 1958. Preceding efforts included the Public Bodies Corrupt Practices Act 1889 and the Prevention of Corruption Act 1906. However, it was not until the creation of the Serious Fraud Office (SFO) that the UK began to take the threat posed by financial crime seriously.[45] The new millenium saw the introduction of the Financial Services and Markets Act 2000 (FSMA 2000) and the statutory objective of the Financial Services Authority to reduce financial crime.[46] This, combined with their investigative and enforcement powers, was an innovative attempt to tackle financial crime that arose from within or targeted the financial corporations. In 2002, the Proceeds of Crime Act 2002 codified the existing anti-money laundering that was originally found in the Drug Trafficking Offences Act 1986 and the Criminal Justice Act 1993 (CJA 1993). The Fraud Act 2006 revamped the common law offence of conspiracy to defraud and the inadequate fraud legislation and this was followed by the extension of the enforcement powers of the Financial Conduct Authority (FCA), by the Financial Services Act 2012. The measures tackled financial crime committed by individuals and not corporations.

The only mechanism to tackle corporate financial crime was the arguably inadequate common law doctrine of corporate criminal liability. In order to address this problem, the Bribery Act 2010 and the Criminal Finances Act 2017 introduced two new corporate criminal offences: failing to prevent bribery[47] and failure to prevent the facilitation of tax evasion.[48]

The doctrine of corporate criminal liability has limited the ability of UK law enforcement and financial regulatory agencies from seeking criminal sanctions against corporations for breaches of financial crime legislation. The UK courts began to consider the restrictive application of criminal law to companies in the nineteenth century, which included cases involving public nuisance, criminal libel and breach of statutory duty.[49] The doctrine was extended by the judiciary in three Court of Appeal decisions in 1944, which concluded that a corporation

[45] CJA 1987, s 1.
[46] FSMA 2000, s 6.
[47] Bribery Act 2010, s 7.
[48] Criminal Finances Act 2017, s 44.
[49] See Ministry of Justice, *Corporate liability for economic crime: call for evidence* (Ministry of Justice, 2017) 11.

could be held directly accountable, as opposed to vicariously liable, for the actions of their employees.[50] The foremost authority on the doctrine of criminal liability of corporations is the House of Lords of decision in *Tesco Supermarkets v Nattrass*.[51] Here, the House of Lords concluded that in order for a company to be criminally liable, a person who has the directing mind of the company and the self-determination of the company must also have criminal intent. This decision in *Tesco* resulted in the creation of the 'identification doctrine', the test to determine whether corporations are to be held liable for breaches of criminal law. The Bribery Act 2010 introduced a novel form of criminal liability where a corporation can be found guilty of an offence if a person associated with the organisation bribes another, intending to obtain or retain business or a business advantage for that organisation.[52] The scope of section 7 is broad, so as to encompass the whole range of individuals who may be committing bribery on behalf of a third party organisation. Under this section, prosecutors must prove a *mens rea* or fault element in addition to the *actus reus* or conduct element. The failing to prevent bribery offence is enforced by the SFO who have used Deferred Prosecution Agreements (DPAs).[53] The SFO obtained its first DPA for breaches of the failing to prevent bribery offence against *Standard Bank Plc*, which were 'ordered to pay financial orders of $25.2m and required to pay the government of Tanzania a further $7m in compensation'.[54] This was followed by a second DPA against *XYX Ltd* who agreed to 'pay financial orders of £6.5m, comprised of a £6.2m disgorgement of gross profits and a £352,000 financial penalty'.[55] In 2017, Rolls Royce agreed to enter into a DPA that 'involve[d] payments of £497m … [and] Rolls-Royce [were] also reimbursing the SFO's costs in full'.[56] In April 2017, the SFO announced that it had entered into a DPA with *Tesco*, which was required to pay a fine of £129m for over stating its profits.[57] Interestingly, in each of the four DPAs

[50] *DPP v Kent and Sussex Contractors Ltd* [1944] 1 KB 146; *R v ICR Haulage Co Ltd* [1944] KB 551 and *Moore v Bresler Ltd* [1972] AC 153.

[51] [1972] AC 153. See Law Commission, *Criminal Liability in Regulatory Contexts* (Law Com No 195, 2010) para 5.34.

[52] Bribery Act 2010, s 7.

[53] Crime and Courts Act 2013, sch 17. The then Coalition Government announced its intention to introduce DPAs in October 2012 and stated that they will 'give prosecutors an effective new tool to tackle what has become an increasingly complex issue … this will ensure that more unacceptable corporate behaviour is dealt with including through substantial penalties, proper reparation to victims, and measures to prevent future wrongdoing'. See HM Government 'New tool to fight economic crime' 23 October 2012, available from www.gov.uk/government/news/new-tool-to-fight-economic-crime, accessed August 5 2017.

[54] Serious Fraud Office 'Standard Bank PLC' 10 December 2015, available from www.sfo.gov.uk/cases/standard-bank-plc/, accessed August 5 2017.

[55] Serious Fraud Office 'SFO secures second DPA' 8 July 2016, available from www.sfo.gov.uk/2016/07/08/sfo-secures-second-dpa/, accessed August 5 2017.

[56] Serious Fraud Office 'Rolls-Royce PLC' 11 September 2014, available from www.sfo.gov.uk/cases/rolls-royce-plc/, accessed August 5 2017.

[57] Serious Fraud Office 'SFO agrees Deferred Prosecution Agreement with Tesco' April 2017, available from www.sfo.gov.uk/2017/04/10/sfo-agrees-deferred-prosecution-agreement-with-tesco/, accessed 18 January 2018.

obtained by the SFO, no criminal prosecutions have been brought against any of the offending corporation's employees or agents. As of July 2019, the offence failure to prevent offences created by the Criminal Finances Act 2017 has not been used. This is largely due to the fact that HM Revenue and Customs have preferred to impose a series of financial penalties on firms and individuals who have dishonestly evaded paying tax.[58]

This section of the chapter considers the ability of the FCA to impose financial penalties for breaches of its financial crime rules and the obligations under the Senior Management Certification Regime. The most frequently used power against corporations for financial crime breaches by the FCA are financial penalties. For example, in January 2017 the FCA imposed a record financial penalty of £163 million on Deutsche Bank for failing to maintain an adequate AML laundering system.[59] The decision by the FCA to impose this record financial penalty can be contrasted with the stance of its predecessor, the Financial Services Authority, towards HSBC when the regulator decided not to take any action. Here, HSBC entered into a DPA with the US Department of Justice in 2012 after admitting breaches of US anti-money laundering and counter-terrorist financing laws.[60] This must be questioned and criticised because HSBC flouted US AML laws and the UN sanctions regime, which resulted in no enforcement action by the FSA. Conversely, Deutsche Bank were fined for not having adequate AML rules as proscribed by the *FCA Handbook*, even though there was no evidence of any money laundering. The FCA has imposed large financial penalties for breaches of its money laundering rules, even though there was no evidence of money laundering. For examples, such fines were imposed on Turkish Bank (UK) Ltd,[61] Habib Bank AG Zurich[62] and Coutts & Company.[63] In none of these cases did the FCA pursue any prosecutions for breaches of the Proceeds of Crime Act 2002 against any employee or agent of the financial institutions. In fact, the FCA has only instigated criminal proceedings for money laundering under the

[58] See HM Revenue and Customers 'Increased penalties for offshore tax evasion', n/d, available from https://assets.publishing.service.gov.uk/government/uploads/system/uploads/attachment_data/file/387346/offshore-penalties.pdf, accessed 20 March 2019.

[59] Financial Conduct Authority, 'FCA fines Deutsche Bank for serious anti-money laundering controls failings' 31 January 2017, available at www.fca.org.uk/news/press-releases/fca-fines-deutsche-bank-163-million-anti-money-laundering-controls-failure.

[60] See *United States of America v HSBC Bank USA* Cr No 12-762.

[61] Financial Services Authority 'Turkish Bank (UK) Ltd: Decision Notice' 26 July 2012, available at http://webarchive.nationalarchives.gov.uk/20130202000754/http://www.fsa.gov.uk/static/pubs/final/turkish-bank.pdf, accessed 3 August 2017.

[62] Financial Services Authority 'FSA fines Habib Bank AG Zurich £525,000 and money laundering reporting officer £17,500 for anti-money laundering control failings' 15 May 2012, available from http://webarchive.nationalarchives.gov.uk/20130201230641/http://www.fsa.gov.uk/library/communication/pr/2012/055.shtml, accessed August 2017.

[63] Financial Services Authority 'Coutts fined £8.75 million for anti-money laundering control failings' 26 March 2012, available from http://webarchive.nationalarchives.gov.uk/20130201230628/http://www.fsa.gov.uk/library/communication/pr/2012/032.shtml, accessed 3 August 2018.

Proceeds of Crime Act 2002 on one occasion.[64] Another example of the ineffectiveness of financial penalties was the £72 million fine imposed on Barclays Bank in November 2015.[65] The FCA concluded that 'Barclays ignored its own process designed to safeguard against the risk of financial crime and overlooked obvious red flags to win new business and generate significant revenue'.[66] Despite the imposition of financial sanctions by the FCA for breaches of its AML rules, the regulator decided against imposing any further sanctions such as a prosecution of the bank's senior management or the money laundering reporting officer. The ability to impose financial penalties in the UK against corporations can be contrasted with the approach in the US approach. The financial penalties imposed by the FCA and its predecessor the FSA are civil and administrative in nature, because they are imposed by a regulator for breaches of the FSMA 2000 or the Handbook. Importantly, there is no criminal liability imposed under these fines imposed by the UK's financial regulatory agency. This is unsurprising given the practical limitations of the common law rules that have attempted to impose criminal liability on corporations in the UK for breaches of its financial crime legislation. This approach is unsatisfactory and there have been two legislative attempts to imposed criminal liability on corporations in the UK – the Bribery Act 2010 and the Criminal Finance Act 2017. Neither pieces of legislation have attached any criminal liability on offending corporations. The financial penalties imposed by the Financial Services Authority and FCA have increased since the onset of the 2007/08 financial crisis. However, it is questionable if the fines have had their desired impact and prevented future misconduct by UK corporations. For example, the first financial penalty imposed by the FSA in relation to the LIBOR scandal was £59.5 million on Barclays Bank in 2012. This fine, amongst other external factors, contributed to Barclay's profits for 2012 falling from £5.9 billion to £246 million.[67] Hence, the fine for the manipulation of LIBOR was proportionate. Conversely, in 2013 Barclays reported that its profits had increased to £2.9 billion.[68] It could be argued that the financial penalties imposed in the UK are not proportionate and only represent a small fraction of the annual profits of offending corporations.[69]

[64] See *R v Rollins* [2010] UKSC 39.

[65] Financial Conduct Authority 'FCA fines Barclays £72 million for poor handling of financial crime risks' 26 November 2015, available from www.fca.org.uk/news/press-releases/fca-fines-barclays-%C2%A372-million-poor-handling-financial-crime-risks, accessed 2 August 2017.

[66] ibid.

[67] BBC News 'Barclays announces 3,700 job cuts' 12 February 2012, available from www.bbc.co.uk/news/business-21423691, accessed 28 January 2019.

[68] BBC News 'Barclays releases profit figures a day early' 10 February 2014, available from www.bbc.co.uk/news/business-26118789, accessed 28 January 2019.

[69] For a more detailed commentary see H Hillman, 'Are the current laws and potential enforcement measures effective in achieving the accountability of bank directors for their actions, or the actions of the banks they manage? A comparison of UK and US approaches' in N Ryder, U Turksen and S Hassler (eds), *Fighting Financial Crime in the Global Economic Crisis* (Routledge Cavendish, 2014).

VI. The United States of America

The US has adopted an aggressive stance towards financial crime sanctions. For example, the US has been at the front of the global efforts to tackle money laundering as part of the 'War on Drugs'. Furthermore, the US was an integral part in the evolution and implementation of the 'Financial War on Terrorism' following the al Qaeda terrorist attacks in September 2001. Additionally, the US has embraced a robust enforcement policy towards fraudulent activities as illustrated following the Savings and Loans Crisis, the collapse of several corporations due to fraud and financial crime associated with the 2007/08 financial crisis. The latter resulted in the Securities and Exchange Commission (SEC) and the Federal Bureau of Investigation (FBI) securing record financial penalties and convictions for fraudulent behaviour. Examples would include the Ponzi fraud convictions of Bernard Madoff and over 1,100 convictions for mortgage fraud.

The US approach towards imposing criminal sanctions on corporations can be traced back to the decision of the Supreme Court in *New York Central & Hudson River Railroad Company v US*.[70] The central point in this was whether the corporation could be held liable for the illegal acts of its agent, who was acting within the scope of his authority. Here, the defendants, in conjunction with an agent of the company, were convicted for breaching the Elkins Act 1903.[71] In its unprecedented judgment, the Supreme Court determined that that 'the old and exploded doctrine that a corporation cannot commit a crime' was no longer appropriate.[72] Specifically, the Supreme Court held that a corporation could be held criminally responsible for the illegal acts of its agent. The US judiciary have adopted the *respondent superior* model to deal with the doctrine of corporate criminal liability.[73] This is a variation of the vicarious liability doctrine, and it allows the extension of civil liability on employers for the actions committed by their agents.[74] The decision of the Supreme Court has since been broadened to comprise the actions of agents of corporations who are acting without authority or breaching specific directions.[75] Therefore, a corporation could be held liable for the conduct of 'low-level employees who acted contrary to the corporate policy and to the compliance program of its firm'.[76]

[70] 212 US 481 (1909).

[71] 32 Stat 847.

[72] 212 US 481 (1909) at 495 per Justice Day.

[73] See generally *Marbury Management Inc v Kohn* (2d Cir 1980) 629 F 2d 705; *Wood, Walker & Co v Marbury Management Inc* 449 US 1011; *Sharp v Coopers & Lybrand* (3d Cir 1981) 649 F 2d 175 *cert denied* 455 US 938 (3d Cir 1981) as cited in N Poser 'Chinese wall or emperor's new clothes? Part 3' (1989) 9 *Company Lawyer* 207.

[74] The evolution of this doctrine has been heavily influenced by three distinct theories that the US judiciary have developed regarding the corporate identity: the artificial theory, the aggregation theory and the real entity. A full discussion of these theories is beyond the scope of this article but see generally D Millon 'Theories of the corporation' (1990) 2 *Duke Law Journal* 201.

[75] See *United States v Hilton Hotels Corp*., 467 F.2d 1000, 1004 (9th Cir 1972).

[76] E Lederman, 'Corporate criminal liability: the second generation' (2016) 46 *Stetson Law Review* 74.

The instigation of criminal proceedings in financial crime cases initially concentrated on persons and not corporations. This was illustrated following the 1980s Savings and Loans Crisis, which resulted in the collapse of over 2,100 financial institutions and losses exceeding $150bn[77] and resulted in over 1,000 senior executives being convicted of fraud and receiving lengthy custodial sentences.[78] However, it was not until later that decade that the Department of Justice (DoJ) began to prosecute corporations for breaches of financial crime legislation. For example, in 1987, the stock brokerage firm EF Hutton, revealed that some of the firm's brokers had laundered money for the Patriarca Crime Family.[79] As a result, EF Hutton was indicted and eventually convicted of 2,000 counts of mail and wire fraud.[80] EF Hutton entered into a plea bargain with the DoJ and it was 'forced to merge with a competitor'.[81] The prosecution of the investment-banking corporation Drexel Burnham Lambert undoubtedly illustrates well the impact of a corporate conviction. After the firm's managing director, Dennis Levine, who had a history of illegal conduct, pleaded guilty to several insider trading charges,[82] the US Attorney for the Southern District of New York launched an investigation into Drexel Burnham Lambert under the Racketeering Influenced and Corruption Organisations Act 1970.[83] As a result of the threat of prosecution, Drexel Burnham Lambert entered into an 'Alford plea'[84] for several market manipulation charges and agreed to pay a fine of $650 million to the SEC.[85] In consequence, Drexel Burnham Lambert was forced to close several of its departments which resulted in the loss of 5,000 jobs.

DPAs in the US are granted for a number of years and once the corporation is able to demonstrate that they have complied with the terms of the DPA, the charges are dropped. Conversely, if a corporation breaches the terms of the

[77] S Smith, 'Reforming the law of adhesion contracts: a judicial response to the subprime mortgage crisis' (2010) *Fall Lewis & Clark Law* 1060.

[78] For the definitive commentary on the Savings and Loans Crisis and its association with control fraud see W Black, *The best way to rob a bank is to own one – how corporate executives and politicians looted the S&L industry* (Texas, University of Texas Press, 2005).

[79] C Golumbie and A Lichy, 'The too big to jail effect and the impact on the Justice Department's corporate charging policy' (2014) 65 *Hastings Law Journal* 1301.

[80] See generally Committee on the Judiciary House of Representatives Hearings before the Subcommittee on Crime of the Committee on the Judiciary House of Representatives on HR 3500 and HR 3911: Major Fraud Act of 1988 (Washington DC, Committee on the Judiciary House of Representatives, 1989).

[81] See Golumbie and Lichy (n 79) 1301–02.

[82] Levine was given a two-year custodial sentence and ordered to pay a fine of $362,000. See T Lueck, 'Levine gets 2-year jail term' 21 February 1987, available from www.nytimes.com/1987/02/21/business/levine-gets-2-year-jail-term.html, accessed 10 November 2017.

[83] Public Law 91-452 and 18 USC ss 1961–1968.

[84] An Alford plea is where a defendant submits a guilty plea but at the same time asserts their innocence. See *North Carolina v Alford* 400 US 25 (1970).

[85] K Eichenwald, 'The collapse of Drexel Burnham Lambert; Drexel, symbol of Wall St, era, is dismantling; bankruptcy filed' 14 February 1990, available from www.nytimes.com/1990/02/14/business/collapse-drexel-burnham-lambert-drexel-symbol-wall-st-era-dismantling-bankruptcy.html?pagewanted=all, accessed 10 November 2017.

agreement the investigation will be restarted. One way to mitigate the impact of corporate conviction is by using DPAs, which was illustrated by the '1990s Treasury Bond scandal'. Here, the investment-banking corporation Salomon Brothers was investigated for breaches of the False Claims Act 1986[86] and the Sherman Act 1890 for making unlicensed bids for Treasury bonds.[87] The corporation submitted to a DPA where it agreed to pay a large fine,[88] to continue assisting investigators and to introduce a new compliance structure.[89] This was followed by the imposition of another DPA on Prudential Securities Incorporated, which defrauded 400,000 investors of $8 billion.[90] Prudential Securities Corporation agreed to pay a $330 million fine, continued to cooperate with the investigation and made several corporate governance alterations including the appointment of an independent director.[91] Here, the aim of DPAs was to discipline the offending corporations and eliminate the financial advantage derived from the illegal conduct. If the financial penalty imposed as part of the DPA is too high or so excessive that the corporation folds, the impact is then on employees, customers and the supply chain. This has been referred to as the collateral consequences (as outlined below) of a corporation losing its licence. These two cases can clearly be contrasted with the damaging impact of the corporate convictions of EF Hutton and Drexel Burnham Lambert.

Undoubtedly the use of DPAs is fraught with legal, ethical and political concerns. It was not until the conviction of Arthur Andersen LLP, one of the 'Big Five' accounting firms, that the DoJ reconsidered the indictment of corporations and fully used DPAs.[92] Arthur Andersen had acted as an outside accountant for Enron, which collapsed in 2001 due to wide scale fraudulent activities.[93] Arthur Andersen was accused of shredding audit documents during the DoJ investigation into Enron's conduct and subsequently agreed to surrender its practising licence as a Certified Public Accountant following its conviction for obstruction

[86] Public Law 99-562, 100 Stat 3153.

[87] 26 Start 209 15 USC ss 1–7.

[88] United States Department of Justice 'Department of Justice and SEC enter $290m settlement with Saloman Brothers in Treasury Securities Case' 20 May 1992, available from www.justice.gov/archive/atr/public/press_releases/1992/211182.htm, accessed 10 November 2017.

[89] See *US v Saloman Brothers Incorporated* 92 Civ 3200 1992.

[90] Also see Securities and Exchange Commission 'Prudential to pay $600 Million in Global Settlement of Fraud Charges in Connection with Deceptive Market Timing of Mutual Funds' 28 August 2006, available from www.sec.gov/news/press/2006/2006-145.htm, accessed 10 November 2017.

[91] See Golumbie and Lichy (n 79) 1302.

[92] Between 2000 and 2016 a total of 457 DPAs were imposed by the DoJ and SEC. See Gibson Gunn, '2017 Mid-Year Update on Corporate Non-Prosecution Agreements (NPAs) and Deferred Prosecution Agreements (DPAs)' 11 July 2017, available from www.gibsondunn.com/2017-mid-year-update-on-corporate-non-prosecution-agreements-npas-and-deferred-prosecution-agreements-dpas/#_ftn3, accessed 26 February 2018.

[93] Two of Enron's directors, Kenneth Lay and Jeffrey Skilling were convicted on multiple counts of securities, wire fraud, money laundering and insider trading. Lay was convicted and sentenced to 45 years in prison, although he died before commencing his sentence. Skilling was sentenced to 24 years' imprisonment, which has since been reduced to ten years on appeal. See *Skilling v United States* (No 08-1394) 554 F 3d, 529.

of justice. Subsequently, Arthur Andersen filed for bankruptcy and approximately 30,000 employees were made redundant. The impact of the conviction on Arthur Andersen was catastrophic and 'there was nothing left of the firm to be salvaged'.[94] Subsequently, the Supreme Court overturned the conviction of Arthur Andersen in 2005 due to inaccurate jury instructions by federal prosecutors.[95,96]

Despite this questionable use of DPAs US federal prosecutors are too scared to indict corporations following the collapse of Arthur Andersen. For example, in December 2012, the DoJ announced that it had reached an agreement with HSBC for violating US AML laws, the United Nations sanctions regime and related criminal offences.[97] In particular, HSBC admitted to breaching the Bank Secrecy Act 1970,[98] the International Emergency Economic Powers Act 1977[99] and the Trading with the Enemy Act 1917.[100] The DoJ noted that 'HSBC's blatant failure to implement proper AML controls facilitated the laundering of at least $881m in drug proceeds through the US … [its] willful flouting of US sanctions laws … resulted in the processing of hundreds of millions of dollars in OFAC-prohibited transactions'.[101] HSBC entered into a five year DPA, agreed to pay a financial penalty of $1.92 billion, introduced a series of measures to improve its compliance procedures and offered an apology.[102] In December 2017, the DoJ announced that it was seeking the dismissal of the charges brought against HSBC and had filed a petition with the US District Court for the Easter District of New York.[103] HSBC responded by announcing that the five-year DPA had expired and the DoJ charges

[94] V Rajah, 'Prosecution of financial crimes and its relationship to a culture of compliance' (2016) 37 *Company Lawyer* 123.

[95] Indeed the Supreme Court unanimously noted that 'jury instructions at issue simply failed to convey the requisite consciousness of wrongdoing'. See *Arthur Andersen LLP v United States*, 544 US 696 (2005).

[96] See Costantino Grasso, 'Peaks and Troughs of the English Deferred Prosecution Agreement: The Lesson Learned From the DPA Between the SFO and ICBC SB Plc.' (2016) 5 *Journal of Business Law* 388.

[97] See United States Department of Justice 'HSBC Holdings Plc and HSBC Bank USA N.A Admit to anti-money laundering and sanctions violations, forfeit $1.256bn in deferred prosecution agreement' 11 December 2012, available from www.justice.gov/opa/pr/hsbc-holdings-plc-and-hsbc-bank-usa-na-admit-anti-money-laundering-and-sanctions-violations, accessed 3 August 2016.

[98] This is also referred to as the Currency and Foreign Transactions Reporting Act, Public Law 91–508.

[99] Public Law 95–223 91 Stat 1626.

[100] 40 Stat 411 12 USC ss 95a and b, 50 USC App ss 1–44.

[101] United States Department of Justice (n 97).

[102] ibid. Also see HSBC, 'HSBC announces settlements with authorities' 11 December 2012, available from www.hsbc.com/news-and-insight/media-resources/media-releases/2012/hsbc-announces-settlements-with-authorities, accessed 6 December 2017.

[103] M Arnold, 'US DoJ seeks dismissal of HSBC deferred criminal charges' 11 December 2017, available from www.ft.com/content/874f90e9-0098-37c6-ba00-10574f66ab65, accessed 21 February 2018.

have been deferred.[104] One of the aims of punishment is deterrence. HSBC, like Arthur Andersen, was a repeat offender who had previously been sanctioned by law enforcement agencies in France,[105] the UK,[106] Switzerland,[107] the US[108] and Hong Kong.[109]

An alternative form of enforcement mechanism to tackle corporate financial crime, the Sentencing Reform Act, was introduced, as part of the Comprehensive Crime Control Act of 1984.[110] Importantly, the Act granted both law enforcement and regulatory agencies with additional powers to tackle corporate economic crime. With this in mind, the SEC has imposed a record number of financial penalties.[111] The Commodities and Futures Trading Commission (CFTC) have adopted a similar enforcement strategy since the introduction of the Sentencing Reform Act 1984.[112] The introduction of the Sentencing Reform Act 1984

[104] HSBC, 'HSBC Holdings plc Expiration of 2012 Deferred Prosecution Agreement' 11 December 2017, available from www.hsbc.com/news-and-insight/media-resources/media-releases/2017/hsbc-holdings-plc-expiration-of-2012-deferred-prosecution-agreement, accessed 18 December 2017.

[105] In November 2017 the Cour d'appel de Paris approved the use of a DPA against HSBC for money laundering and tax evasion charges. See Ministère de la Justice, 'Convention judiciaire d'intérêt public between the National Financial Prosecutor of the Paris first instance court and HSBC Private Bank (Suisse) SA' 14 November 2017, available from www.economie.gouv.fr/files/files/directions_services/afa/CJIP_English_version.pdf, accessed 6 December 2017.

[106] Financial Conduct Authority, 'Final Notice HSBC' 11 November 2014, available from www.fca.org.uk/publication/final-notices/final-notice-hsbc.pdf, accessed 6 December 2017.

[107] J Titcomb, 'HSBC to pay £28m after money laundering investigation' 4 June 2015, available from www.telegraph.co.uk/finance/newsbysector/banksandfinance/11652093/Swiss-authorities-fine-HSBC-after-money-laundering-investigation.html, accessed 6 December 2017.

[108] Federal Reserve, 'Federal Reserve Board fines HSBC Holdings plc and HSBC North America Holdings Inc. $175 million for unsafe and unsound practices in FX trading' 29 September 2017, available from www.federalreserve.gov/newsevents/pressreleases/enforcement20170929a.htm, accessed 6 December 2017.

[109] The Securities and Futures Commission, 'HSBC Private Bank (Suisse) SA fined HK$400 million for systemic failures in selling structured products' 21 November 2017, available from www.sfc.hk/edistributionWeb/gateway/EN/news-and-announcements/news/doc?refNo=17PR138, accessed 6 December 2017.

[110] Pub L 98–473.

[111] eg, in 2012 the SEC announced that it had 'obtained orders in fiscal year 2012 requiring the payment of more than $3bn in penalties and disgorgement for the benefit of harmed investors'. In 2015, the SEC filed over 800 enforcement actions and 'obtained orders totalling approximately $4.2bn in disgorgement and penalties'. A year later the SEC announced that it had filed over 860 enforcement actions and obtained orders totalling more than $4bn. More recently, the SEC has obtained 754 enforcement activities and has imposed financial penalties totalling $3.8bn. See Securities and Exchange Commission, 'SEC's Enforcement Program Continues to Show Strong Results in Safeguarding Investors and Markets' 14 November 2012, available from www.sec.gov/News/PressRelease/Detail/PressRelease/1365171485830, accessed 11 August 2013; Securities and Exchange Commission, 'SEC Announces Enforcement Results For FY 2015' 22 October 2015, available from www.sec.gov/news/pressrelease/2015-245.html, accessed 18 December 2017; Securities and Exchange Commission, 'SEC Announces Enforcement Results For FY 2016' 11 October 2017, available from www.sec.gov/news/pressrelease/2016-212.html, accessed 18 December 2017 and Securities and Exchange Commission, 'SEC Enforcement Division Issues Report on Priorities and FY 2017 Results' 15 November 2017, available from www.sec.gov/news/press-release/2017-210, accessed 18 December 2017.

[112] In 2013 its Division of Enforcement filed 82 enforcement actions including financial penalites of $1.5bn. In 2015, the CFTC stated it had filed 69 actions which included financial penalites exceeding $3bn. In 2017, the CFTC announced that it had filed 49 financial actions and imposed financial

has permitted law enforcement and financial regulation agencies to impose a number of large financial penalties on corporations who have breached financial crime legislation. This is the most frequently used enforcement power against corporations in the US and it is regularly used in association with a DPA, as was illustrated in the HSBC case outlined above.

Another important legislative measure that has been used against corporations is the Financial Institutions Reform, Recovery and Enforcement Act 1989.[113] The Act was introduced as a response to the Savings and Loans crisis in the 1980s and permits law enforcement and financial regulatory agencies to instigate civil proceedings against corporations for a wide range of financial crimes. This includes mail fraud, wire fraud, providing false statements and bank fraud. The 1989 Act provides that prosecutors are only required to illustrate a civil burden of proof and not a criminal burden in order to impose civil liability on the offending corporation.[114] This civil measure has been used by the DoJ on numerous occasions for corporate financial crime offences and it has generated billions of dollars in financial penalties and compensation for victims where identifiable. For example, the DoJ reached an agreement with Bank of America who settled the 'the largest civil settlement ($16.65bn) with a single entity in American history' under the 1989 Act.[115] Other examples include the largest settlement for robo-signing,[116] fair lending settlements with Countrywide Financial Corporation[117] and Wells Fargo Bank.[118]

penalites totalling £413m. See Commodities Futures Trading Commission, 'CFTC Releases Enforcement Division's Annual Results for 2013' 24 October 2013, available from www.cftc.gov/PressRoom/PressReleases/pr6749-13, accessed 18 December 2017; Commodities Futures Trading Commission, 'CFTC Releases Enforcement Division's Annual Results for 2015' 6 November 2015, available from www.cftc.gov/PressRoom/PressReleases/pr7274-15, accessed 18 December 2017 and Commodities Futures Trading Commission, 'CFTC Releases Enforcement Division's Annual Results for 2017' 22 November 2017, available from www.cftc.gov/PressRoom/PressReleases/pr7650-17, accessed 18 December 2017. The Federal Trade Commission has imposed large financial penalties on firms who have participated in predatory lending practices which includes Ameriquest, Household International, Bear Stearns and EMC Mortgage. A full list of the enforcement activities of the Federal Trade Commission can be found at Federal Trade Commission 'Enforcement', n/d, available from www.ftc.gov/enforcement, accessed 19 December 2017.

[113] Pub L 101–73.

[114] Financial Institutions Reform, Recovery and Enforcement Act 1989, s 951.

[115] United States Department of Justice, 'Bank of America to pay $16.65 billion in historic Justice of Department settlement for financial fraud leading up to and during the financial crisis' 21 August 2014, available from www.justice.gov/opa/pr/bank-america-pay-1665-billion-historic-justice-department-settlement-financial-fraud-leading, accessed 7 August 2017.

[116] Department of Justice, '$25 Billion Mortgage Servicing Agreement Filed in Federal Court' 12 March 2012, available from www.justice.gov/opa/pr/2012/March/12-asg-306.html, accessed 2 October 2013.

[117] Department of Justice, 'Justice Department Reaches $335 Million Settlement to Resolve Allegations of Lending Discrimination by Countrywide Financial Corporation' 21 December 2011, available at www.justice.gov/opa/pr/justice-department-reaches-335-million-settlement-resolve-allegations-lending-discrimination.

[118] Department of Justice, 'Manhattan U.S. Attorney Files Mortgage Fraud Lawsuit Against Wells Fargo Bank, N.A. Seeking Hundreds of Millions of Dollars in Damages for Fraudulently Certified Loans' 9 October 2012, available at www.justice.gov/archive/usao/nys/pressreleases/October12/WellsFargoLawsuitPR.html.

The importance of the 1989 Act is further illustrated by figures published by the DoJ in December 2016 when it announced that it had collected more than $15.3bn in civil sanctions.[119] The introduction of financial penalties and civil proceedings are to be broadly welcomed, as these measures have imposed some form of liability on corporations for financial crime breaches. Then again, the impact of financial penalties on corporations is negligible as they are often smaller than administrative actions and related civil actions and therefore did little to prevent misconduct.[120]

The financial penalties imposed in the US by its financial regulatory and law enforcement bodies are administrative in nature, thus adopting a similar approach to that used in the UK. However, the difference in the financial penalties imposed in the US when compared to the UK, is the frequency of fines and the amount of the fine. For example, in 2014, the total monetary value of the fines imposed in the UK by the FCA was £1.4bn.[121] However, this figure is insignificant when compared to some of the financial penalties imposed by US authorities. For example, in August 2014 the DoJ imposed its largest financial penalty on Bank of America ($16.65bn) for fraud during the 2007/08 financial crisis.[122] This one financial penalty is 400 per cent more than the total financial value of fines imposed by the UK's financial regulatory agencies since 2002.[123] Therefore, the fines imposed in the US, when compared to the UK, could be regarded as disproportionate.

VII. Conclusion

This chapter has set out to discuss the use of sanctions in the context of market abuse, and the purpose was to show the often delicate yet functional approach to sanctions which often seem to be criminal law but are still labelled by the legislator as administrative or civil law. This is particularly evident in the EU context where Article 49 of the EU Charter on the need for proportionate sanctions only apply to criminal law. Likewise, given the history of the development of EU sanctions,

[119] United States Department of Justice, 'Justice Department collects more than $15.3bn in civil and criminal cases in fiscal year 2016' 14 December 2016, available from www.justice.gov/opa/pr/justice-department-collects-more-153-billion-civil-and-criminal-cases-fiscal-year-2016.

[120] Gabriel Markoff, 'Arthur Andersen and the Myth of the Corporate Death Penalty: Corporate Criminal Convictions in the Twenty-First Century' (2013) 15 *University of Pennsylvania Journal of Business Law* 803.

[121] Financial Conduct Authority, 'Fine table 2014' 31 August 2016, available from www.fca.org.uk/news/news-stories/2014-fines, accessed 28 January 2019. A total of 40 financial penalties were imposed by the FCA in 2014.

[122] United States Department of Justice, 'Bank of America to pay $16.65bn in historic Justice Department Settlement for financial fraud leading up to and during the financial crisis' 21 August 2014, available from www.justice.gov/opa/pr/bank-america-pay-1665-billion-historic-justice-department-settlement-financial-fraud-leading, accessed 28 January 2019.

[123] The total amount of fines imposed in the UK is approximately £3.7bn.

the legislator has had a very restricted competence in criminal law matters, and thereby opted for the administrative pathway often contrary to Article 6 ECHR. Furthermore in the EU context, the effectiveness and loyalty obligation towards the EU has often required Member States to adopt harsh sanctions, but the enforcement of those sanctions has been left to the Member States and sometimes lacked effectiveness.

Moreover, this chapter has then adopted a more practical stance and looked at both the UK and US and how these countries have adopted similar enforcement models towards financial crime and have favoured imposing financial penalties. UK efforts to tackle financial crime concentrated on targeting individuals as opposed to corporations. The unsatisfactory nature of this stance led to the introduction of the failure to prevent bribery corporate offence. This has secured several DPAs against corporations, but there have been no related prosecutions and UK authorities have adopted a similar approach to their counterparts in the US. The ability of the FCA to instigate financial penalties draws unfavourable comparisons with the provisions in the US and it is recommended that the UK should impose higher financial penalties. The US judiciary has adopted a flexible and innovative approach towards the doctrine of corporate criminal responsibility, which can be contrasted with the UK. The DoJ initially targeted prosecuting employees rather than corporations as illustrated following the Savings and Loans Crisis and have subsequently secured the conviction of several corporations for fraud. However, each case has illustrated the collateral consequences of obtaining a criminal corporate conviction. These collateral consequences resulted in the DoJ abandoning its prosecution of corporations in favour of DPAs. DPAs are aimed at preventing collateral consequences but they have done little to deter future criminal misconduct by corporations, as illustrated by HSBC. The DoJ declined to prosecute any staff in either HSBC or Arthur Andersen, who had been associated with major financial crime breaches committed by both of these companies. Therefore, DPAs must be used in conjunction with the prosecution of employees who are responsible for the implementation of a corporation's financial crime obligations. The additional value presented by financial penalties is minimal because they are often less than the illegal gains made by the corporation.

A major difference between the EU and the UK on the one hand and the US on the other hand is the use of proportionality under EU law that seems often absent in US law. The US also uses more administrative law, while the UK uses civil law penalties. The EU in turn often uses a double approach by legislating on both administrative and criminal law sanctions and thereby questioning the effective use of the EU principle of proportionality.

The book will now turn to the EU's wider fight against financial crimes and its relevance for understanding the suppression of market abuse before investigating the system of the UK and the USA in this regard.

4

Market Abuse and the Wider EU Fight Against Financial Crimes

I. Introduction

The aim of this chapter is to broaden the discussion and look at the EU framework for combatting market abuse in the context of the EU's wider fight against financial crime. Specifically, the chapter is concerned with the links between the EU market abuse regime and other EU financial crimes areas such as the fight against money laundering and the suppression against EU fraud. In addition, the chapter will investigate the establishment of the European Public Prosecutor's Office (EPPO) and discuss its relevance for understanding EU market abuse. In so doing the chapter discusses also the question as to whether this prosecutor will have a role to play in the EU fight against market abuse. The chapter will also briefly discuss broader issues of subsidiarity, accountability for EU agencies as well as EU fundamental rights and data protection. Thus, the aim of the chapter is to zoom out and discuss market abuse in the broader framework of the EU current strategies to fight financial crimes. As explained in the previous chapters, market abuse is generally considered to hamper confidence in the market. In the EU context, there seems however to be no general definition of 'confidence' in the market but rather the issue becomes perhaps a question of whether one could envisage the need to ensure confidence as a reason for legislation, and to what extent the effectiveness requirement in terms of the 'general good' should prevail over the autonomy of the individual.[1] Financial crimes are generally any kind of criminal conduct relating to money or to financial services or markets, indicating the wide ranging and potentially broad zone of what could be categorised as 'white-collar crime'.[2]

[1] For a discussion of these issues, see eg Ester Herlin-Karnell, 'Is there more to it than the fight against "Dirty Money"? Art 95 EC and the Criminal Law' (2008) 19 *European Business Law Review* 558, with further references.

[2] See FSMA 2000, www.legislation.gov.uk/ukpga/2000/8/contents (last accessed November 2018). The term 'white collar crime' was famously used by Professor Edwin Sutherland in his seminal paper. See Edwin Sutherland, 'White-collar criminality' (1940) 5(1) *American Sociological Review*.

II. The Wider Area of Financial Crimes: Money Laundering and Fraud

Understanding market abuse and the EU's strategies to fight it, as it is suggested in this book, requires us to place it in the broader context of the EU's fight against financial crimes. As was discussed in chapter two above, the EU has, since the early days, linked the fight against financial crimes with the establishment of the EU market.[3]

As Richard Alexander explains, it is difficult to demarcate insider dealing and market abuse from other categories of financial crimes such as money laundering.[4] For example, market abuse and insider dealing give rise to proceeds of crime which can subsequently be used for money laundering and fraud. In addition, the EU fight against corruption is related to the fight against fraud as forming part of this wide category of white collar crime and other irregularities that the EU seeks to fight.[5] The EU's approach here is often described as consisting of three parts.[6] Initially, the policy was directed at protecting Community finances from corruption from within the EU's own institutions. The second objective was to provide EU citizens with a high level of safety in the AFSJ, devoid of criminal activity. The third rationale for EU anti-corruption measures relates to the internal market and, more specifically, to linking the elimination of corruption to market integration.[7] As will be explored in this chapter, these broader policies are highly relevant to the anti-market abuse grid.

A. EU Anti-Money Laundering Legislation

As noted, the occurrence of market abuse is often difficult to demarcate from other forms of financial crimes as many of the crimes are overlapping. In this regard, the money laundering Directives offer further interesting examples with

[3] Niamh Moloney, *EU Securities Regulation* (Oxford, Oxford University Press, 2014) ch 8.

[4] Richard Alexander, *Insider Dealing and Money Laundering in the EU: Law and Regulation* (Abington, Routledge, 2016) ch 1. See also Council Decision 2007/845/JHA of 6 December 2007 concerning cooperation between Asset Recovery Offices of the Member States in the field of tracing and identification of proceeds from, or other property related to, crime.

[5] See generally European Commission 'Corruption', n/d, available from https://ec.europa.eu/home-affairs/what-we-do/policies/organized-crime-and-human-trafficking/corruption_en (last accessed 30 November 2018).

[6] ibid.

[7] Sope Williams, 'The Mandatory Exclusions for Corruption in the New EC Procurement Directives' (2006) 31 *European Law Review* 711. Commission, 'Fighting Corruption in the EU' (Communication), COM (2011) 308 final. See Council Document 17024/09, adopted by the European Council on 10/11 December 2009 (OJ C115, 1). See also the Resolution of the Council 6902/05, adopted on 14 May 2005, which called upon the Commission to also consider the development of a mutual evaluation and monitoring mechanism.

regard to the imposition of sanctions and thus the EU largely follows the international trend in the fight against dirty money and terrorist financing.[8] It should be remembered that the first Money Laundering Directive was adopted in 1991.[9] This Directive was subsequently amended in 2001[10] and then replaced by a Third Directive in 2005,[11] while the Commission has now introduced a Fourth and subsequently a Fifth Directive.[12] The Fourth Directive and Fifth Directives illustrate an impressive and ambitious attempt by the Commission to address many of the challenges neglected in the previous Directives, such as the definition of a predicate offence.[13] The Fourth Directive claimed to follow the international trend by including a specific reference to tax crimes within the serious crimes that can be considered as predicate offences to money laundering. Thus, the Directive stresses the importance of highlighting that 'tax crimes' relating to direct and indirect taxes are included in the broad definition of 'criminal activity' in this Directive, in line with the revised Financial Action Task Force (FATF) Recommendations.[14] Hence Member States should allow, to the greatest extent possible under their national law, the exchange of information or the provision of assistance between EU Financial Intelligence Units. So while not directly requiring a tax crime competence at the EU level, it does so indirectly by allocating enforcement powers to the EU.[15]

Recently, the EU adopted a proposal for a Sixth Directive based on Article 83 TFEU that lists money laundering as an EU crime.[16] The Directive was originally

[8] Fourth Money Laundering Directive, Directive of the European Parliament and of the Council on the Prevention of the Use of the Financial System for the Purpose of Money Laundering and Terrorist Financing, Directive (EU) 2015/849. See also the European security agenda COM (2015) 185 final and proposal for a Directive on Combating terrorism and replacing Council Framework Decision 2002/475/JHA, COM (2015) 625 final.

[9] Directive 91/308/EEC OJ 1991 L 166/77.

[10] Directive 2001/97/EC of the European Parliament and of the Council amending Directive 91/308/EEC on the prevention of the use of the financial system for the purpose of money laundering OJ L344, 28 December 2004.

[11] Directive 2005/60/EC OJ L309/15, 25 November 2005.

[12] Directive 2015/849 of the European Parliament and of the Council of 20 May 2015 on the Prevention of the use of the Financial System for the Purposes of Money Laundering or Terrorist Financing, Amending Regulation No 648/2012 of the European Parliament and of the Council, 2015 OJ (L 141) 73. Directive (EU) 2018/843 of the European Parliament and of the Council of 30 May 2018 amending Directive (EU) 2015/849 on the prevention of the use of the financial system for the purposes of money laundering or terrorist financing, and amending Directives 2009/138/EC and 2013/36/EU, 2018 OJ (L 156) 43–74.

[13] Money laundering is by definition based on another crime termed a predicate offence, which gives rise to the laundering in question.

[14] Given that different tax offences may be designated in each Member State as constituting 'criminal activity' punishable by means of the sanctions as referred to in point (4)(f) of Article 3 of this Directive, national law definitions of tax crimes may diverge.

[15] Article 57 states 'Differences between national law definitions of tax crimes shall not impede the ability of FIUs to exchange information or provide assistance to another FIU, to the greatest extent possible under their national law'.

[16] European Parliament legislative resolution of 12 September 2018 on the proposal for a directive of the European Parliament and of the Council on countering money laundering by criminal law (COM (2016)0826 C8 0534/2016 2016/0414 (COD)).

proposed to complement the Fourth Directive adopted under Article 114 TFEU. The proposed Directive states that the definition of criminal activities which constitute predicate offences for money laundering should be sufficiently uniform in all Member States. Member States should ensure that all offences that are punishable by a term of imprisonment as set out in this Directive are considered predicate offences for money laundering. Moreover, to the extent that the application of those penalty thresholds does not already do so, Member States should include a range of offences within each of the categories of offences listed in this Directive. In that case, Member States should be able to decide how to delimit the range of offences within each category.

Similarly to the market abuse regime approach with parallel instruments (Market Abuse Directive (MAD) and Market Abuse Regulation (MAR)), in the area of anti-money laundering legislation the EU has also adopted a Regulation related to the suppression of money laundering, based on Article 114 TFEU, regulating the transfer of funds.[17] This is linked to the EU's internal security strategy and focuses on ensuring the payer's information is made immediately available to law enforcement and prosecutorial authorities. Curiously, while largely overlapping with the Directive, the Regulation points out that it may not always be possible in criminal investigations to identify the relevant data or the person concerned until long after the original transfer took place. Consequently, a preventive approach should be adopted and information stored to facilitate investigation. The Regulations affirm that information on the payer and the payee shall not be retained for longer than strictly necessary. Payment service providers of the payer and of the payee shall retain records of the information (Articles 4–7 of the Regulation) for a period of five years.

This raises several questions. Is the retention of data for five years proportionate? Would it stand a proportionality test on the necessity of keeping the data for that long?[18] As noted in chapter two, within such a risk-based approach to money laundering, private actors, such as lawyers and banks, are expected to make risk assessments of their customers and divide them into low and high-risk. The rationale for actively engaging the private sector in the anti-money laundering process is to make them collect the appropriate information. Therefore, and as explained in chapter two, this is commonly referred to as a 'risk-based approach' because private actors are required to pass on sensitive information based on a risk assessment of their clients.[19] But the risk-based approach could also be seen in a broader governing context of risk regulation at the EU (criminal law) level. Thus, the question of the governing of risk connects to the justification of

[17] Regulation (EU) 2015/847 on information accompanying transfers of funds, OJ L 141, 5.6.2015, pp 1–18.

[18] See Case C-293/12 and C-594/12, Digital rights, judgment of 8 April 2014 and Case C-362/14, Schrems, judgment delivered on 6 October 2015.

[19] See eg Nicholas Ryder, *Money laundering – an endless cycle? A comparative analysis of the anti-money laundering policies in the United States of America, the United Kingdom, Australia and Canada* (London, Routledge, 2012).

EU legislative action in the first place. Furthermore, as is well known the FATF has issued several guidance notes for the private sector that seek to incorporate the risk-based approach.[20] The Money Laundering Directives also provide that customer due diligence comprises 'identifying, where applicable, the beneficial owner and taking risk-based and adequate measures to verify his identity so that the institution or person covered by this Directive is satisfied that it knows who the beneficial owner is, including, as regards legal persons, trusts and similar legal arrangements, taking risk-based and adequate measures to understand the ownership and control structure of the customer'.[21]

In addition, the recent Anti-Money Laundering Directives have sought to establish an increased focus on risk assessment at the national level. Such a risk assessment is to be carried out in liaison with various agencies that should provide guidance for the Member States as to how to carry out risk assessments and where European Supervisory Authority (ESA) plays a key role. The ESA is being asked to provide regulatory technical standards where needed for financial institutions to adapt their internal controls to deal with specific situations.

It should be remembered that the *Meroni* doctrine holds that only executive powers can be delegated from the EU institutions to agencies and their use must be entirely subject to the supervision of the delegating institution.[22] Moreover, the European Securities and Markets Authority (ESMA) case,[23] is interesting here as it concerned Regulation No 236/2012, which lays down a common regulatory framework with regard to the requirements and powers relating to short selling and credit default swaps to ensure greater coordination and consistency between Member States and which granted ESMA powers to supervise the area. In this case, the UK challenged this on the basis that it had not intended to authorise ESMA to take individual measures directed at natural or legal persons. The Court of Justice of the EU upheld the Regulation. It stated that

> the EU legislature, in its choice of method of harmonisation and, taking account of the discretion it enjoys with regard to the measures provided for under Article 114 TFEU, may delegate to a Union body, office or agency powers for the implementation of the harmonisation sought. That is the case in particular where the measures to be adopted are dependent on specific professional and technical expertise and the ability of such a body to respond swiftly and appropriately.[24]

Hence, the outsourcing of responsibility is a phenomenon in EU law that is becoming more and more common, and will be addressed in further detail below.

[20] This includes eg guidance for the financial sector, accountants, the legal profession and casinos.

[21] eg Directive (EU) 2018/843 (n 12).

[22] Case C-9/56 and C-10/56, *Meroni & Co, Industrie Metallurgiche s.p.a. v High Authority* [1957–1958] ECR 133; Marta Simoncini, 'Legal Boundaries of European Supervisory Authorities (ESAs) in the Financial Markets Tensions in the Development of True Regulatory Agencies' (2015) *Yearbook of European Law* 1–32, see also Pierre Schammo, 'EU day-to-day supervision or intervention-based supervision: Which way forward for the European system of financial supervision?' (2012) 32 *Oxford Journal of Legal Studies* 771.

[23] C-270/12, *UK v Council and European Parliament*, judgment of 7 March 2014.

[24] ibid.

B. Fraud against the EU's Budget

The EU fights fraud at a number of levels. For example, the EU has a new Directive in place.[25] The question of enforcement of EU anti-fraud policies seems still largely left to the EU Court of Justice through its case law. According to the well-established case law starting with the Greek Maize[26] case, as mentioned above, Member States have to protect EU interest the same way as it protects national interests. Specifically, this case concerned fraud against the EU where the Court held that:

> … the Member States must ensure that infringements of EU law are penalised under conditions, both procedural and substantive, which are analogous to those applicable to infringements of national law of a similar nature and importance and which, in any event, make the penalty effective, proportionate and dissuasive.

There are a number of legislative instruments to fight fraud against the EU budget. The first relevant anti-fraud measures in this area were adopted in 1995 with the Convention for the protection of the financial interests of the European Communities (the PIF Convention).[27] Against that background, the Directive on the fight against fraud to the Union's financial interests by means of criminal law was recently adopted.[28] The Directive is based on Article 325 TFEU and seeks to suppress fraud against the EU's budget and at first instance this appears to be a significant development in the evolution of the EU's counter fraud strategy. The scope of the Directive is limited to fraud committed against the financial interests of the EU where the instrument establishes minimum rules concerning the definition of criminal offences and sanctions with regard to combatting fraud and other illegal activities affecting the Union's financial interests. The idea is that the framework for combatting fraud is supplemented by general Union criminal law measures for the fight against certain illegal activities particularly harmful to the EU's financial interests, such as money laundering and corruption.

As mentioned above, the question of enforcement of EU anti-fraud policies seems then largely left to the CJEU through its case law. The case law on the equivalent protection and effectiveness of the EU system as developed by the CJEU, and as discussed more fully in chapter three above, has been supplemented by a number of legislative instruments to fight fraud against the EU budget. Thus, largely in line with this legislative measure the CJEU has recently in the *Taricco* judgment held that national rules on prescription periods, which hinder

[25] Directive (EU) 2017/1371 of the European Parliament and of the Council of 5 July 2017 on the fight against fraud to the Union's financial interests by means of criminal law, OJ L 198, 28.7.2017, pp 29–41. This is a very important development in the EU's policy towards fraud which has previously attracted a great deal of criticism. See eg, Nicholas Ryder, *Financial Crime in the 21st Century: Principles and Policies* (Edward Elgar, 2011).

[26] Case C-68/88 *Commission v Greece* [1989] ECR 1-2965, paragraph 24.

[27] Convention of 26 July 1995 (OJ C 316, 27.11.1995, p 49).

[28] Directive (EU) 2017/1371 of the European Parliament and of the Council of 5 July 2017 on the fight against fraud to the Union's financial interests by means of criminal law.

prosecutions of VAT fraud against the national budget, infringe EU law.[29] The Court held that 'The provisions of Article 325(1) and (2) TFEU therefore have the effect, in accordance with the principle of the precedence of EU law, in their relationship with the domestic law of the Member States, of rendering automatically inapplicable, merely by their entering into force, any conflicting provision of national law.'[30] The Court asserted that this approach was in line with the Charter of Fundamental Rights and the guarantees set out in Article 49 on proportionality of a sanction. While this case does not seem too controversial in the light of the spirit of EU law, it could nonetheless be argued that the division between the Union's financial interests and the Member States' interests does not make much sense when viewed in the light of the EU's market regulation powers. Of course, Article 325 TFEU only empowers the EU to fight fraud against its own budget. As will be shown below though with regard to the broader picture of market regulation and the construction of an AFSJ, the EU has largely transgressed the division of competence with regard to EU and Member States' finances and fiscal powers. Therefore, it is suggested that the limitation set out in Article 325 TFEU entails a rather cosmetic rule since the overall approach adopted by the EU seems not to be limited to fight fraud against the EU but also sets out to regulate the Member States as a result of the financial crisis.

Important here is also the Anti-Fraud Office (OLAF).[31] In short, OLAF concentrates on frauds committed against the EU and by monitoring its institutions, and it does not impose any anti-fraud obligations on Member States as such. The origins of its strategy can be traced to the creation of the Common Agricultural Policy which resulted in the number of allegations of fraud increasing.[32] OLAF was born in 1999 and investigates fraud against the EU budget, corruption and serious misconduct within the European institutions, and it develops anti-fraud policy for the European Commission.[33]

Generally, OLAF's function is to assist EU institutions to combat fraud and other financial indiscretions.[34] OLAF is responsible for the 'fraud-proofing of EU legislation',[35] and it has the ability to conduct administrative investigations,[36] which are defined as inspections and other appropriate measures performed by

[29] Case C-105/14, *Taricco* delivered on 8 September 2015, see also *Taricco II*, case C-42/17, judgment of 5 December 2017.

[30] ibid, at para 52.

[31] Regulation 883/2013 of the European Parliament and of the Council of 11 September 2013 concerning investigations conducted by the European Anti-Fraud Office (OLAF) and repealing Regulation (EC) No 1073/1999 of the European Parliament and of the Council and Council Regulation (Euratom) No 1074/1999.

[32] Dick Ruimschotel, 'The EC budget: ten percent fraud? A policy analysis approach' (1994) 32(3) *Journal of Common Market Studies* 320.

[33] https://ec.europa.eu/anti-fraud/about-us/history_en.

[34] Commission Decision of 28 April 1999 establishing the European Anti-Fraud Office (OLAF) (OJ 1999 L136).

[35] House of Lords European Union Committee, *Strengthening OLAF, the European Anti-Fraud Office* (London, House of Lords European Union Committee, 2004) 11.

[36] Johan Vlogaert and Michal Pesta, 'OLAF fighting fraud and beyond' in Steven Brown (ed), *Combating international crime – the longer arm of the law* (London, Routledge, 2008) 77–87.

OLAF staff to determine the quality of the allegation under investigation. There are two types of investigations – internal and external. Internal investigations relate to the financial indiscrepancies of EU and alleged staff misconduct,[37] while external investigations relate to activities that occur outside the EU. The effectiveness of these investigations is limited due to OLAF's inability to independently initiate them,[38] although it is permitted (though seemingly not encouraged) to assist other Member States by sharing information and financial intelligence. Due to these shortcomings a European Public Prosecutor's Office (EPPO) was proposed to offer a more effective EU cooperation model.

III. The European Public Prosecutor's Office and EU Agencies

The idea of establishing an EPPO is one of the most contested EU criminal law measures in recent years (based on Article 86 TFEU).[39] While EPPO currently does not have competences to prosecute market abuse or financial crimes in general but only crimes against the EU budget, there is a possibility for this prosecutor to have a wider competence. The establishment of EPPO emanates from the longstanding project of creating a comprehensive EU anti-fraud regime and has been extensively debated for over two decades, with the EPPO representing something of a jewel in the crown. As such the EPPO project represents a follow-up to the previous *Corpus Juris* venture.[40]

The EPPO has very limited enforcement powers, however. This is because EPPO is a centralised decision-making EU institution with a de-centralised enforcement structure of national authorities that investigates, prosecutes, and brings to judgment offences against the EU financial interests.[41] As Jürg Monar points out, the Member States have kept the law enforcement powers and have not delegated such powers to the AFSJ Agencies, with the exception of Frontex in the area of migration law policies.[42] Yet Europol has been given extended powers to supervise the EU crime-fighting agenda within the AFSJ.[43] This has resulted in a

[37] ibid, at 79.

[38] ibid.

[39] Regulation (EU) 2017/1939, implementing enhanced cooperation on the establishment of the European Public Prosecutor's Office, OJ L 283, 31.10.2017, pp 1–71.

[40] Mireille Delmas-Marty and John Vervaele (eds), *The Implementation of the Corpus Juris in the Member States* (Antwerp, Intersentia, 2000).

[41] Carlos Gómez-Jara Díez and Ester Herlin-Karnell, 'Prosecuting EU Financial Crimes: The European Public Prosecutor's Office in Comparison to the US Federal Regime' (2018) 19 *German Law Journal* 1191–1220.

[42] See generally, Jürg Monar, *Experimentalist Governance in Justice and Home Affairs, in Experimentalist Governance in the European Union* in Jonathan Zeitlin and Charles Sabel (eds), (2010).

[43] Regulation (EU) 2016/794 of the European Parliament and of the Council of 11 May 2016 on the European Union Agency for Law Enforcement Cooperation (Europol) and replacing and repealing Council Decisions 2009/371/JHA, 2009/934/JHA, 2009/935/JHA, 2009/936/JHA and 2009/968/JHA.

complex relationship between AFSJ legislation and the role played by Europol in, for example, the financial tracking programme and those legislative acts such as the numerous Money Laundering Directives, mentioned above, that are part of the internal market *acquis*. As for those instruments adopted within the internal market, the ESMA is responsible for any supervision. The ESMA Regulation contains a review clause that grants the CJEU the power to review the fines imposed by this agency. But it is not clear to what extent Europol and Eurojust can be held to account for their actions.[44] The same holds true for EPPO, which will have far-reaching competences yet limited enforcement powers to investigate EU financial crimes, as discussed below.[45]

Thus, EPPO is responsible for investigating, prosecuting and bringing to judgment, where appropriate in liaison with Europol, the perpetrators of and accomplices to offences against the Union's financial interests, as determined by the regulation provided for in Article 86 TFEU. The establishment of an EPPO has however met some serious opposition.[46] Considering the fact that during the legislative process for the adoption of EPPO, 11 Member States voted against the proposal through the yellow card procedure, one would have thought that the enhanced cooperation mechanism was the only venue available now. Instead the Commission has maintained essentially intact its proposal notwithstanding only the second use of the yellow card subsidiarity procedure since the procedure's inclusion in the Lisbon Treaty.[47] The Regulation was subsequently redrafted exactly so as to avoid this fragmented scenario taking place. But this was exactly what happened: the EPPO regulation was recently adopted, but prior to its enactment, it had triggered two yellow cards in the legislative process with regard to the earlier proposals for this legislation.[48] Eventually the EU Commission resorted to enhanced cooperation, a flexible mode of integration where not all Member States participate in the legislative measure – but at least nine Member States do – and this has attracted a lot of attention and debate in EU law scholarship.[49]

[44] On Agencies see Magdalena Busuioc, Deidre Curtin and Martin Groenleer, 'Agency Growth Between Autonomy and Accountability: The European Police Office as a "Living Institution"' (2011) 18(6) *Journal of European Public Policy* 848–67. See also Pierre Schammo, 'The European Securities and Market Authority: Lifting the Veil on the Allocation of Powers' (2011) *Common Market Law Review* 1887.

[45] Gerard Conway, 'Holding to Account A Possible European Public Prosecutor: Supranational Governance and Accountability Across Diverse Legal Traditions' (2013) *Criminal Law Forum* 24.

[46] See Katlin Ligeti (ed), *Toward a Prosecutor for the European Union Volume 1* (Oxford, Hart Publishing, 2012); Gerard Conway, 'The Future of a European Public Prosecutor' in Maria Fletcher, Ester Herlin-Karnell and Claudio Matera (eds), *The European Union as an Area of Freedom, Security and Justice* (Routledge, 2016) and Marienne Wade, 'A European Public Prosecutor: Potential and Pitfalls' (2013) 59 *Crime, Law & Social Change* 439.

[47] ibid.

[48] Treaty of Lisbon Amending the Treaty on European Union and the Treaty Establishing the European Community art. 12(b), 13 December 2007, 2007 OJ (C 306) (providing for a competence of national Parliaments to see that the principle of subsidiarity is respected in accordance with Protocol No. 2) [hereinafter Treaty of Lisbon].

[49] Lennert Erkelens, Pim Geelhoed and Arian Meij (eds), *The Establishment of the European Public Prosecutor's Office (EPPO): 'State of Play and Perspectives'* (The Hague, Springer, 2017) and Jacob Öberg,

In short, most arguments against the previous proposals for an EPPO concerned the inaccuracy of the figures presented by the Commission as well as the lack of added value of EPPO investigations.[50] It was also argued that its establishment had a possible detrimental impact on the existing actors in the area and their future cooperation with non-EPPO Member States.[51] The main argument as presented by the Commission is that Eurojust and Europol have a general mandate to facilitate the exchange of information and coordinate national criminal investigations and prosecutions, but lack the power to carry out acts of investigation or prosecution themselves. According to the Commission, action by national judicial authorities remains often slow, prosecution rates on the average low and results obtained in the different Member States over the Union as a whole unequal.[52] For this reason, the judicial action undertaken by Member States against fraud may currently not be considered as effective, equivalent and a deterrent as required under the Treaty. A potential problem with EPPO is that it is difficult to separate on the one hand rules relating to investigations and prosecutions, at the EU level, and on the other hand, trials at Member State level. According to Peers, for example, the Commission should have considered other possibilities of more limited measures to achieve the same objectives such as the harmonisation of the national prosecution rules in this area.[53]

Indeed, Article 86(4) provides the opportunity for a future European Council to adopt a decision amending the competences of such a prosecutor to include serious crime with a cross-border dimension in the broader sense. Whether Eurojust would simply be transformed into an EPPO or would be used to assist the formation of an EPPO is an open question on the basis of the phrasing in Article 86(1). Accordingly, today the EPPO currently has the competence to prosecute offences against the EU financial interests. Yet, Article 86(4) TFEU specifically enables the European Council – by way of a unanimous decision – to extend the powers of EPPO to include serious cross-border criminality.[54]

Limits to EU Powers: A Case Study of EU Regulatory Criminal Law (Oxford, Hart Publishing, 2017) ch 7. Carlos Gómez-Jara Díez and Ester Herlin-Karnell, 'Prosecuting EU Financial Crimes: The European Public Prosecutor's Office in Comparison to the US Federal Regime' (2018) 19 *German Law Journal* 1191–1220.

[50] Andreas Csuri, 'The Proposed European Public Prosecutor's Office – from a Trojan Horse to a White Elephant?' (2016) *Cambridge Yearbook of European Legal Studies* 1–30.

[51] ibid.

[52] Proposal for a Council Regulation on the Establishment of the European Public Prosecutor's Office, COM (2013) 0534 final (7 July 2013). See eg the contributions in Lennert Erkelens, Pim Geelhoed and Arian Meij (eds), *The Establishment of the European Public Prosecutor's Office (EPPO): 'State of Play and Perspectives'* (The Hague, Springer, 2017).

[53] Steve Peers, *EU Justice and Home Affairs Law* (Oxford, Oxford University Press, 2011) 858–60.

[54] The European Council may – at the same time or subsequently – adopt a decision amending paragraph one in order to extend the powers of the European Public Prosecutor's Office to include serious crime having a cross-border dimension and amending accordingly paragraph two as regards the perpetrators of, and accomplices in, serious crimes affecting more than one Member State. The European Council shall act unanimously after obtaining the consent of the European Parliament and after consulting the Commission.

Most importantly, EPPO is interesting also as regards the future operation of the EU Market Abuse Directive and Regulation.[55] As spelled out elsewhere there are three potential avenues for expanding EPPO powers:[56] (a) those areas already subject to EU criminal harmonisation on the basis of serious cross-border criminality – contained in Article 83.1 TFEU; (b) those cases subject to EU criminal harmonisation on the basis of a need to implement an EU policy, that additionally affect more than one Member State; and (c) those cases not subject to EU criminal harmonisation, but that are governed by EU law and affect more than one Member State.[57] One way would be to determine which type of financial crime – in a broad sense – has already been subject to EU harmonisation pursuant to the clause included in Article 83.1 TFEU. When market abuse and insider dealing affect more than one Member State it would seem reasonable that the EPPO could have jurisdiction. Moreover, it cannot be ruled out that there could be a potential extension of the EPPO's powers to areas related to banking supervision and the resolution of credit institutions. This, again, holds especially true when in some instances EU legislation is already imposing the obligation on EU institutions to ensure that individuals and companies are held criminally accountable, and Member States are obliged to impose 'effective, proportionate and dissuasive' sanctions for not complying with the obligations of EU legislation as discussed in chapters two and three above. In this sense – in the context of the resolution of credit institutions by the Single Resolution Mechanism – Regulation 806/2014[58] establishes as a general principle a governing resolution – Article 15 – that the Board, the Council and the Commission ensure that natural and legal persons are made liable, subject to national law, under civil or criminal law, for their responsibility for the failure of the institution under resolution.

Interestingly, in September 2018 in the 'State of the Union' yearly speech, Commission President Junker stated that 'we are proposing to extend the tasks of the newly established European Public Prosecutor's Office to include the fight against terrorist offences. We need to be able to prosecute terrorists in a more coordinated way, across our Union. Terrorists know no borders. We cannot allow ourselves to become unwitting accomplices because of our

[55] Directive 2014/57/EU of the European Parliament and of the Council of 16 April 2014 on criminal sanctions for market abuse (market abuse directive), OJ L 173, 12.6.2014, pp 179–89 (hereafter MAD), Regulation (EU) No 596/2014 on market abuse (market abuse regulation) and repealing Directive 2003/6/EC of the European Parliament and of the Council and Commission Directives 2003/124/EC, 2003/125/EC and 2004/72/EC, OJ L 173, 12.6.2014, pp 1–61 (hereafter MAR).

[56] Carlos Gómez-Jara Díez and Ester Herlin-Karnell, 'Prosecuting EU Financial Crimes: The European Public Prosecutor's Office in Comparison to the US Federal Regime' (2018) 19 *German Law Journal* 1191–1220.

[57] ibid.

[58] See Regulation 806/2014 of the European Parliament and of the Council of 15 July 2014, establishing Uniform Rules and a Uniform Procedure for the Resolution of Credit Institutions and Certain Investment Firms in the Framework of a Single Resolution Mechanism and a Single Resolution Fund and amending Regulation 1093/2010, 2014 OJ (L 225), pp 1–90; Directive 2014/59, of the European Parliament and of the Council of 15 May 2014, Establishing a Framework for the Recovery and Resolution of Credit Institutions and Investment Firms, art. 34, 2014 OJ (L 173), pp 190–348.

inability to cooperate'.[59] According to Junker, the link to the EU budget is not necessarily the most central element of EPPO: the fight against terrorism is a measure to enhance security in the EU and to increase consumer confidence in the market and already the Money Laundering Directive and its inclusion of terrorist financing is an example of the nexus between security and market law. Yet how does a possible extended jurisdiction of the EPPO correspond with the EU idea of subsidiarity and better regulation?

Moreover, the key question is perhaps whether the EPPO represents 'Better Regulation' at all? In its Better Regulation Agendas of 2016 and 2017 the Commission points out that where regulatory costs are found to be disproportionate to the goals pursued, alternative approaches to achieving the same goals will be explored.[60] A key question is also what happens when EU law is not enforced. The Communication 'EU law: Better results through better application' sets out a more strategic approach to the Commission's infringement policy, focusing on systemic problems, where the Commission's enforcement action can make a real difference.[61] The priority will be to investigate cases where Member States incorrectly transpose EU law into national law or fail to do so at all. The importance the Commission attaches to the timely transposition of Union law is reflected in its strengthened approach to financial sanctions for such cases.

Arguably, the EPPO project and the priorities to get it adopted seem closely connected to the reformation of the EU regulatory system for market regulation and as such in line with the recent Market Abuse and Money Laundering Directives and the new Fraud Directive and other measures. But the EPPO's biggest challenge is not what happens in the EU's institutions but what happens on the 'field'. It is the Member States and the Council who are to decide the fate of the EPPO with the consent of the European Parliament.

IV. Subsidiarity Questions and Accountability with Broader Relevance for the EU Market Abuse Regime

According to the EU idea of subsidiarity, Member States should have the first option to legislate themselves, if it is feasible, as action should only be taken at

[59] https://ec.europa.eu/commission/sites/beta-political/files/soteu2018-speech_en_0.pdf published September 2018 (last accessed 18 November 2018).

[60] Better Regulation 2016 and Better Regulation 2017 COM(2017) 651 final Completing the Better Regulation Agenda: Better solutions for better results. Ester Herlin-Karnell, 'The Establishment of a European Public Prosecutor's Office: Between "Better Regulation" and Subsidiarity Concerns' ch in Erkelens et al (n 48) ch 5.

[61] Better Regulation 2017 COM(2017) 651 final.

the EU level when it is needed.[62] Applying the principles of better regulation will ensure that measures are evidence-based, well designed and deliver tangible and sustainable benefits for citizens, business and society as a whole.

Subsidiarity has of course been in the limelight for a long time and remained a contested concept in mainstream EU constitutional law due to its political nature. Protocol No 2 on the Application of the Principles of Subsidiarity and Proportionality is attached to the Lisbon Treaty and is of crucial importance here. Briefly, this important protocol declares that the Commission must consult widely when proposing legislation and that it must furnish reasons as to why an objective is better achieved at the EU level which is supported by qualitative and, wherever possible, quantitative indicators.[63]

For the purpose of discussing the concept of subsidiarity a number of 'better criteria' are available. This is reflected in the so-called efficiency check of proposed legislation, which requires a comparative evaluation of the costs and benefits of action at Union and national level. This 'better criteria' analysis is commonly described as the comparative efficiency test, according to which EU action must be, to put it simply, more effective than action at the national level. More specifically, the Union should act only if the action in question cannot be achieved by the individual Member States and the EU can better achieve the desired result because of its effects or scale.[64] A well-known difficulty is that the notion of effectiveness suggests in itself various other criteria, such as whether a given level of government is in the best position to act from a geographical point of view or in terms of access to information.[65] However, part of the difficulty appears to be that there will be many areas in which the comparative efficiency test comes out in favour of EU action, as the very *raison d'être* of the EU will often demand supranational action to ensure the 'effectiveness' of EU law.

Recently, the EU Commission initiated a new Task Force on Subsidiarity, Proportionality and 'Doing Less More Efficiently' which was established by the President Juncker in November 2017.[66] In a similar fashion as the previous EU motto on being 'big on big things and small on small things', the Task Force represented an EU attempt to focus on important matters. The question arises perhaps whether subsidiarity is to be conceived in a different manner in the present context of the EU fight against financial crimes as compared to EU law in general?

[62] Nicholas Emiliou, 'Subsdiarity: An Effective Barrier against 'the Enterprise of Ambition' (1992) 17 *European Law Review* 383.

[63] Moreover, the Commission must submit an annual report to the Council, the European Council and the EP.

[64] ibid.

[65] Grainne de Búrca, 'Reappraising subsidiarity's significance after Amsterdam' *Jean Monnet paper* 7/1999.

[66] Subsidiarity and Proportionality: Task Force presents recommendations on a new way of working to President Juncker, Brussels 10 July 2018: see http://europa.eu/rapid/press-release_IP-18-4393_en.htm (last accessed 30 November 2018).

Indeed, Article 69 TFEU emphasises the importance of subsidiarity in chapters 4 and 5 of title V on the AFSJ concerning EU criminal law cooperation and police cooperation.[67] Does that mean that subsidiarity is not as important in the other policy fields of the AFSJ? The ordinary rules on subsidiarity monitoring including the Protocols No 1 and 2 apply to all legislation. As noted above, and as discussed by other authors in this volume, the EPPO has triggered not only one yellow card but two. That is very unusual and it indicates the delicate nature of the matter.[68]

At the very least Article 69 TFEU singles out the need for subsidiarity in the areas of criminal law and police cooperation and thereby confirms the sensitive nature of EU action in these areas.

A. Outsourcing of Responsibility?

A general trend in EU law is the outsourcing of responsibility in various sectors. For example, as indicated above, the Fourth and Fifth Money Laundering Directives contain several areas where work by the European Supervisory Authorities is envisaged as raising crucial issues with respect to the relationship between this agency and other AFSJ agencies such as Europol and Eurojust. This complex interaction of AFSJ policies and financial regulation at the heart of the internal market is intensified by the fact that the European Banking Authority has been asked to carry out an assessment of the money laundering and terrorist financing risks facing the EU. Yet the greater emphasis on the risk-based approach requires an enhanced degree of guidance for Member States and financial institutions on the factors to be taken into account when applying simplified and enhanced customer due diligence and when applying a risk-based approach to supervision. It is technocratic in the sense that the framework for fighting financial crimes is regulated in a way similarly to that of medical issues and risk regulation in environmental law.

Moreover, while the AFSJ agencies of Europol and Eurojust do not have direct regulatory enforcement powers, as mentioned above, they are increasingly important players in the AFSJ regulatory machinery. However, the Member States

[67] Article 69 TFEU states that: National Parliaments ensure that the proposals and legislative initiatives submitted under Chapters 4 and 5 comply with the principle of subsidiarity, in accordance with the arrangements laid down by the Protocol on the application of the principles of subsidiarity and proportionality.

[68] On 28 October 2013, the second yellow card ever was activated. Katlin Ligeti (ed), *Toward A Prosecutor For The European Union*, (Oxford, Hart Publishing, 2012); Diane Fromage, 'The Second Yellow Card on the EPPO Proposal: An Encouraging Development for Member State Parliaments?' (2016) 35(1) *Yearbook of European Law* 5–27; Andreas Csúri, 'The Proposed European Public Prosecutor's Office – from a Trojan Horse to a White Elephant?' (2016) *Cambridge YB of Eur Legal Stud* 1–30; Irene Wieczorek, 'The EPPO Draft Regulation Passes the First Subsidiarity Test: An Analysis and Interpretation of the European Commission's Hasty Approach to National Parliaments' Subsidiarity Arguments' (2016) *German Law Journal* 1247.

themselves have retained law enforcement powers and have not delegated such powers to the AFSJ agencies, with the exception of Frontex in the area of migration law policies.[69] Specifically, the possibilities of judicial review seem unclear, as it remains somewhat vague as to how an individual could challenge a decision of an Agency. Also EPPO has far-reaching powers to investigate financial crimes and with very little transparency as to how it could be held accountable.[70] There is a clear accountability deficit, therefore, with regard to the role and function of agencies as key agents in the sanctions game. It asks fundamental questions about the legitimacy of any enforcement of sanctions that are enforced through Agencies.[71]

Accordingly, the outsourcing of responsibility in the fight against financial crimes has several dimensions. For example, Europol plays an increasingly important role as a global information hub and information centre. The agency collects proceeds, retains and exchanges data in an unprecedented way.[72] For example, Europol was involved in the EU–US Agreement on the Terrorist Financing Tracking Programme.[73] Consequently, Europol assesses whether the data requested in any given case are necessary for the fight against terrorism and its financing. In addition, the interpretation of the data allows Europol to pinpoint the areas, activities or populations which are at risk and should be given priority in the fight against organised crime at the EU level.[74] Yet the new powers granted to Agencies, as noted, raise familiar questions not only about the accountability of these actors but also about the desirability of outsourced enforcement powers from the perspective of judicial review.[75]

As for accountability, the ESMA is responsible for any supervision. When it comes to judicial review, the ESMA contains a review clause that grants the CJEU the power to review the fines imposed by this agency. But as noted, it is not clear to what extent Europol and Eurojust can be held to account for their actions.

[69] Jürg Monar, 'Experimentalist Governance in Justice and Home Affairs' in Jonathan Zeitlin and Charles F Sabel (eds), *Experimentalist Governance in the European Union*, (Oxford, Oxford University Press, 2010) ch 10.

[70] Proposal for a Council Regulation on the establishment of the European Public Prosecutor's Office, Brussels, 17.7.2013, COM(2013) 534 final 2013/0255 (APP) and Gerard Conway, 'The European Public Prosecutor – Holding to Account a Possible European Public Prosecutor' (2013) *Criminal Law Forum* 1.

[71] In a different context, Ari Dorfman & Alon Harel, 'Against Privatization as Such' (2016) 36(2) *Oxford Journal of Legal Studies* 400.

[72] Carol Harlow and Richard Rawlings, *Process and Procedure in EU Administration* (London, Hart, 2014).

[73] (2010) L195/5, Agreement between the European Union and the United States of America on the processing and transfer of Financial Messaging Data from the European Union to the United States for the purposes of the Terrorist Finance Tracking Program.

[74] Helena Carrapiço and Florian Trauner, *Europol and its Influence on EU Policy-making on Organized Crime, Perspectives on European Politics and Society* (2013) 14 *European Politics and Society* 357–71.

[75] See Dorfman and Harel (n 71).

The same holds true for EPPO, which as explained, has far-reaching powers to prosecute financial crimes committed against the EU budget.[76]

V. Fundamental Rights and Data Protection

While the discussion of the increased involvement of Agencies as monitors of financial crimes poses well known questions about accountability, it also poses more general questions of fundamental rights protection in the EU. Specifically, the discussion of the EU's regulatory endeavours to fight fraud and money laundering, pose some intriguing questions with regard to the adequate protection of personal data and applicable human rights protection. Indeed, there are some difficulties ahead for the EU and the Member States when it comes to ensuring a uniform standard of human rights protection. Directive 2016/680 is important here.[77] The Directive lays down rules for competent authorities for the purposes of the prevention, investigation, detection or prosecution of criminal offences or the execution of criminal penalties, and on the free movement of such data.

As for data protection matters, plenty is happening in this area. The EU Commission recently proposed a new Regulation and Directive on the use of e-evidence in criminal investigations.[78] The aim is to create a European Production Order which will allow a judicial authority in one Member State to obtain electronic evidence in another Member State. In addition, a European Preservation Order will allow a judicial authority in one Member State to request that a service provider or its legal representative in another Member State preserves specific data with a view to a subsequent request to produce this data via mutual legal assistance, a European Investigation Order (EIO) or a European Production Order (EPO). In an elaborated assessment of the proposed legislation setting out to explain why the new legislation is needed, the Commission explains that as some crimes cannot be effectively investigated and prosecuted in the EU because of challenges in cross-border access to electronic evidence, public authorities need effective and timely access to it to be able to prosecute criminals and prevent future crimes.[79] As more and more countries join the technology revolution and more people around the world get connected to the Internet, the need to access

[76] see n 68.

[77] Directive 2016/680 on the protection of natural persons with regard to the processing of personal data by competent authorities for the purposes of the prevention, investigation, detection or prosecution of criminal offences or the execution of criminal penalties, and on the free movement of such data, and repealing Council Framework Decision 2008/977/JHA.

[78] Proposal for a Regulation of The European Parliament And Of The Council on European Production and Preservation Orders for electronic evidence in criminal matters, COM/2018/225 final – 2018/0108.

[79] See, eg, Els De Busser, 'EU-US Digital Data Exchange to Combat Financial Crime: Fast is the New Slow' (2018) 19 *German Law Journal* 1251.

evidence across borders rapidly increases according to the EU legislator. As the Commission stresses, globalisation also implies globalisation of criminal evidence. The proposed instruments are based on Article 82 TFEU (services). Part of the problem is, as the Commission argues, that there are no mandatory data retention rules in the US (where some of the most important service providers are based) or at EU level, since the Data Retention Directive was declared invalid in the Digital Rights case in 2014.[80]

In short, the proposal on e-evidence aims to makes it easier to secure and gather electronic evidence for criminal proceedings stored or held by service providers in another jurisdiction. The EIO Directive, which has to a large extent replaced the Convention on Mutual Assistance in Criminal Matters, covers any investigative measure. This includes access to electronic evidence but the EIO Directive does not contain any specific provisions on this type of evidence. The new instrument will not replace the EIO for obtaining electronic evidence but provides an additional tool for authorities. There may be situations, for example, when several investigative measures need to be carried out in the executing Member State, where the EIO may be the preferred choice for public authorities. Creating a new instrument for electronic evidence may be a better alternative than amending the EIO Directive because of the specific challenges inherent in obtaining electronic evidence which do not affect the other investigative measures covered by the EIO Directive.[81] It is important to emphasise that the General Data Protection Regulation of 2016 lays down general rules to protect natural persons in relation to the processing of personal data and to ensure the free movement of personal data within the Union.[82]

Likewise, although Article 52 of the EU Charter of Fundamental Rights sets out the possibility to derogate from Charter rights when complied with proportionality, as discussed in chapters two and three the applicable human rights standard needs to be sufficiently high. Yet there is reason to believe that the principle of proportionality as a guarantee of fundamental rights could have a significant impact in the area of the EU's suppression of financial crimes. A recent ground-breaking decision where the principle of proportionality was applied to strike down a legal measure on the retention of data is the Digital Rights case. The Court annulled the 2006 Data Retention Directive, which was aimed at fighting crime and terrorism and which allowed data to be stored for up to two years.[83] It concluded that the

[80] Digital Rights Ireland and Seitlinger and others, Judgment of the Court (Grand Chamber) Case C-293/12,of 8 April 2014.

[81] Proposal for a Regulation of The European Parliament And of The Council on European Production and Preservation Orders for electronic evidence in criminal matters, COM/2018/225 final – 2018/0108.

[82] Regulation (EU) 2016/679 of the European Parliament and of the Council of 27 April 2016 on the protection of natural persons with regard to the processing of personal data and on the free movement of such data, and repealing Directive 95/46/EC (General Data Protection Regulation), OJ L 119/1.

[83] Directive 2006/24/EC of the European Parliament and of the Council of 15 March 2006 on the retention of data generated or processed in connection with the provision of publicly available electronic communications services or of public communications networks and amending Directive 2002/58/EC.

measure breached proportionality on the grounds that the Directive had a too sweeping generality and therefore violated, inter alia, the basic right of data protection as set out in Article 8 of the Charter of Fundamental Rights. If the Court is to develop criteria for the increasing use of proportionality as a balancing principle in connection with the Charter, this will arguably confirm a more robust view of fundamental rights protection in the AFSJ context.

As was mentioned in chapter two, the Market Abuse Regulation and the Market Abuse Directive each contain clauses setting out the listing of market abuse and publication of infringements. This raises, for natural reasons, some questions. In addition, the EPPO Regulation discussed above touches upon delicate questions on data protection.[84] Data protection is a fundamental EU right as it is stated in Article 7–8 of the Charter of Fundamental Rights, Article 16 TFEU, and Article 8 ECHR.[85] In addition, recital 27 of the Market Abuse Directive states that:

> This Directive respects the fundamental rights and observes the principles recognised in the Charter of Fundamental Rights of the European Union (the Charter) as recognised in the TEU. Specifically, it should be applied with due respect for the right to protection of personal data (Article 8), the freedom of expression and information (Article 11), the freedom to conduct a business (Article 16).

Article 52 of the EPPO Regulation is interesting here. The provision makes it clear that if it emerges that incorrect operational personal data has been transmitted, or operational personal data has been unlawfully transmitted, the recipient shall be notified without delay. In such a case, the operational personal data shall be rectified, erased, or processing shall be restricted in accordance with Article 61 stating that, inter alia, the data subject shall have the right to obtain from the EPPO without undue delay the rectification of inaccurate operational personal data relating to him or her. Also, Article 56 of the EPPO Regulation is interesting in this respect concerning 'automated individual decision-making, including profiling'. It stated that:

> The data subject shall have the right not to be subject to a decision of the EPPO based solely on automated processing, including profiling, which produces legal effects concerning him/her or similarly significantly affects him/her. As a general rule, the controller shall provide the information in the same form as the request.[86]

[84] Directive (EU) 2016/680 of the European Parliament and of the Council of 27 April 2016, on the Protection of Natural Persons with Regard to the Processing of Personal Data by Competent Authorities for the Purposes of the Prevention, Investigation, Detection or Prosecution of Criminal Offenses or the Execution of Criminal Penalties, and on the Free Movement of such Data, and Repealing Council Framework Decision, 2008/977/JHA, 2016 OJ (L 119) 89–131.

[85] *Digital Rights Ireland and Seitlinger and others*, Judgment of the Court (Grand Chamber) Case C-293/12, of 8 April 2014, nyr and *Maximillian Schrems v Data Protection Commissioner*, Judgment of the Court (Grand Chamber) of 6 October 2015.

[86] Articles 56–65 of the EPPO Regulation.

Of central importance to the processing of data is also who is to be counted as a processor. Article 65 of the Regulation regulates the notion of processing. Specifically, it stipulates that:

> Where processing is to be carried out on behalf of the EPPO, the EPPO shall use only processors providing sufficient guarantees to implement appropriate technical and organisational measures in such a manner that processing will meet the requirements of this Regulation and ensure the protection of the rights of the data subject.

Yet the definition of what processing means remains somewhat unclear, as well as who is a reliable 'processor' in this context.

This is largely uncharted territory and the cooperation with Europol, and other EU key agents, regarding the processing of data and what is considered 'proportionate' will have a very interesting future ahead of it. Moreover, in the Preamble – recital nr 98 of the EPPO Regulation – it is stated that the European Data Protection Supervisor should have the tasks laid down in the EPPO Regulation and should give effective powers, including investigative, corrective, and advisory powers to the EPPO which constitute the necessary means to perform those tasks. This seems welcome. In addition, the EPPO is already bound by the provision in Article 5 of the Regulation, and by EU principles in general on fundamental rights that it must confirm with proportionality and the rule of law.

VI. Conclusion

This chapter has placed the EU's fight against market abuse in the broader context of the combat of financial crimes and highlighted some associated questions of crucial importance such as fundamental rights protection. The chapter has tried to demonstrate the close links between the interlinked crimes of market abuse, money laundering and other white-collar crimes. This chapter has also discussed the establishment of the EPPO and the role of Agencies in the EU machinery. Thereafter, the chapter highlighted the often complex relationship between the principle of subsidiarity and that of effective EU action. In addition, the chapter has discussed some of the current issues with the evolving regulation of data protection as part of the EU fundamental rights *acquis* and how it can be upheld while fighting crime effectively

While financial regulation and the fight against financial crime is still at the heart of the EU's 'getting tough on crime' approach, the old internal market endeavours in this area are now much more complex than they used to be and confirm an intersectoral competence between the internal market and that of the AFSJ. In particular, the extended powers granted to EU Agencies ask difficult questions about the democratic oversight of the AFSJ. Events such as Brexit and other national sentiments across Europe predict a difficult future ahead for the EPPO, despite the urgency of its proper functioning. In these post-Brexit decision days, it is to be hoped that when it comes to the EPPO and the fight against financial crimes in general in the EU context the Member States will understand that joint business and freedoms also imply that it is necessary to embrace the full package of cooperation, including fully shaped defence rights and protection of the individual. It remains to be seen whether the EPPO in future will have the authority to prosecute EU market abuse that is not directly related to the EU budget but has an impact on consumer confidence in the EU market. It largely depends on the political willingness of the Member States.

5

The United Kingdom

I. Introduction

The aim of this chapter is to undertake a detailed analysis of how the United Kingdom (UK) has tackled the problems associated with insider dealing and market abuse in light of the 2007/08 financial crisis. Therefore, it is divided into two parts. The first part concentrates on the legislative provisions that tackle insider dealing, as contained in the Criminal Justice Act 1987 (CJA 1987) and the Market Abuse Regime under the Financial Services and Markets Act 2000 (FSMA 2000). The chapter briefly refers to the implementation of the EU Market Abuse Regulation (MAR) and then moves on to critically analyse the enforcement of the insider dealing criminal law provisions and the civil market abuse statutory provisions in light of the misconduct of financial institutions and related individuals associated with the 2007/08 financial crisis. Specifically, this second part of the chapter focuses on the enforcement response by the Serious Fraud Office (SFO), the Financial Services Authority and the Financial Conduct Authority (FCA) towards the manipulation of the London Inter-bank Offered Rate (LIBOR) and the Foreign Exchange Market (FOREX)

II. Insider Dealing

Insider dealing can be defined as the illegal trading in shares or securities by someone, or at the instigation of someone, with inside knowledge of unpublished business data or information that would affect the price of shares being bought or sold.[1] The UK criminalised insider dealing following the enactment of CJA 1993.[2] A person commits a criminal offence if they have information, as an insider, that relates to securities in a regulated market.[3] Furthermore, a person commits

[1] See Kern Alexander, *Insider dealing and market abuse: the Financial Services and Markets Act 2000*, ESRC Centre for Business Research, University of Cambridge, Working Paper No. 222 (Cambridge, University of Cambridge, 2001) 4.

[2] CJA 1993, s 52.

[3] For the purpose of this Act, a regulated market is defined as 'any market, however operated, which, by an order made by the Treasury, is identified (whether by name or by reference to criteria prescribed by the order) as a regulated market for the purposes of this Part'. See CJA 1993, s 60(1).

a criminal offence if they have inside information, and they encourage another person to deal in securities, or the person discloses such information that breaches the contractual employment.[4] The UK has opted out from the Market Abuse Directive (MAD) under Article 83 Treaty on the Functioning of the European Union (TFEU). The UK participates in the Market Abuse Regulation adopted under Article 114 TFEU, concerning administrative sanctions. The UK criminal law regulating market abuse is still heavily influenced by EU law and especially the 1989 Insider Dealing Directive, which created three criminal offences that are commonly referred to as dealing, encouraging another to deal and disclosing information.[5] In order for a person to be convicted, inside information must be present,[6] and the UK interpretation is fundamentally based on the interpretation provided by the Insider Dealing Directive.[7] In order for the criminal offences to have been committed, the information must have been made public,[8] and only a fragment of the public needs to be aware of this information.[9] Additionally, the term 'insider' must be defined in order for the criminal offences to apply. Under the CJA 1993, a person is deemed to have information as an insider if '(a) it is, and he knows that it is, inside information … (b) he has it, and knows that he has it, from an inside source'.[10] Furthermore, the Act provides that 'a person has information from an inside source if and only' they are acting as a '(i) director, employee or shareholder of an issuer of securities; or (ii) having access to the information by virtue of his employment, office or profession; or (b) the direct or indirect source of his information is a person within paragraph (a)'.[11] It is important to note that these criminal offences cannot be committed by a corporation.[12]

A person is not deemed to have information as an insider due to the fact that the information was obtained from a confidential source. The prosecution must be able to establish that the accused had actual knowledge of both of these aspects. Securities for the purpose of the offence relate to price-affected securities, with the inside information in question needing to have a 'significant effect on the price [or value] of the securities'[13] involved, therefore making the inside information

[4] CJA 1993, s 52(2).

[5] [1989] OJ L 334 (Insider Dealing Directive 89/592). The power to ban individuals who have abused the insider dealing provisions of the CJA 1993 has been used by the Financial Services Authority/Financial Conduct Authority. See FSMA 2000, s 56.

[6] Insider information is defined as information that 'relates to particular securities or to a particular issuer of securities or to particular issuers of securities and not to securities generally or to issuers of securities generally; is specific or precise; has not been made public; and if it were made public would be likely to have a significant effect on the price of any securities'. See CJA 1993, s 56.

[7] Insider Dealing Directive (n 5).

[8] CJA 1993, s 58.

[9] CJA 1993, s 58(3).

[10] CJA 1993, s 57(1). See *Hannam v Financial Conduct Authority* [2014] UKUT 233 (TCC); [2014] WLUK 916; [2014] Lloyd's Rep FC 704 (UT) (Tax).

[11] CJA 1993, s 57(2).

[12] For a more detailed explanation of the problems associated with the application of the criminal law to corporations in the UK, see ch 3.

[13] CJA 1993, s 56(2).

price sensitive. Examples of relevant securities include shares, debt securities, warrants, depositary receipts, options, futures and contracts for differences.[14] Furthermore, a regulated market is one which has been identified as such for the purposes of the CJA 1993 by HM Treasury.[15] Therefore, in order for a person to be convicted of insider dealing in the UK, the prosecutor must demonstrate that the individual was within the UK at the time of the dealing; the regulated market is one which has been defined as regulated in the UK by HM Treasury; if the offence involved a professional intermediary, he too was within the UK at the time of the dealing; and finally, if the offence involves encouraging another to deal, the discloser and recipient of the information and/or encouragement are within the UK when the information or encouragement is given and received.[16]

The first offence is committed if a person using inside information deals in price-affected securities on a regulated market. The person involved can either be relying on a professional intermediary or acting as a professional intermediary themselves.[17] Dealing in securities includes conduct that is acquiring or disposing of securities or procuring, directly or indirectly an acquisition or disposal of the securities by another person.[18] Acquiring includes entering into a contract in order to create a security or making an agreement that a security will be acquired.[19] Furthermore, disposing involves bringing to an end such a contract or entering into an agreement that a security will be disposed of.[20] There is no requirement to establish a causal link between the held information and the dealing; although, it is a defence if the trader can prove that he would have dealt in the same way regardless of the inside information. Examples of this behaviour include where the inside information is that a publicly listed company is about to be taken over, which would usually result in the price of its shares increasing. By buying shares before this information is made public the likely result is a large profit for the insider. Conversely, the inside information could be that a publicly listed company is about to issue a profit warning and before this information is widely known the insider sells his shares to avoid losses. The criminal offence of encouraging another to deal applied to situations where the person with the inside information encourages another to deal with securities on any regulated market on the basis of this information and the insider knows or has reasonable cause to believe that

[14] CJA 1993, sch 2.

[15] CJA 1993, s 60.

[16] CJA 1993, s 62.

[17] CJA 1993, s 52(1) and s 52(3). See *Patel v Mirza* [2013] EWHC 1892 (Ch); [2013] 7 WLUK 187; [2013] Lloyd's Rep FC 525; [2013] WTLR 1755; [2014] LLR 110; [2013] 2 P & CR DG23 (CHD) and *R v Rollins* (Neil) [2011] EWCA Crim 1825; [2011] 6 WLUK 701; [2012] 1 Cr App R (S) 64; [2011] Crim LR 896 (CA (Crim Div)).

[18] CJA 1993, s 55(1).

[19] CJA 1993, s 55(2).

[20] CJA 1993, s 55(3).

such dealing will take place.[21] The final offence is committed where an individual who has inside information discloses this to another person and he has reasonable cause to believe that they will use this information to deal in price affected securities on any regulated market or as a professional intermediary or through a professional intermediary.[22] The CJA 1993 provides a number of defences for those accused of insider dealing.[23] For instance, the offences will not be committed if the accused is able to demonstrate that at the time of the dealing, he did not expect to make a profit,[24] had reasonable grounds for believing that the information on which the dealing was based was widely known,[25] or that he would have acted in the way that he did even if he had not known about the insider information.[26] If a person discloses insider information, they are not guilty by virtue of this disclosure of information if they are able to illustrate '(a) that he did not at the time expect any person, because of the disclosure, to deal in securities', and '(b) that, although he had such an expectation at the time, he did not expect the dealing to result in a profit attributable to the fact that the information was price-sensitive information in relation to the securities'.[27] The CJA 1993 also provides a number of 'special defences'.[28]

These criminal offences are enforced by a number of different agencies, most notably by the Financial Services Authority, now the FCA.[29] The FCA's ability to prosecute insider dealing cases is confirmed by the FSMA 2000.[30] For example, between 2009 and 2011, the Financial Services Authority obtained a total of 10 convictions.[31] In July 2014, the FCA reported that it had obtained 23 convictions for insider dealing offences since 2004.[32] In March 2015 this figure had risen to 27 convictions.[33] Between 2016 and 2017, the FCA secured six convictions for insider dealing.[34] There was no reference to any insider dealing convictions in the FCA's 2017/2018 Annual Enforcement report.[35] These figures have attracted a

[21] CJA 1993, s 52(2)(a).
[22] CJA 1993, s 52(2)(b).
[23] CJA 1993, s 53.
[24] CJA 1993 s 53(6).
[25] CJA 1993, s 53(1)(b).
[26] CJA 1993, s 53(1)(c).
[27] CJA 1993, s 53(3).
[28] CJA 1993, sch 1.
[29] The Financial Services Authority was replaced as the City Regulator in April 2013 by virtue of the Financial Services Act 2012, s 6. Also see FSMA 2000, s 1A.
[30] FSMA 2000, s 402(1(a).
[31] Financial Services Authority, 'Investment banker and two associates charged with insider dealing', 4 August 2011, available at www.fsa.gov.uk/pages/Library/Communication/PR/2011/069.shtml.
[32] Financial Conduct Authority, *Why has the FCAs market cleanliness statistic for takeover announcements decreased since 2009?* (Financial Conduct Authority, 2014) 20.
[33] Financial Conduct Authority, 'Former senior trader sentenced for insider dealing', 19 March 2015, available at: www.fca.org.uk/news/former-senior-trader-sentenced-for-insider-dealing.
[34] Financial Conduct Authority, *Enforcement annual performance accounts Annual Account 2016/2017* (Financial Conduct Authority, 2017) 12.
[35] ibid.

great deal of criticism and it has been suggested that between 2013 and 2018, the FCA only prosecuted eight cases of insider dealing and obtained 12 convictions.[36] Despite the low number of criminal convictions, the FCA initiated a record number of insider dealing investigations in 2017. However, it is essential to remember that insider dealing, like other types of financial crime, is very complex and lengthy, thus limiting the ability of the FCA to obtain more criminal convictions.

Examples of criminal prosecutions include Christopher McQuoid,[37] who was given an eight month custodial term for using inside information to make a profit of almost £50,000.[38] Additionally, McQuoid was subjected to a criminal confiscation order under the Proceeds of Crime Act 2002. In 2014, Neel and Matthew Uberoi were sentenced to prison terms of two years and one year respectively for insider dealing trades worth a benefit of £288,050.[39] Whilst this was more punitive than previous cases, it is lenient when compared to the conviction of Asif Butt,[40] who was initially sentenced to five years imprisonment for conspiracy to commit insider dealing. Butt made £388,488 profit for his investment bank (Credit Suisse); equating to £237,000 in personal benefit. However, the Court of Appeal reduced the sentence to four years. Recently, Malcolm Calvert was sentenced to 21 months in prison for insider dealing after making an illegal profit of £103,883.[41] Neil Rollins was initially sentenced to 27 months imprisonment, but this was reduced by the Court of Appeal to 18 months.[42] Christian Littlewood was sentenced to three years and four imprisonment for insider dealing. The co-defendant Helmy Omar Sa'aid received two years imprisonment and a confiscation order of £640,000.[43] In May 2015, Martyn Dodgson and Andrew Hind were sentenced to three and a half and four and a half years imprisonment following their conviction for insider dealing.[44] Pegden J described the conduct of the defendants as 'persistent, prolonged, deliberate, dishonest behavior'.[45] The FCA stated this case

[36] Ben Chapman, 'FCA: City watchdog secures just 12 insider trading convictions in five years', 19 January 2018, available at www.independent.co.uk/news/business/news/fca-city-london-insider-trading-convictions-five-years-financial-conduct-authority-a8167486.html.

[37] *Regina v Christopher McQuoid* [2009] EWCA Crim 1301.

[38] Financial Services Authority, 'Solicitor and his father-in-law found guilty in FSA insider dealing case' 27 March 2009, available at www.fsa.gov.uk/Pages/Library/Communication/PR/2009/042.shtml.

[39] Financial Services Authority, 'Corporate broker intern and his father receive 12 and 24 month prison sentences respectively for insider dealing' 10 December 2010, available at www.fsa.gov.uk/library/communication/pr/2009/149.shtml.

[40] *R v Butt (Asif Nazir)* [2006] 2 Cr App R (S) 44.

[41] Financial Services Authority, 'Former Cazenove broker sentenced to 21 months in prison for insider dealing' 11 March 2010, available at www.fsa.gov.uk/pages/Library/Communication/PR/2010/043.shtml.

[42] Financial Services Authority, 'Neil Rollins update' 30 June 2011, available at www.fsa.gov.uk/pages/Library/Communication/Statements/2011/neil_rollins.shtml.

[43] Financial Services Authority, 'Investment banker, his wife and family friend sentenced for insider dealing' 2 February 2011, available at www.fsa.gov.uk/pages/Library/Communication/PR/2011/018.shtml.

[44] Financial Conduct Authority, 'Insider dealers sentenced in Operation Tabernula trial' 12 May 2015, available at www.fca.org.uk/news/press-releases/insider-dealers-sentenced-operation-tabernula-trial.

[45] ibid.

'involved serious offending over a number of years, conducted in a sophisticated way using deliberate techniques to avoid detection. Dodgson was … entrusted by his employer with sensitive and valuable information. He betrayed that trust by exploiting the information for his own benefit, conspiring with Hind to deceive the market'.[46] In 2016, Mark Lyttleton (Lyttleton) was convicted on two counts of insider dealing and sentenced to 12 months imprisonment and subject to a criminal confiscation order of £149,861.[47] In sentencing Lyttleton, Goymer J stated that 'insider dealing is not a victimless crime, I regard these offences as pre-meditated and blatantly dishonest'. The FCA stated that 'Lyttleton's insider dealing involved a gross abuse of the trust placed in him as a senior fund manager'.[48] In January 2017, Manjeet Mohal was convicted on two counts of insider dealing, and was sentenced to ten months imprisonment, which was suspended for two years.[49] The number of insider dealing convictions obtained by the FCA clearly illustrate the difficulty in investigating and pursuing white collar criminals. Therefore, in order to overcome these problems the FCA has prioritised pursuing administrative financial penalties.

In addition to the ability of the FCA to commence criminal proceedings, it has the ability to impose unlimited administrative financial sanctions on corporations and/or individuals for insider dealing.[50] For example, the Financial Services Authority imposed its then largest financial penalty against an individual, fining Philippe Jabre £750,000 for insider dealing as part of its credible deterrence strategy.[51] Furthermore, the Financial Services Authority fined Mark Lockwood £20,000 for failing to prevent insider dealing.[52] In March 2015, the FCA fined Kenneth Carver £35,212 for insider dealing.[53] These examples would suggest that the FCA and are trying to project the deterrent image that insider dealing is a serious offence and is just as serious as other financial crimes. However, this is arguably not being mirrored in practice, with some serious and dishonest offences being met with fairly low level or suspended sentences. When the maximum penalty for the offence is seven years imprisonment, how large must the benefit be before a reasonably serious sentence is passed, whether that be through the civil or criminal routes.

[46] Financial Conduct Authority (n 44).

[47] Financial Conduct Authority, 'Mark Lyttleton sentenced to 12 months imprisonment for insider dealing' 21 December 2016, available at www.fca.org.uk/news/press-releases/mark-lyttleton-sentenced-12-months-imprisonment-insider-dealing.

[48] ibid.

[49] Financial Conduct Authority, 'Two sentenced in insider dealing case' 13 January 2017, available from www.fca.org.uk/news/press-releases/two-sentenced-insider-dealing-case.

[50] FSMA 2000, s 206(1).

[51] Financial Services Authority, 'FSA fines GLG Partners and Philippe Jabre £750,000 each for market abuse' 1 August 2006, available at www.fsa.gov.uk/pages/Library/Communication/PR/2006/077.shtml.

[52] Financial Services Authority, 'FSA fines broker for failing to prevent insider dealing' 2 September 2009, available at www.fsa.gov.uk/pages/Library/Communication/PR/2009/115.shtml.

[53] Financial Conduct Authority, 'Kenneth Carver fined £35,212 for insider dealing' 30 March 2015, available at www.fca.org.uk/news/kenneth-carver-fined-for-insider-dealing.

III. Market Abuse

Market abuse is defined as trading on the basis of inside information; disclosing inside information otherwise than in the proper course of employment; trading which gives misleading or false impressions; trading which uses deception or fictitious devices; the disclosing of information which leads to a misleading or false impression; and behaviour which is likely to distort the market.[54] The Market Abuse Directive is divided into two areas – inside information is defined as 'information that is precise, non-public and likely to have a significant impact on the price of a financial instrument'.[55] Market manipulation encompasses transactions and orders to trade that give false or misleading signals or secure the price of a financial instrument at an artificial level, transactions or orders to trade that employ fictitious devices; and distribution of information likely to give false or misleading signals. Importantly, market abuse is not a criminal offence, although offences do exist, within FSMA 2000 and the Financial Services Act 2012. The criminal offences created by FSMA 2000 include misleading the FCA or the Prudential Regulation Authority (PRA)[56] and misleading the Competition and Markets Authority (CMA).[57] FSMA 2000 also used to include an offence of misleading statements and practices,[58] but this was repealed in April 2013 by the Financial Services Act 2012, which also creates three further offences: misleading statements,[59] misleading impressions[60] and misleading statements/impressions in relation to benchmarks.[61]

FSMA 2000 contains two misleading offences. The first is in relation to any dealings with the FCA or PRA under the Act and is made out where a person who is required to comply with an obligation under the Act recklessly or knowingly 'gives a regulator information which is false or misleading in a material particular'.[62] The second misleading offence refers to any action which misleads the CMA.[63] The first criminal offence under the Financial Services Act 2012 relates to a situation where a person knowingly or recklessly makes a misleading statement or where he/she dishonestly conceals material facts when a statement is made,[64] with the intention to induce (or being reckless as to whether this may induce) another person to enter into market activity.[65] An offence under section 90 is committed

[54] FSMA 2000, s 118.
[55] ibid.
[56] FSMA 2000, s 398.
[57] FSMA 2000, s 399.
[58] FSMA 2000, s 397.
[59] Financial Services Act 2012, s 89.
[60] Financial Services Act 2012, s 90.
[61] Financial Services Act 2012, s 91.
[62] FSMA 2000, s 398(1).
[63] FSMA 2000, s 399.
[64] Financial Services Act 2012, s 89(1)(a)–(c).
[65] See *Financial Conduct Authority v Capital Alternatives Ltd* [2018] 3 WLUK 623 (ChD).

where a person intentionally creates a misleading impression as to the price or value of a relevant investment or as to the market in general, and the situation falls within either or both of subsections (2) and (3).[66] Section 90(2) covers the event where a person has intentionally created the misleading impression so as to induce another person into market activity. This can include acquiring, disposing of, subscribing to or underwriting investments or refraining from undertaking these activities; or, exercising or refraining from exercising rights conferred by the investments.[67] Section 90(3) is relevant where the person knowingly or recklessly makes a false or misleading impression and through creating this impression intends to either make a gain (for him/herself or for another person) or cause loss to another person.[68] The offence can also be committed where the person does not necessarily intend the aforementioned results, but is aware that by creating the false or misleading impression it is likely that such results will occur.[69] For the purposes of this offence, gain can include 'getting what one does not have'[70] in addition to 'keeping what one [does] have'.[71] Likewise, loss includes 'parting with what one has'[72] in addition to 'not getting what one might get'.[73] The final offence relates to the creation of a false or misleading impression or the making of a false or misleading statement, in connection with the setting of a specified benchmark. In terms of a false or misleading statement, an offence is made out where a person makes such a statement in the course of setting a benchmark; he/she intends that the statement is used for that purpose; and, knows or is reckless to the fact that the statement is false or misleading.[74] For false and/or misleading impressions, a person commits a criminal offence where he/she intends to create the impression; knowing or being reckless as to the fact that it is false or misleading; that impression may affect the setting of a benchmark; and, the person is aware that the impression may affect the setting of that said benchmark.[75] A benchmark in this context is defined under section 93 of the Act as 'a benchmark of a kind specified in an order made by the Treasury'.[76] Definitions relevant to other phrases used within these three offences can also be found in section 93.

For all market abuse offences, the activity must occur within the UK. For the purposes of market manipulation, it must be in relation to qualifying investments which are either 'admitted to trading on a prescribed market'[77] operating in the

[66] Financial Services Act 2012, s 90(1). For a brief discussion see *United States v Sarao* [2016] 3 WLUK 680; [2016] Lloyd's Rep FC 339 (MC).

[67] Financial Services Act 2012, s 90(2).

[68] Financial Services Act 2012, s 90(4).

[69] Financial Services Act 2012, s 90(3).

[70] Financial Services Act 2012, s 90(7).

[71] Financial Services Act 2012, s 90(7).

[72] Financial Services Act 2012, s 90(8).

[73] Financial Services Act 2012, s 90(8).

[74] Financial Services Act 2012, s 91(1).

[75] Financial Services Act 2012, s 91(2).

[76] Financial Services Act 2012, s 93(4).

[77] FSMA 2000, s 118A(1)(b)(i).

UK or for 'which a request for admission to trading on such a prescribed market has been made'.[78] For these purposes, investments which are 'related investments' in such a prescribed market will also fall under such behaviour.[79] In this context, behaviour is defined as 'action or inaction'[80] and so includes the situation where either the trader should have alerted the market to a problem and neglected to do so, or created a reasonable expectation that he would act in a particular way and again failed to do so. In relation to the criminal offences under the Financial Services Act 2012, the person making the statement or creating the impression must be within the UK and either the person who is induced must also be within the UK or the intended agreement would have been exercised within the UK.[81] Defences for market abuse are reliant on the suspected market manipulator proving a number of elements. First, the accused must illustrate that they believed that they were not engaging in market abuse, and that the belief was objectively reasonable. There must be sufficient evidence of this for the defence to work. The accused must illustrate to the FCA that they took all reasonable precautions and exercised all due diligence in performing the transactions in question. A defence can also be relied on, if it can be established that the disclosure was protected.[82] Defences are offered by the Financial Services Act 2012.[83]

Market abuse is not a criminal offence under FSMA 2000 and a civil regime has been introduced to enforce this provision. The aim of the civil regime is to avoid the problems associated with criminal cases of insider dealing, as outlined above, which will provide the FCA with greater enforcement powers. An integral part of the civil regime is the Code of Market Conduct (the Code) of the *FCA Handbook*, which was amended to include examples of what does amount to market abuse, thus giving clear guidelines to market participants of the types of behaviour to avoid. The Code provides assistance and guidance in ascertaining whether certain behaviour amounts to market abuse. While the Code is important in tackling market abuse, the FCA also relies on High Level Standards such as Principles of Business, and Senior Management Arrangement, Systems and Controls, and specific Handbooks such as Supervision, Decision Procedures and Penalties Manual, Disclosure Rules and Transparency Rules and the Listing Rules.

An important amendment to the UK's efforts to tackle market abuse was introduced in 2016 in the shape of the Market Abuse Regulation,[84] which aim to

[78] FSMA 2000, s 118A(1)(b)(ii).
[79] FSMA 2000, s 118A(1)(b)(iii).
[80] FSMA 2000, s 130A(3).
[81] Financial Services Act 2012, s 89(4) and s 90(10).
[82] FSMA 2000, s 131A(1)–(4).
FSMA 2000, s 131A(2).
FSMA 2000, s 131A(3).
FSMA 2000, s 131A(4).
[83] Financial Services Act 2012, s 89(3).
[84] [2014] OJ 173/1 (MAR).

'increase market integrity and investor protection, enhancing the attractiveness of securities markets for capital raising'.[85] MAR applies to financial instruments traded on a regulated market, financial instruments traded to a multilateral trading facility, financial instruments traded on an organised trading facility and financial instruments not covered. The Market Abuse Regulation contains several important requirements that include inside information and disclosure, insider dealing and unlawful disclosure, market manipulation, market soundings, buyback programmes and stabilisation measures, accepted market practices, insider lists, suspicious transaction and order reports, managers' transactions, investment recommendations and whistle blowing.[86]

A person found guilty of any of the new criminal offences under the Financial Services Act 2012 is liable to a term of imprisonment not exceeding seven years, an unlimited fine, or both.[87] For misleading the FCA or PRA, the maximum penalty is a fine,[88] while for misleading the CMA, the maximum penalty is increased to a term of custody not exceeding two years and/or a financial penalty.[89] Even though market abuse is not defined as a criminal offence under the FSMA 2000, as detailed above the majority of market abusers are dealt with using financial penalties under the civil market abuse regime rather than through a criminal route. These enforcement powers are contained in Part XI of the FSMA 2000, which allows the investigating authorities to appoint professionals to undertake 'general'[90] or 'particular'[91] investigations. For the purpose of this part of the Act, investigating authorities refers to the FCA, the PRA and in some limited circumstances the Secretary of State.[92] Investigations into particular cases include instances of suspected insider dealing[93] and market abuse.[94] To bring a disciplinary action the FCA must be satisfied that a person has either engaged in market abuse,[95] or has encouraged or required another person to undertake behaviour which if he had engaged in such action, would amount to market abuse.[96] The outcome of such investigations is sent to the Regulatory Decisions Committee, an administrative decision maker, to decide whether or not to bring disciplinary actions against an individual. Before a fine can be imposed, the FCA must prepare and issue a statement of its intention to fine, known as a statement of policy.[97] Before this is issued,

[85] Financial Conduct Authority, 'Market Abuse Regulation' 4 May 2015, available at www.fca.org.uk/markets/market-abuse/regulation.

[86] ibid.

[87] Financial Services Act 2012, s 92.

[88] FSMA 2000, s 398(3).

[89] Competition Act 1998, s 44(3).

[90] FSMA 2000, s 167.

[91] FSMA 2000, s 168.

[92] FSMA 2000, s 168(6).

[93] FSMA 2000, s 168(2)(a).

[94] FSMA 2000, s 168(2)(d).

[95] FSMA 2000, s 123(1)(a).

[96] FSMA 2000, s 123(1)(b).

[97] FSMA 2000, s 124.

a draft version is published and the public are invited to make representations.[98] Such statements will be taken into account when setting the level of fine. When the level has been decided upon, the FCA must then issue a warning notice which will state the amount involved.[99] It is at this point that the named individual or company will be able to argue any relevant defences. If, having taken any representations into account, a financial penalty is still deemed appropriate; the FCA will finally issue a decision notice which will contain the final decision regarding the level of fine.[100] An important check and balance here is that if the FCA decides to take action against a person, that person may refer the matter to the Financial Services and Markets Tribunal, an independent Tribunal set up to hear appeals against FCA decisions and if necessary can appeal this decision to the Court of Appeal, as long as this appeal is on a point of law.

Where market abuse has been proved, the FCA has a number of options, dependent on the severity of the abuse. For instance, through the FSMA 2000, the Financial Services is authorised to impose 'a penalty of such amount as it considers appropriate'.[101] In determining what this amount should be, the FCA must have regard to:

(a) whether the behaviour in respect of which the penalty is to be imposed had an adverse effect on the market in question and, if it did, how serious that effect was;
(b) the extent to which that behaviour was deliberate or reckless; and
(c) whether the person on whom the penalty is to be imposed is an individual.[102]

In addition to these guidelines the FCA also has a financial penalties policy which provides a framework for calculating the size of fines and which is contained within its Handbook. This penalty setting regime is based on three principles – disgorgement, discipline and deterrence.

Fines made against firms follow a similar structure. Instead of individual income however, the FCA will take into account the amount of revenue generated by the firm, with the fine representing a percentage of this revenue.

The above framework has led to quite sizeable penalties being imposed, many of which have been in relation to incidences whereby individuals or companies have failed to submit accurate and/or timely suspicious transaction reports. For example in 2010, the Financial Services Authority fined the London branch of Société Générale £1.5 million,[103] the London branch of Commerzbank AG

[98] FSMA 2000, s 125.
[99] FSMA 2000, s 126(3).
[100] FSMA 2000, s 127.
[101] FSMA 2000, s 123(1).
[102] FSMA 2000, s 124(2).
[103] Financial Services Authority, 'FSA fines Société Générale £1.575 million for failures in transaction reporting' 25 August 2010, available at www.fca.org.uk/news/press-releases/fsa-fines-soci%C3%A9t%C3%A9-g%C3%A9n%C3%A9rale-%C2%A31575-million-failures-transaction-reporting.

£595,000,[104] Credit Suisse £1.75 million,[105] Getco Europe Limited £1.4 million[106] and Instinet Europe Limited £1 million for such offences.[107] In 2009 Barclays Capital Securities Limited and Barclays Bank plc were fined £2.4 million.[108] Large fines were also issued by the Financial Services Authority in 2012. For example, in February 2012, the Financial Services Authority imposed a financial penalty on David Einhorn of £3.63 million for engaging in market abuse.[109] His firm, Greenlight Capital Inc, was also fined £3.6 million.[110] When the FCA took over in 2013, it continued using the civil regime and imposed three financial penalties for market abuse, under the heading of market manipulation. Michael Coscia was fined £597,993,[111] Stefan Chaligne £900,000 and ordered to pay a disgorgement of €362,950[112] and Patrick Sejean £650,000.[113] Furthermore in 2014, Ian Hannam was fined £450,000 by the FCA for engaging in two instances of market abuse[114] and '7722656 Canada Inc' formerly trading as Swift Trade Inc was fined £8 million for engaging in market abuse to create a false or misleading impression in order to achieve a profit.[115] In 2015, the FCA imposed six financial penalties for breaches of its market abuse regime including Da Vinci Invest Ltd £1.46 million;[116] Mineworld Ltd £5 million;[117] Gyorgy Szabolcs £290,000;[118] Szabolcs Banya £410,000;[119]

[104] Financial Services Authority, 'FSA fines Commerzbank for failures in transaction reporting' 27 April 2010, available at www.fca.org.uk/news/press-releases/fsa-fines-commerzbank-failures-transaction-reporting.

[105] Financial Services Authority, 'FSA issues fines totaling £4.2m for transaction reporting failures' 8 April 2010, available at www.fca.org.uk/news/press-releases/fsa-issues-fines-totalling-%C2%A342m-transaction-reporting-failures.

[106] ibid.

[107] See Financial Services Authority (n 105).

[108] Financial Services Authority, 'Transaction reporting cases' n/d, available at www.fsa.gov.uk/pages/About/What/financial_crime/market_abuse/library/index.shtml.

[109] Financial Services Authority, 'Final Notice: David Einhorn' 15 February 2012, available at http://webarchive.nationalarchives.gov.uk/20130301170532/http://www.fsa.gov.uk/static/pubs/final/david-einhorn.pdf.

[110] ibid.

[111] Financial Conduct Authority, 'Final Notice: Michael Coscia' 3 July 2013, available at www.fca.org.uk/your-fca/documents/final-notices/2013/michael-coscia.

[112] Financial Conduct Authority, 'Final Notice: Stefan Chaligne' 21 January 2013, available at www.fca.org.uk/your-fca/documents/final-notices/2013/fsa-final-notice-2013-stefan-chaligne.

[113] Financial Conduct Authority, 'Final Notice: Patrick Sejean' 24 January 2013, available at www.fca.org.uk/your-fca/documents/final-notices/2013/fsa-final-notice-2013-stefan-chaligne.

[114] Financial Conduct Authority, 'Final Notice: Ian Hannam' 22 July 2014, available at www.fca.org.uk/news/fca-publishes-final-notice-for-ian-hannam.

[115] Financial Conduct Authority, 'Final Notice: 7722656 Canada Inc' 24 January 2014, available at www.fca.org.uk/your-fca/documents/final-notices/2014/7722656-canada-inc.

[116] Financial Conduct Authority, 'Final Notice: Da Vinci Invest Ltd' 12 August 2015, available at www.fca.org.uk/news/fca-secures-high-court-judgment-awarding-injunction-and-over-7-million-in-penalties.

[117] Financial Conduct Authority, 'Final Notice: Mineworld Ltd' 12 August 2015, available at www.fca.org.uk/news/fca-secures-high-court-judgment-awarding-injunction-and-over-7-million-in-penalties.

[118] Financial Conduct Authority, 'Final Notice: Gyorgy Szabolcs Brad' 12 August 2015, available at www.fca.org.uk/news/fca-secures-high-court-judgment-awarding-injunction-and-over-7-million-in-penalties.

[119] Financial Conduct Authority, 'Final Notice: Szabolcs Banya' 12 August 2015, available at www.fca.org.uk/news/fca-secures-high-court-judgment-awarding-injunction-and-over-7-million-in-penalties.

Tamas Pornye £410,000;[120] and Kenneth George Carver £35,212.[121] In May 2016, the FCA fined and banned Mark Taylor for a period of two years for engaging in market abuse.[122] Later that year, the FCA fined Gavin Breeze approximately £60,000 for engaging in market abuse.[123] In 2017, the FCA imposed four financial penalties on Tejoori Limited,[124] Paul Axel Walter,[125] Lukhvir Thind[126] and Niall O'Kelly.[127] The FCA only imposed one financial penalty in 2018, Interactive Brokers (UK) was fined £1 million.[128] In addition to issuing financial penalties, the FCA also has the power to publicly censure market participants by publishing a statement that a person has engaged in market abuse;[129] presumably to damage his/her reputation and standing. In some cases this 'naming and shaming' will be sufficient punishment and deterrence. Additionally, it can either apply to the courts for restitution or it can order restitution itself.[130] Furthermore, the FCA can also suspend or restrict the future business activities of individuals who it has found guilty of market abuse. This option is seen as an additional disciplinary measure and may include a limit on a regulated activity or a restriction on a person's 'performance of their controlled functions'.[131] The fines imposed by the FCA for market abuse have been used in conjunction with the insider dealing provisions under the CJA 1993. The impact of the fines on corporations can be questioned as they are significantly smaller than those imposed in the US, as will be outlined in chapter seven. The effectiveness of financial penalties has done little to limit future instances of market abuse. Conversely, the financial penalties imposed on individuals will have had a significant impact on countering market abuse.

[120] Financial Conduct Authority, 'Final Notice: Tamas Pornye' 12 August 2015, available at www.fca.org.uk/news/fca-secures-high-court-judgment-awarding-injunction-and-over-7-million-in-penalties.

[121] Financial Conduct Authority, 'Final Notice: Kenneth George Carver' 20 March 2015, available at www.fca.org.uk/news/kenneth-carver-fined-for-insider-dealing.

[122] Financial Conduct Authority, 'FCA fines and bans financial adviser for insider dealing' 13 May 2015, available at www.fca.org.uk/news/press-releases/fca-fines-and-bans-financial-adviser-insider-dealing.

[123] Financial Conduct Authority, 'The FCA fines, publicly censures and orders Jersey resident to pay restitution for insider dealing and improper disclosure' 15 July 2016, available at www.fca.org.uk/news/press-releases/fca-fines-publicly-censures-and-orders-jersey-resident-pay-restitution-insider.

[124] Financial Conduct Authority 'AIM Investment Company fined for failing to disclose inside information as soon as possible' 14 December 2017, available from www.fca.org.uk/news/press-releases/aim-investment-company-fined-failing-disclose-inside-information-soon-possible, accessed 14 December 2018.

[125] Financial Conduct Authority, 'FCA fines bond trader £60,000 for market abuse' 22 November 2017, available at www.fca.org.uk/news/press-releases/fca-fines-bond-trader-60k-market-abuse.

[126] Financial Conduct Authority, *Final Notice – Lukhvir Thind* (Financial Conduct Authority, 2017).

[127] Financial Conduct Authority, *Final Notice – Niall Stephen Patrick O'Kelly* (Financial Conduct Authority, 2017).

[128] Financial Conduct Authority, 'FCA fines Interactive Brokers (UK) Limited £1,049,412 for poor market abuse controls and failure to report suspicious client transactions' 25 January 2018, available at www.fca.org.uk/news/press-releases/fca-fines-interactive-brokers-uk-limited.

[129] FSMA 2000, s 123.

[130] FSMA 2000, s 384.

[131] Financial Conduct Authority, 'FCA Handbook DEPP A.1.3' available at www.handbook.fca.org.uk/handbook/DEPP/6A/1.html.

IV. The 2007/08 Financial Crisis, Market Manipulation and the Enforcement Response

This part of the chapter provides a detailed review of the enforcement response to market manipulation that is associated with the 2007/08 financial crisis. In particular, this section of the chapter focuses on the response by the FCA and SFO and illustrates how the FCA has concentrated on imposing financial penalties, while the SFO have targeted individuals.

V. The Serious Fraud Office

The SFO is the principal law enforcement agency to tackle market manipulation that is associated with the 2007/08 financial crisis. In relation to the LIBOR scandal, there was initially some uncertainty as to whether the SFO or Financial Services Authority was able, or willing, to prosecute those accused of market manipulation. For example, the Financial Services Authority has the ability to prosecute for a wide range of criminal activities,[132] including their ability to commence criminal proceedings for insider dealing,[133] money laundering[134] and terrorist financing.[135] However, there was both hesitation and vagueness if the Financial Services Authority was able to instigate criminal proceedings for fraud. For instance, the Financial Services Authority stated 'we cannot prosecute most types of fraud and dishonesty'.[136] This clarification was reiterated by Lord Turner, the former Chairman of the Financial Services Authority.[137] Further uncertainty was also expressed by the Financial Services Authority who stated that they were not a 'fraud prosecutor'.[138] However, evidence suggests that the Financial Services Authority is able to prosecute allegations of fraud.[139] Nonetheless, the SFO became the lead agency and targeted traders who had been accused of market manipulation.

One of the first prosecutions brought by the SFO was Tom Hayes, a derivative trader who worked with Citibank and UBS. Following an investigation by the SFO, Hayes was arrested by the SFO and City of London Police in December 2012. Hayes participated in a number of 'scoping interviews' following an agreement

[132] FSMA 2000, ss 401 and 402.
[133] FSMA 2000, s 402 (1)(a).
[134] FSMA 2000, s 402 (1)(b).
[135] FSMA 2000, s 402 (1)(c).
[136] Financial Services Authority, *Developing our policy on fraud and dishonesty – discussion paper 26* (London, Financial Services Authority, 2003) 18.
[137] HM Treasury Select Committee, *Fixing LIBOR: some preliminary findings* (London, HM Treasury, 2012) 102.
[138] ibid.
[139] Financial Services Authority, 'Fake stockbroker sentenced to 15 months' 13 February 2008, available at www.fsa.gov.uk/library/communication/pr/2008/011.shtml.

with the SFO.[140] During these interviews Hayes admitted that he had attempted to manipulate the LIBOR rate and that he had acted dishonestly. In his defence, Hayes unsuccessfully argued that such behaviour was common within the sector and that his line manager knew of his conduct. Subsequently, Hayes was convicted in August 2015 on eight counts of conspiracy to defraud and sentenced to 14 years imprisonment. Hayes appealed against the length of his sentence and this was reduced to 11 years. Additionally, Tom Hayes was ordered to pay a confiscation order of £878,806, which was satisfied on 31 October 2016, and in November 2017 the FCA decided to prohibit Hayes from 'performing any function in relation to any regulated activity in the financial services industry' following his conviction for conspiracy to defraud.[141] In February 2014, Peter Charles Johnson, Jonathan James Mathew and Stylianos Contogoulas were charged with the conspiracy to defraud. Two months later, Jay Vijay Merchant, Alex Pabon and Ryan Michael Reich were also charged with the conspiracy to defraud following an investigation into the alleged manipulation of the US Dollar LIBOR. Johnson pleaded guilty to conspiracy to defraud in October 2014 and was sentenced to four years imprisonment. Upon sentencing, Leonard J stated that 'you [Johnson] played a leading role as the senior submitter for Dollar Libor … you abused your position of trust as the Libor submitter who should have put in a rate uninfluenced by the requests of the traders … the offending was carried out of over a significant period of time'.[142] Additionally, Johnson was ordered to pay a criminal confiscation order under the Proceeds of Crime Act 2002 amounting to £114,501 and was prohibited from 'performing any function in relation to any regulated activity carried on by any authorised or exempt person, or exempt professional firm'.[143] Subsequently, Mathew, Merchant and Pabon were convicted by a jury. Leonard J stated that Mathew 'abused your position of trust as the Libor submitter who should have put in a rate uninfluenced by the requests of the traders … [the manipulation] required you to make careful calculations of what the rate should be and involved sophistication and planning … the offending was carried out of over a significant period of time, and there was a large number of victims'.[144] Mathew was sentenced to four years imprisonment, ordered to pay a criminal confiscation order totalling £34,700 and prohibited from 'performing any function in relation to any regulated activity carried on by any authorised or exempt person, or exempt professional firm'.[145]

[140] Serious Organised Crime and Police Act 1971, s 71.

[141] Financial Conduct Authority, 'FCA decides to ban Tom Hayes' 8 November 2017, available at www.fca.org.uk/news/press-releases/fca-decides-ban-tom-hayes.

[142] *R v Peter Johnson, Jonathan Mathew, Jay Vijay Merchant and Alex Pabon*, Sentencing Remarks of HHJ Anthony Leonard QC Southwark Crown Court 8 July 2016, available at www.judiciary.uk/wp-content/uploads/2016/07/r-v-johnson-and-others-sentencing.pdf.

[143] Financial Conduct Authority, *Final Notice – Peter Charles Johnson* (Financial Conduct Authority, 2016).

[144] See *R v Peter Johnson, Johnathan Mathew, Jay Vijay Merchant and Alex Pabon* (n 142).

[145] Financial Conduct Authority, *Final Notice – Jonathan Mathew* (Financial Conduct Authority, 2018).

Following his conviction and sentence, it was suggested that Mathew had challenged his conviction and that it would be reviewed by the Criminal Cases Review Commission.[146] However, in September 2018, the Criminal Cases Review Commission announced that it had closed the case without sending it back to the Appeal Courts.[147] Merchant was given a custodial sentence of six years, Leonard J stated that 'of all the defendants, to bear the greatest responsibility for what happened … The evidence of the way in which manipulation of the rate began in earnest after you arrived in New York was compelling … it was under your leadership on the desk that the requests to the Libor submitters really took off'.[148] Merchant and Mathew had their convictions upheld by the Court of Appeal in February 2017, but Merchant's sentence was reduced to five and a half years. Parbon was sentenced for two years and nine months and ordered to pay a criminal confiscation order of £2,300. The jury were unable to come to a decision on the alleged conduct of Contogoulas and Reich and they were subsequently acquitted at Southwark Crown Court in April 2017.[149]

VI. The Financial Conduct Authority

The purpose of FSMA 2000 is to provide a single legal framework for the Financial Services Authority, now FCA, replacing the different frameworks under which the various regulators operated. The Act has a number of distinct features. For example, it provides the FCA with four statutory objectives and requires them to adopt an open and responsive approach. In order to meet this requirement the FCA has established a Consumer Panel,[150] with a brief to monitor the extent to which the FCA is meeting its objectives in relation to consumers. The FSMA 2000 created an independent Practitioner Forum, which publishes its views on the work of the FCA.[151] The FCA has the power to grant,[152] refuse,[153] withdraw the authorisation,[154] or restrict the business of firms.[155] The FCA also has five main types of standard setting powers – to make rules,[156] which are applicable to regulated firms, to state principles in the form of a code of practice, to make

[146] Kristen Ridley, 'Second British Libor trader to have conviction examined' 9 November 2017, available at https://uk.reuters.com/article/us-libor-appeal-conviction/second-british-libor-trader-to-have-conviction-examined-idUKKBN1D92IL.

[147] ibid.

[148] See *R v Peter Johnson, Johnathan Mathew, Jay Vijay Merchant and Alex Pabon* (n 142).

[149] Serious Fraud Office, 'Two acquitted in Libor trial' 6 April 2017, available at www.sfo.gov.uk/2017/04/06/two-acquitted-libor-trial/.

[150] FSMA 2000, s 10.

[151] FSMA 2000, s 9.

[152] FSMA 2000, s 42.

[153] FSMA 2000, s 54.

[154] FSMA 2000, s 33.

[155] FSMA 2000, s 48.

[156] FSMA 2000, s 138.

evidential provisions, which will assist to demonstrate observance or breach of binding requirements, to endorse codes of regulated firms and to issue guidance. The Financial Services Authority also has the ability to fine firms for breaches of its rules and procedures, which this chapter now turns to.

The first UK bank fined for market manipulation was Barclays Bank, which was fined £59.5 million, the then largest fine ever imposed by the Financial Services Authority, in June 2012 for misconduct relating to LIBOR and EURIBOR.[157] The Financial Services Authority noted that Barclay's misconduct related to false submissions made by traders who were motivated by securing profits.[158] They concluded that 'Barclays' misconduct was serious, widespread and extended over a number of years. The integrity of benchmark reference rates such as LIBOR and EURIBOR is of fundamental importance to both UK and international financial markets'.[159] In December 2012, the UBS AG (UBS) were fined £160 million for manipulating both LIBOR and EURIBOR.[160] The Financial Services Authority identified a plethora of misconduct by a large number of employees in UBS between 2005 and 2010.[161] They noted that 'UBS traders and managers … manipulated UBS's submissions in order to benefit their own positions and to protect UBS's reputation … [its] misconduct was all the more serious because of the orchestrated attempts to manipulate the JPY LIBOR submissions of other banks as well as its own and the collusion with interdealer brokers and other panel banks in coordinated efforts to manipulate the fix'.[162]

In September 2013, ICAP Europe Limited (ICAP) became the first broking firm to be fined (£14 million) for transgressions relating to the manipulation of LIBOR.[163] The FCA concluded that the illegal conduct took place between October 2006 and November 2010 and included attempts by ICAP traders, in conjunction with UBS traders, to manipulate the JPY LIBOR (Japanese Yen). ICAPs brokers intentionally circulated inaccurate LIBOR submissions and requested Panel Banks to make specific JPY LIBOR submissions which resulted in one broker receiving corrupt bonus payments. A month later, the FCA fined Coöperatieve Centrale Raiffeisen-Boerenleenbank BA (Rabobank) £105 million for 'serious, prolonged and widespread misconduct relating to the LIBOR'.[164] Following its investigation,

[157] Financial Conduct Authority, 'Final notice Barclays Bank Plc' 27 June 2012, available at www.fca.org.uk/publication/final-notices/barclays-jun12.pdf.

[158] ibid.

[159] Financial Conduct Authority (n 157).

[160] Financial Services Authority, 'FSA Final notice UBS AG' 19 December 2012, available at http://webarchive.nationalarchives.gov.uk/20130202001303/http://www.fsa.gov.uk/static/pubs/final/ubs.pdf.

[161] ibid.

[162] Financial Services Authority (n 160).

[163] Financial Conduct Authority, 'ICAP Europe Limited fined £14 million for significant failings in relation to LIBOR' 25 September 2013, available at www.fca.org.uk/news/press-releases/icap-europe-limited-fined-%C2%A314-million-significant-failings-relation-libor.

[164] Financial Conduct Authority, 'The FCA fines Rabobank £105 million for serious LIBOR-related misconduct' 29 October 2013, available at www.fca.org.uk/news/press-releases/fca-fines-rabobank-%C2%A3105-million-serious-libor-related-misconduct.

the FCA determined that between 2005 and 2011 Rabobank permitted its traders to 'make, or influence others at the bank to make LIBOR submissions that benefitted trading positions linked … LIBOR … collude with individuals at other LIBOR panel banks and interdealer firms to influence … LIBOR submissions … collude with individuals at other LIBOR banks and interdealer broker firms who sought to influence Rabobank's JPY LIBOR submissions'.[165] The FCA concluded that Rabobank 'failed to act with due skill care and diligence … breached three of the FCA's fundamental principles for businesses … [identified] over 500 instances of attempted LIBOR manipulation, directly or indirectly involving at least 9 managers and 19 other individuals based across the world'.[166] Rabobank's poor internal controls encouraged collusion between traders and LIBOR submitters and allowed systematic attempts at benchmark manipulation. Rabobank did not fully address these failings until August 2012, despite assuring the FCA in March 2011 that suitable arrangements were in place. The FCA's director of enforcement and financial crime said 'Rabobank's flawed assurances and failure to get a grip on what was going on in its business were extremely disappointing'.[167]

In May 2014, the FCA imposed its smallest fine £630,000 on Martin Brokers (UK) Ltd (Martins) for the manipulation of LIBOR.[168] The FCA determined that over a three-year period, Martin Brokers conspired with a UBS trader to illegally influence the JPY Libor (Japanese Yen) rates. It was during this period that Martins intentionally circulated a deceptive and distorted LIBOR submission. In particular, the FCA stated that Martins and the UBS trader manipulated the submissions by 'communicating skewed suggestions to some Panel Banks as to where they believed the published JPY LIBOR rate would set for a particular day … creating false orders, with the aim of influencing Panel Banks' views of the cash market so that they would make JPY LIBOR submissions at levels that benefitted the UBS trader; and requesting certain Panel Banks to make specific JPY LIBOR submissions'.[169] The FCA stated:

> Interdealer brokers are expected to act as trusted intermediaries and are key conduits of market information. Martins abused this position of trust by providing false information to Panel Banks, with no regard for the integrity of the market. This is unacceptable behaviour from any market participant.[170]

A mere eight days after Martins was fined, the FCA sanctioned Barclays Bank in May 2015. The FCA concluded that David James Plunkett had manipulated flaws within Barclays' systems and controls and attempted to illegally affect the

[165] ibid.
[166] Financial Conduct Authority (n 164).
[167] ibid.
[168] Financial Conduct Authority, 'Martin Brokers (UK) Limited fined £630,000 for significant failings in relation to LIBOR' 15 May 2014, available at www.fca.org.uk/news/press-releases/martin-brokers-uk-limited-fined-%C2%A3630000-significant-failings-relation-libor.
[169] ibid.
[170] Financial Conduct Authority (n 168).

Gold Fixing, thus personally benefiting (£1.75 million) at the customer's expense. Consequently, Barclays was not obligated to make a £3.9 million payment to the customer, who was eventually recompensed. Subsequently, Plunkett was fined £95,600 and banned from undertaking any regulated activity.[171] Barclays was fined £26 million for 'failing to adequately manage conflicts of interest between itself and its customers as well as systems and controls failings, in relation to the Gold Fixing'.[172] The FCA said:

> A firm's lack of controls and a trader's disregard for a customer's interests have allowed the financial services industry's reputation to be sullied again. Plunkett has paid a heavy price for putting his own interests above the integrity of the market and Barclays' customer. Traders who might be tempted to exploit their clients for a quick buck should be in no doubt – such behaviour will cost you your reputation and your livelihood. Barclays' failure to identify and manage the risks in its business was extremely disappointing. Plunkett's actions came the day after the publication of our LIBOR and EURIBOR action against Barclays. The investigation and outcomes in that case meant that the firm, and Plunkett, were clearly on notice of the potential for conflicts of interests around benchmarks. We expect all firms to look hard at their reference rate and benchmark operations to ensure this type of behaviour isn't being replicated. Firms should be in no doubt that the spotlight will remain on wholesale conduct and we will hold them to account if they fail to meet our standards.[173]

In July 2014, the FCA imposed a financial penalty of £105 million on Lloyds Bank plc (Lloyds) and Bank of Scotland plc (BoS), for misconduct that related to the Special Liquidity Scheme (SLS), the Repo Rate benchmark and LIBOR.[174] Here, the FCA noted that between 2008 and 2009, both Lloyds and BoS unlawfully influenced the Repo Rate to reduce the fees they paid to the Bank of England. The FCA concluded that four people (two from each firm), collectively conspired to manipulate the Repo Rate and described the conduct as 'an extremely serious failing'.[175] In relation to the manipulation, the FCA determined that the manipulation occurred between 2006 and 2009. The FCA noted that Lloyds had conspired with Rabobank to manipulate the JPY LIBOR, and both Lloyds and BoS had actively attempted to 'force LIBOR' to affect the LIBOR submissions of other LIBOR banks to benefit their trading position. A total of 16 employees of both firms were involved in the manipulation of LIBOR, seven were managers. The FCA stated:

> The firms were a significant beneficiary of financial assistance from the Bank of England through the SLS. Colluding to benefit the firms at the expense, ultimately, of the

[171] Financial Conduct Authority, 'Final notice – Daniel James Plunkett' 23 May 2014, available at www.fca.org.uk/publication/final-notices/daniel-james-plunkett.pdf.

[172] Financial Conduct Authority, 'Barclays fined £26m for failings surrounding the London Gold Fixing and former Barclays trader banned and fined for inappropriate conduct' 23 May 2014, available at www.fca.org.uk/news/press-releases/barclays-fined-%C2%A326m-failings-surrounding-london-gold-fixing-and-former-barclays.

[173] ibid.

[174] Financial Conduct Authority, 'Lloyds Banking Group fined £105m for serious LIBOR and other benchmark failings' 28 July 2015, available at www.fca.org.uk/news/press-releases/lloyds-banking-group-fined-%C2%A3105m-serious-libor-and-other-benchmark-failings.

[175] ibid.

> UK taxpayer was unacceptable. This falls well short of the standards the FCA and the market is entitled to expect from regulated firms. The abuse of the SLS is a novel feature of this case but the underlying conduct and the underlying failings – to identify, mitigate and monitor for obvious risks – are not new. If trust in financial services is to be restored then market participants need to ensure they are learning the lessons from, and avoiding the mistakes of, their peers. Our enforcement actions are an important source of information to help them do this.[176]

In November 2014, the FCA imposed a financial penalty on five banks totaling £1.1 billion for 'failing to control business practices in their G10 spot foreign exchange (FX) trading operations'.[177] In total, five banks were subjected to a then record financial penalty from the FCA. Citibank NA were fined £225.5 million,[178] HSBC Bank Plc £216.3 million,[179] JPMorgan Chase Bank NA £222.1 million,[180] The Royal Bank of Scotland Plc £217 million[181] and UBS AG £233.8 million.[182] Because of its investigation, the FCA determined that between January 2008 and October 2013, the banks 'failed to implement adequate and effective controls over their G10 spot FX trading businesses'.[183] These weaknesses resulted in an inappropriate 'tight knit' culture within the banks which contributed towards the traders distributing information to assist their trading strategies, which ultimately included the attempted manipulation of currency rates. Martin Wheatley, the then Chairman of the FCA stated:

> The FCA does not tolerate conduct which imperils market integrity or the wider UK financial system. Today's record fines mark the gravity of the failings we found and firms need to take responsibility for putting it right. They must make sure their traders do not game the system to boost profits or leave the ethics of their conduct to compliance to worry about. Senior management commitments to change need to become a reality in every area of their business. But this is not just about enforcement action. It is about a combination of actions aimed at driving up market standards across the industry. All firms need to work with us to deliver real and lasting change to the culture of the trading floor. This is essential to restoring the public's trust in financial services and London maintaining its position as a strong and competitive financial centre.[184]

[176] Financial Conduct Authority (n 174).

[177] Financial Conduct Authority, 'FCA fines five banks £1.1 billion for FX failings and announces industry-wide remediation programme' 12 November 2015, available at www.fca.org.uk/news/press-releases/fca-fines-five-banks-%C2%A311-billion-fx-failings-and-announces-industry-wide.

[178] Financial Conduct Authority, 'Final Notice – Citi Bank NA' 11 November 2015, available at www.fca.org.uk/publication/final-notices/final-notice-citi-bank.pdf.

[179] Financial Conduct Authority, 'Final Notice – HSBC Bank Plc' 11 November 2015, available at www.fca.org.uk/publication/final-notices/final-notice-hsbc.pdf.

[180] Financial Conduct Authority, 'Final Notice – JPMorgan Chase Bank N.A' 11 November 2015, available at www.fca.org.uk/publication/final-notices/final-notice-jpm.pdf.

[181] Financial Conduct Authority, 'Final Notice – The Royal Bank of Scotland Plc' 11 November 2015, available at www.fca.org.uk/publication/final-notices/final-notice-rbs.pdf.

[182] Financial Conduct Authority, 'Final Notice – UBS AG' 11 November 2018, available at www.fca.org.uk/publication/final-notices/final-notice-rbs.pdf.

[183] Financial Conduct Authority (n 177).

[184] ibid.

In April 2015, Deutsche Bank was fined £227 million by the FCA for LIBOR and EURIBOR failings and for misleading the regulator.[185] Here, the FCA determined that over a five-year period (between 2005 and 2010), Deutsche Bank trading desks engineered its LIBOR submissions. The manipulation of the LIBOR submissions involved 29 employees of Deutsche Bank, based in the UK (London), Germany (Frankfurt), Japan (Tokyo) and the US (New York). The traders adopted a 'three pronged' approach towards the attempted manipulation of EURIBOR. Firstly, the traders attempted to 'influence Deutsche Bank's submitters to alter the Bank's EURIBOR submissions'. Secondly, the traders conspired with other banks and asked them to change this their submissions. Thirdly, the traders offered a 'cash bid' to indicate an alteration in the supply of funding. This conduct was unimpeded due to the weak and defective systems and controls of Deutsche Bank. The FCA stated:

> This case stands out for the seriousness and duration of the breaches by Deutsche Bank – something reflected in the size of today's fine. One division at Deutsche Bank had a culture of generating profits without proper regard to the integrity of the market. This wasn't limited to a few individuals but, on certain desks, it appeared deeply ingrained. Deutsche Bank's failings were compounded by them repeatedly misleading us. The bank took far too long to produce vital documents and it moved far too slowly to fix relevant systems and controls. This case shows how seriously we view a failure to cooperate with our investigations and our determination to take action against firms where we see wrongdoing.[186]

In May 2015, the FCA fined Barclays Bank £284.4 million for 'failing to control business practices in its foreign exchange (FX) business in London'.[187] The FCA determined that between January 2008 and October 2013, Barclays' systems and control were deficient and several traders were able to exploit them for the benefit of the of their employer. The traders were 'inappropriately sharing information about clients' activities and attempting to manipulate spot FX currency rates, including in collusion with traders at other firms, in a way that could disadvantage those clients and the market'.[188] The FCA stated:

> This is another example of a firm allowing unacceptable practices to flourish on the trading floor. Instead of addressing the obvious risks associated with its business Barclays allowed a culture to develop which put the firm's interests ahead of those of its clients and which undermined the reputation and integrity of the UK financial system.

[185] Financial Conduct Authority, 'Deutsche Bank fined £227 million by Financial Conduct Authority for LIBOR and EURIBOR failings and for misleading the regulator' 23 April 2015, available at www.fca.org.uk/news/press-releases/deutsche-bank-fined-%C2%A3227-million-financial-conduct-authority-libor-and-euribor.

[186] ibid.

[187] Financial Conduct Authority, 'FCA fines Barclays £284,432,000 for forex failings' 20 May 2015, available at www.fca.org.uk/news/press-releases/fca-fines-barclays-%C2%A3284432000-forex-failings.

[188] ibid.

> Firms should scrutinise their own systems and cultures to ensure that they make good on their promises to deliver change.[189]

In January 2018, the FCA imposed a financial penalty of £250,000 on Neil Danzinger and banned him from performing any function in the regulated financial activity.[190] In this instance, the FCA concluded that between 2007 and 2010, Danzinger had routinely made requests to RBS's primary submitters, intending to benefit the trading positions for which he and other derivatives traders were responsible; took those trading positions into account when acting as a substitute submitter; and on two occasions, obtained a broker's assistance to attempt to manipulate the JPY LIBOR submissions of other banks. In addition, between 19 September 2008 and 25 August 2009, Mr Danziger entered into 28 wash trades – risk free trades, with the same party, in pairs that cancelled each other out and for which there was no legitimate commercial rationale. The purpose of these wash trades was to make or facilitate brokerage payments to two firms of brokers in recognition of his receipt of personal hospitality. The FCA found he acted recklessly, and therefore with a lack of integrity, in deliberately closing his mind to the risk that his actions were improper. Here, the FCA determined that Danzinger 'was knowingly concerned in RBS's failure to observe proper standards of market conduct and has determined that he is not a fit and proper person because he acted recklessly and lacks integrity'. The FCA stated:

> Proper standards of market conduct reflect the interests of the whole community in the well-being of our financial markets. Mr Danziger's reckless disregard of these standards has no place in the financial services industry. Market participants cannot turn a blind eye to what the community, through its laws and regulations, expects nor apply their own, lower standards. This substantial fine and ban should reinforce that message.[191]

Additionally, the FCA fined Guillaume Adolph (Adolph) £180,000 and banned him from performing any function in relation to any regulated financial activity.[192]

VII. Conclusion

The UK has attempted to adopt a tough enforcement stance towards insider dealing and market abuse and it is very dependent on the provisions of the Insider Dealing Directive and Market Abuse Regime. However, the ineffectiveness of the enforcement stances towards insider dealing is evident due to the low level

[189] Financial Conduct Authority (n 187).

[190] Financial Conduct Authority, 'FCA fines and bans former RBS trader, Neil Danziger' 8 January 2018, available at www.fca.org.uk/news/press-releases/fca-fines-and-bans-former-rbs-trader-neil-danziger.

[191] ibid.

[192] Financial Conduct Authority, 'FCA fines and bans former Deutsche Bank trader, Guillaume Adolph' 5 March 2018, available at www.fca.org.uk/news/press-releases/fca-fines-and-bans-former-deutsche-bank-trader-guillaume-adolph.

of criminal convictions following the introduction of the CJA 1993. The criminalisation of insider dealing in the UK is a failure as a result of the high burden of proof required in such difficult evidentiary cases. The attempt to address this perceived failure has come in the form of a civil regime enacted as part of FSMA 2000. The Financial Services Authority and the FCA are now being more aggressive, but it is difficult to judge, if the financial penalties will have the desired impact to prevent future misconduct. The level of fines for the LIBOR scandal have been higher in comparison to those imposed for insider dealing and market abuse. However, these fines are significantly smaller when compared to those imposed in the US. Therefore, the UK has adopted an almost identical stance towards market manipulation as that adopted by the EU. However, at the time of writing this chapter, the future relationship with the EU legislation on market manipulation is uncertain.[193] Given the UK's robust stance towards enforcing the insider dealing law's market abuse provisions it seems unlikely that Brexit will initially have any drastic impact. The only financial crime related law that specifically addresses Brexit is the Sanctions and Anti-Money Laundering Act 2018.

The next chapter focuses on the approach adopted in the US towards the regulation of market manipulation.

[193] European Union (Withdrawal) Act 2018, s 1.

6

The United States of America

I. Introduction

The purpose of this chapter is to critically comment on the regulation of market manipulation and insider trading in the United States of America (US). The chapter begins by initally concentrating on the US legislative provisions that criminalise insider trading and it then moves on to undertake a comparable commentary on the US approach towards market manipulation. The remainder of the chapter adopts a similar structure to that adopted in the United Kingdomn UK) chapter. For example, it concentrates on the association between market manipulation and the 2007/08 financial crisis and focuses on the enforcement reponse by the Securities and Exchange Commission (SEC), the US Department of Justice (DoJ) and the Commodities Futures and Trading Commission (CFTC). The chapter concludes that the US has adopted an identical enforcement policy towards market manipulation to that used in both the EU and UK, thus favouring imposing administrative financial penalties as opposed to instigating criminal proceedings.

II. Insider Trading

The US legislative efforts to tackle insider trading were largely introduced following the Wall Street Crash in October 1929 and the consequent Great Depression.[1] The criminalisation of insider trading was introduced by the Securities and Exchange Act 1934, which created the SEC.[2] However, it is interesting to note that before insider trading became a federal criminal offence, it was initially criminalised under State legislation.[3] In addition to the ability of US law enforcement

[1] The link between the Wall Street Crash and financial crime was highlighted following the publication of the Pecora Commission. See the Committee on Banking and Currency, *Stock Exchange Practices* (The Committee on Banking and Currency, 1934).

[2] See Securities and Exchange Commission, 'What we do' n/d, available at www.sec.gov/Article/whatwedo.html.

[3] However, several US authors say that State legislation has played a minor role in the regulation of insider trading. See eg Victor Brudney, 'Insiders, Outsiders, and Informational Advantages Under the Federal Securities Law' (1979) 93 *Harvard Law Review* 322 and Joel Seligman, 'The Reformulation of Federal Securities Law Concerning Non-public Information' (1985) 73 *The Reformulation of Federal Securities Law Concerning Nonpublic Information* 1083.

and financial regulatory agencies to instigate criminal proceedings for alleged breaches of the Securities and Exchange Act 1934, the SEC instigated civil actions under the 1934 Act. As will be outlined later in the chapter, the Division of Enforcement recommends the type of enforcement action that the SEC should pursue against alleged violators of the Securities and Exchange Act 1934.[4] The SEC has two options available. First, a civil action where the SEC files a grievance with a US District Court seeking a penalty or remedy. Secondly, an administrative action which is before an independent Administrative Judge, who will grant a decision which includes a recommended sanction. The Securities and Exchange Act 1934 criminalised insider trading by virtue of sections 10(b) and 16(b), yet neither provision expressly states a prohibition against insider trading. This uncertainty was identified by Bainbridge who concluded that neither section of the Securities and Exchange Act 1934 criminalised insider trading.[5] Indeed, sections 10(b) and 16(b) are counter-fraud provisions, which have been widely interpreted by the SEC to include a prohibition against insider trading. This is not surprising given the very wide interpretation and use of US fraud legislation, particularly the Mail Fraud Statute[6] and Wire Fraud Statute.[7] Both of these laws are used for a wide range of financial crimes offences including money laundering.[8] However, these sections are benign without the support of specific rules implemented by the SEC, such as Rule 10(b).[9] Despite its criminalisation, insider trading was ignored until several high profile instances of insider trading in the 1980s and 1990s. These include, for example, Ivan Boesky,[10] Dennis Levine,[11] Salim Lewis[12] and Michael Milken,[13] which prompted the US government to introduce stronger counter measures to tackle insider trading.[14] In response to the legislative silence on insider trading, the US judiciary has played an active role in criminalising insider trading and the US courts determined that 'private citizens could maintain civil suits against insider traders upon demonstrating a loss due to the violation'.[15]

[4] See Securities and Exchange Commission, 'Division of Enforcement' n/d, available at www.sec.gov/page/enforcement-section-landing.

[5] Stephen Bainbridge, 'The insider trading prohibition: a legal and economic enigma' (1986) *University of Florida Law Review* 38.

[6] 18 USC § 1341.

[7] 18 USC § 1343.

[8] See generally Nicholas Ryder, *Financial Crime in the 21st Century Law and Policy* (Edward Elgar, 2011) 103–11.

[9] See Securities and Exchange Commission, 'Final Rule: Selective Disclosure and Insider Trading' 23 October 2000, available at www.sec.gov/rules/final/33-7881.htm.

[10] See *United States of America v Ivan F Boesky* 1987 86 Cr 378 (MEL).

[11] See *New York Times*, 'Levine Gets 2-Year Jail Term' 21 February 1987, available at www.nytimes.com/1987/02/21/business/levine-gets-2-year-jail-term.html.

[12] See *New York Times*, 'Timeline: A History of Insider Trading' 6 December 2016, available at www.nytimes.com/interactive/2016/12/06/business/dealbook/insider-trading-timeline.html.

[13] ibid.

[14] Marleen O'Connor, 'Toward a more efficient deterrence of insider trading: the repeal of section 16(b)' (1989) 58 *Fordham Law Review* 309.

[15] See in particular *Kardon v National Gypsum Co*, 69 F Supp 512 (ED Penn, 1946), affirmed, and *Superintendent of Insurance v Bankers Life & Cas Co* 404 US 6 (1971).

In order to address the weakness of the criminalisation of insider trading under the Securities and Exchange Act 1934, the Insider Trading Sanction Act 1984 aimed to improve the enforcement performance of the SEC.[16] Subsequently, the SEC granted more enforcement powers under the Insider Trading and Securities Fraud Enforcement Act of 1988. For example, the SEC can impose financial penalties three times the profit of illegal trades, convicted insider traders face up to five years imprisonment[17] and financial penalties of up to $1 million can be imposed. Furthermore, the 1988 Act 'offered informants a "bounty" in the amount of ten percent of civil penalties recovered from insider traders apprehended on the basis of the informant's information'.[18]

The US courts 'defined insider trading to encompass a broad range of activity. In the 1970s, the courts initially proposed the "possession theory" to define the offence'.[19] Even then progress was slow and it was not until 1961 that the US properly started out on the road of prohibiting insider trading when in *Re Cady Roberts & Co* the SEC expressed its view that corporate officers not only owe a duty to the company but also to shareholders.[20] However, the SEC properly came down against insider trading in the landmark judgment in *SEC v Texas Gulf Sulphur* that stated that anyone who possesses material non-public information had two options, disclose it, or abstain.[21] The *Texas Gulf Sulphur* decision was dealt a blow by the US Supreme Court in 1980, in rejecting the equality of access basis that *Texas Gulf Sulphur* was founded upon. In *Chiarella v US*, the Supreme Court brought the law back to its fiduciary duty origins, so it seemed that only those with a true fiduciary duty to the company could be caught by the insider trading prohibition.[22] The solution to this problem according to Rakoff and Easton was the 'development of the so-called "misappropriation theory" of Rule 10(b)-5 liability, which separates the "fraud" and the "trading" aspects of insider trading into two distinct components. Under this theory, any person who steals or misappropriates inside information from anyone to whom he owes a fiduciary duty also thereby commits a fraud, by not disclosing the theft'.[23] In *Dirks v SEC*,

[16] Pub L No 98–376.

[17] United States Department of Justice, 'Former Amazon Financial Analyst Sentenced to Prison for Insider Trading' 8 December 2017, available at www.justice.gov/usao-wdwa/pr/former-amazon-financial-analyst-sentenced-prison-insider-trading.

[18] Thomas Joo, 'Legislation and legitimation: Congress and insider trading in the 1980s' (2007) 82 *Indiana Law Journal* 578. For a list of payments received by whistle-blowers by the SEC for insider trading cases see Securities and Exchange Commission, 'Office of the Whistleblower' n/d, available at www.sec.gov/whistleblower/pressreleases. The largest award issued by the SEC as of December 2018 was $50 million. See Securities and Exchange Commission, 'SEC Announces Its Largest-Ever Whistle-blower Awards' 29 March 2018, available at www.sec.gov/news/press-release/2018-44.

[19] John Naylor, 'The use of criminal sanctions by UK and US authorities for insider trading: how can the two systems learn from each other? Part 2' (1990) 11 *The Company Lawyer* 84.

[20] (1961) 40 SEC 907 (1961).

[21] 401 F 2d 833 2nd Cir 1968.

[22] 445 US 222 (1980).

[23] Jed Rakoff and Joanne Easton, 'How effective is US enforcement in deterring insider trading?' (1996) 6(3) *Journal of Financial Crime* 283.

the Supreme Court noted that the prohibition did extend beyond just those in a fiduciary relationship, to the so-called 'tippee' in so much that the information in the tippee's possession comes from a person who is in a fiduciary relationship with the company whose securities are involved.[24] Bainbridge took the view that 'the decision's limited practical impact on enforcement, its unique facts, and its focus on objective criteria convinced the committee [SEC] that *Dirks* would not adversely affect enforcement if construed narrowly by the courts'.[25] Nonetheless, US legislature introduced the ITSA and the Insider Trading and Securities Fraud Enforcement Act of 1988 to alter the focus of the definition.[26] Neither the 1984 nor the 1988 legislation clarified the definition of insider trading. Therefore, the different approaches resulted in Naylor concluding 'the statute, regulations, and court cases still fail to provide a precise definition of what constitutes insider trading'.[27] As Bainbridge notes, *Dirks* did not fully answer the question of how far the US prohibition truly extends, when the information is from a non-insider, and is non-public and material.[28] Thus illustrating their commitment to tackle insider trading the SEC began to develop the misappropriation theory. This theory has found favour with the US Supreme Court. For example, in *US v O'Hagan* where a lawyer was not in a fiduciary position, he was convicted of the criminal offence because he still owed a fiduciary duty to the source of the information and had misappropriated it for his own profit.[29] This of course opens up a much wider class of people who could fall within the insider trading prohibition. Mistry argues that the misappropriation theory makes the US enforcement of insider trading more effective as it provides for a more elastic relationship between insider and issuer than the UK regime requires.[30] To clarify the position in respect of insider dealing the SEC has created Rules 10b5-1 and 10b5-2. The first of these provides that a person breaches the insider trading provisions if they trade on the basis of material non-public information if a trader is aware of the material non-public information when making the purchase or sale. The second covers the misappropriation theory position and provides that a person receiving confidential information under circumstances specified in the rule would owe a duty of trust or confidence and thus could be liable under the misappropriation theory. It is evident from a discussion about the US position that the SEC as regulatory body and the US courts, including the Supreme Court, have played an enormous role in prohibiting insider trading even though it is arguable that

[24] 462 US 646 (1983).
[25] See Bainbridge (n 5) 483.
[26] See Naylor (n 19) 84.
[27] ibid.
[28] Bainbridge (n 5) 456.
[29] Alexander Loke, 'From the fiduciary theory to information abuse: the changing fabric of insider trading law in the UK, Australia and Singapore' (2006) 54(1) *The American Journal of Comparative Law* 123.
[30] 521 US 642 (1997).

Congress in 1934 did not have such a prohibition in mind, and in the face of strong intellectual argument against such a prohibition.

Due to the inadequacies of the insider trading laws as outlined above, the SEC has used several other legislative measures to improve its enforcement performance. For example, the Racketeer Influence and Corrupt Organizations Act 1970 (RICO) provided that it was only necessary for prosecutors to illustrate that 'a defendant committed securities fraud twice within any ten-year period. Prosecutors also favoured the stiff penalties imposed for a RICO conviction'.[31] O'Connor argued that 'securities violations and mail and wire fraud violations may serve as predicate acts to establish a pattern of racketeering activity under RICO'.[32] Furthermore, the Mail and Wire Fraud Statutes have provided prosecutors with extensive enforcement powers that have been used in instances of insider trading. The Sarbanes-Oxley Act 2002 introduced a new insider-trading embargo that 'is linked to trading blackouts affecting a significant percentage of US participants in individual account retirement plans that hold employer equity securities. Additionally, the Act requires that new blackout notices be provided to defined contribution retirement plan participants and beneficiaries even when insiders are not restricted from trading and even though the retirement plan holds no employer securities'.[33] Like other regulatory agencies, the SEC is permitted to seek equitable relief for the benefit of investors by virtue of the Securities and Exchange Act 1934 and the Securities Enforcement Remedies and Penny Stock Reform Act 1990.[34] Despite the rigorous approach adopted by the SEC toward enforcing the insider trading provisions a number of concerns have been raised regarding their 'over enthusiasm' demonstrated during their investigations.[35] Furthermore, the SEC needs to rebuild its reputation after failing to act on numerous complaints alleging misconduct by convicted fraudster Bernard Madoff.[36] The effectiveness of the initial US enforcement strategy towards insider trading has been limited by a number of factors including the courts' inconsistent interpretation of 'insider trading' and an initial reluctance by the SEC to pursue the offences outlined above. Nonetheless, the early enforcement stance has altered with the increased coverage and exposure of insider trading since the 1980s. The next section of the chapter focuses on the US approach towards market manipulation and concentrates on its association with the 2007/08 financial crisis.

[31] 84 Stat 922-3 aka 84 Stat 941; 18 USC §§ 1961–1968.

[32] See O'Connor (n 14) 340.

[33] Pub L 107–204, 116 Stat 745.

[34] PL 101–429.

[35] Thomas Newkirk, 'Conflicts between public accountability and individual privacy in SEC enforcement actions' (2001) 8(4) *Journal of Financial Crime* 319.

[36] Julian Harris, 'Getting over Madoff: how the SEC must restore its credibility' (2010) 31(2) *Company Lawyer* 33.

III. Market Manipulation

The SEC defines market manipulation as 'manipulation is intentional conduct designed to deceive investors by controlling or artificially affecting the market for a security'.[37] Market manipulation includes a variety of illegal activities which includes mechanisms that are 'spreading false or misleading information about a company; improperly limiting the number of publicly-available shares; or rigging quotes, prices or trades to create a false or deceptive picture of the demand for a security. Those who engage in manipulation are subject to various civil and criminal sanctions'.[38] This chapter follows a similar structure to that adopted in previous chapters in that it illustrates the link between market manipulation and the 2007/08 financial crisis. Here, we concentrate on the manipulation of LIBOR, EURIBOR and FOREX.

IV. The 2007/08 Financial Crisis, Market Manipulation and the Enforcement Response

The association between the financial crisis and market manipulation can be divided into three subdivisions: concealment of investor risks, terms and improper pricing; misleading disclosures; and hazardous mortgage-related investments.[39] One of the highest profile actions instigated by the SEC was against Goldman Sachs, who were accused of defrauding investors by misleading and excluding important pieces of information about how certain financial commodities that were linked to subprime mortgages as the housing market stumbled.[40] In July 2010, Goldman Sachs admitted that their marketing materials 'contained incomplete information' and that they 'regretted that the marketing materials did not contain that disclosure'.[41] Therefore, they agreed to pay a record financial penalty of $550 million and agreed to alter their business practices.[42] The SEC stated that:

> Half a billion dollars is the largest penalty ever assessed against a financial services firm in the history of the SEC … this settlement is a stark lesson to Wall Street firms that no

[37] Securities and Exchange Commission, 'Manipulation' n/d, available at www.sec.gov/fast-answers/answerstmanipulhtm.html.

[38] ibid.

[39] Securities and Exchange Commission, 'SEC Enforcement addressing misconduct that led or arose from the financial crisis' n/d, available at www.sec.gov/spotlight/enf-actions-fc.shtml#keyStatistics.

[40] Securities and Exchange Commission, 'SEC Charges Goldman Sachs With Fraud in Structuring and Marketing of CDO Tied to Subprime Mortgages' 16 April 2010, available at www.sec.gov/news/press/2010/2010-59.htm.

[41] Securities and Exchange Commission, 'Goldman Sachs to pay record $500 million to Settle SEC Charges Related to Subprime Mortgage CDO' 15 July 2010, available at www.sec.gov/news/press/2010/2010-123.htm.

[42] ibid.

> product is too complex, and no investor too sophisticated, to avoid a heavy price if a firm violates the fundamental principles of honest treatment and fair dealing.[43]

Another example of conduct of concealment from investors related to JP Morgan Securities, who were charged with misleading investors in a multifaceted mortgage securities contract when the US housing sector began to fall.[44] The SEC stated that:

> J.P Morgan marketed highly-complex CDO investments to investors with promises that the mortgage assets underlying the CDO would be selected by an independent manager looking out for investor interests … J.P. Morgan failed to tell investors was that a prominent hedge fund that would financially profit from the failure of CDO portfolio assets heavily influenced the CDO portfolio selection. With today's settlement, harmed investors receive a full return of the losses they suffered.[45]

JP Morgan Securities consented to the final judgment, but without admitting or denying the charges, and agreed to pay $153.6 million. The SEC has also utilised its enforcement powers where financial institutions have provided misleading disclosures to investors. For example, Citigroup were accused by the SEC of deliberately misleading investors over its exposure to subprime mortgage assets.[46] Citigroup agreed to settle the allegations and paid a $75 million penalty, while its former chief financial officer paid $100,000, and its former head of investor relations agreed to pay $80,000.[47] The fine imposed on Citigroup and two of its former senior corporate officials draws favourable comparisons with the enforcement activity of the enforcement activity of the Financial Conduct Authority (FCA) in the UK, as part of its credible deterrence strategy.[48] Another example related to the enforcement activities pursued by the SEC against employees of American Home Mortgage. Here, the SEC charged the employees with accountancy fraud and deliberately misleading investors about their worsening financial predicament due to its exposure to the subprime crisis. In its press release, the SEC stated 'these senior executives did not just occupy a front row seat to the mortgage meltdown – they were part of the show … as the housing market imploded, these executives kept secret that the company's holdings were collapsing like a house of cards'.[49] As a result, the former employees of the firm agreed to pay a settlement worth $2.45 million and were prohibited from working as a directors for

[43] Securities and Exchange Commission (n 41).

[44] Securities and Exchange Commission, 'J.P. Morgan to Pay $153.6 Million to Settle SEC Charges of Misleading Investors in CDO Tied to U.S. Housing Market' 21 June 2011, available at www.sec.gov/news/press/2011/2011-131.htm.

[45] ibid.

[46] Securities and Exchange Commission, 'SEC Charges Citigroup and Two Executives for Misleading Investors About Exposure to Subprime Mortgage Assets' 29 July 2010, available at www.sec.gov/news/press/2010/2010-136.htm.

[47] ibid.

[48] For a more detailed discussion see ch 5.

[49] Securities and Exchange Commission (n 46).

a period of five years.[50] The financial penalties imposed by the SEC on the former employees of American House Mortgage are significantly higher than any financial penalty imposed on an individual in the UK, thus supporting our contention that the FCA needs to adopt a more aggressive stance towards enforcing its market manipulation provisions. One of the largest settlements reached by the SEC was against Credit Suisse and JP Morgan, who were charged with 'misleading investors in offerings of residential mortgage-backed securities'.[51] Both JP Morgan ($296.9 million) and Credit Suisse ($120 million) agreed to settle the SEC accusations.[52] Here, the SEC took the view that:

> In many ways, mortgage products such as RMBS were ground zero in the financial crisis … misrepresentations in connection with the creation and sale of mortgage securities contributed greatly to the tremendous losses suffered by investors once the U.S. housing market collapsed. Today's actions involving RMBS securities are a continuation of the SEC's strong efforts to pursue wrongdoing committed in connection with the financial crisis.[53]

The concealment of risky mortgage-related and other investments is illustrated by the enforcement activities of the SEC against Bear Stearns. In June 2008, the SEC decided to indict two former managers of the ailing financial institution for fraudulently misleading investors about the monetary state of two of their biggest hedge funds and their risk of exposure during the financial crisis.[54] In June 2012, a court approved the SEC settlement with the two former employees of Bear Stearns, Ralph Cioffi and Matthew Tannian, who were ordered to pay $1.05 million.[55] Once again, the enforcement actions of the SEC are favourable when compared to those imposed in the UK by the FCA. Another example of a firm providing misleading statements to investors was Charles Schwab, who settled charges in 2011 and agreed to a financial sanction of $118 million.[56] Here, the SEC stated that:

> All financial firms and professionals – including large mutual fund providers – must be vigilant in accurately describing the risks of the products they sell to the public,

[50] Securities and Exchange Commission, 'SEC Charges Former American Home Mortgage Executives for Misleading Investors About Company's Financial Condition' 28 April 2009, available at www.sec.gov/news/press/2009/2009-92.htm.

[51] Securities and Exchange Commission, 'SEC Charges J.P. Morgan and Credit Suisse With Misleading Investors in RMBS Offerings' 16 November 2012, available at www.sec.gov/news/press/2012/2012-233.htm.

[52] Securities and Exchange Commission 'Remarks During News Conference Call About Enforcement Actions Against J.P. Morgan and Credit Suisse' 16 November 2012, available at www.sec.gov/news/speech/2012/spch111612rk.htm.

[53] ibid.

[54] Securities and Exchange Commission, 'SEC Charges Two Former Bear Stearns Hedge Fund Managers With Fraud' 19 June 2008, available at www.sec.gov/news/press/2008/2008-115.htm.

[55] Securities and Exchange Commission, 'Court Approves SEC Settlements with Two Former Bear Stearns Hedge Fund Portfolio Managers; SEC Bars Managers from Regulated Industries' 25 June 2012, available from www.sec.gov/litigation/litreleases/2012/lr22398.htm.

[56] Securities and Exchange Commission, 'SEC Charges Schwab Entities and Two Executives With Making Misleading Statements' 11 January 2011, available at www.sec.gov/news/press/2011/2011-7.htm.

> especially the widely-held mutual funds that are the bread-and-butter investments of retail investors … Schwab marketed the fund as a cash alternative with only slightly more risk than a money market fund even though, at one point, half of the fund's assets were invested in private-issuer, mortgage-backed and other securities with maturities and credit quality that were significantly different than investments made by money market funds.[57]

Therefore, the next section of the chapter critically considers the enforcement stance of US financial regulatory and law enforcement agencies towards tackling market manipulation in light of the 2007/08 financial crisis.

V. The Securities and Exchange Commission

The SEC was initially designed to act as an 'economic watchdog'.[58] Its mission is to protect 'investors, maintain fair, orderly, and efficient markets, and facilitate capital formation'.[59] The SEC is 'responsible for the enforcement and regulation of the US securities market … it is charged with regulating all companies that hold and trade public stock'.[60] The most pertinant part of the SEC for this chapter is its Division of Enforcement, which was established in August 1972. The Division of Enforcement undertakes investigations for alleged breaches of securities legislation and prosecutes the SEC's civil suits.[61] Common remedies pursued include injunctions, financial penalties and the suspension or prohibition of people acting in certain positions. The SEC is also permitted to provide compensation for the victims of fraud[62] and generate administrative proceedings before an SEC Administrative Law Judge. There are several different categories of proceedings that the SEC could pursue against wrongdoers including a cease and desist order, a disgorgement order, the revocation of a licence or registration or even suspension. The Division of Enforcement seeks to support and advise the SEC in 'executing its law enforcement function by recommending the commencement of investigations of securities law violations, by recommending that the Commission bring civil actions in federal court or as administrative proceedings before an administrative law judge, and by prosecuting these cases on behalf of the Commission'.[63] The SEC investigates a wide range of white-collar crime activities including allegations of misrepresentation, market manipulation, insider trading

[57] ibid.

[58] Daniel Huynh, 'Pre-emption v. punishment: a comparative study of white-collar crime prosecution in the United States and the United Kingdom' (2010) 9 *Journal of International Business and Law* 108.

[59] Securities and Exchange Commission, 'The Investor's Advocate: How the SEC Protects Investors, Maintains Market Integrity, and Facilitates Capital Formation' n/d, available at www.sec.gov/about/whatwedo.shtml.

[60] See Huynh (n 58).

[61] ibid, at 109.

[62] Sarbanes Oxley Act 2002, s 308.

[63] Securities and Exchange Commission (n 4).

and selling unregistered securities.[64] From an enforcement perspective, it is very important to note that the SEC has an extensive array of civil enforcement powers, but it has no authority to instigate criminal proceedings. The SEC has imposed a record number of financial sanctions since the onset of the financial crisis.[65] Despite having an arsenal of enforcement powers, the regulatory performance of the SEC during the financial crisis has been overshadowed and perhaps permanently tarnished as a result of the actions of Bernard Madoff.[66] In 2008, Bernard Madoff was arrested and accused of orchestrating one of the largest Ponzi frauds ever encountered in the US. In 2009, Bernard Madoff pleaded guilty to wire fraud, securities fraud, money laundering, mail fraud and perjury and was sentenced to 150 years imprisonment.[67]

One can see the strong role that market manipulation played in the 2008 financial crisis by examining the increase in enforcement actions in the US. For example, since the start of the financial crisis the SEC has charged 161 companies and individuals (including 66 senior corporate officials with related offences), while 37 individuals have either been barred from acting as company directors or suspended from doing so. The SEC has also imposed penalty orders of $1.53 billion, enforced disgorgement orders totalling $800 million, obtained $400 million compensation for affected investors; the total amount of penalties amounts to $2.73 billion.

The enforcement stance of the SEC has continued to focus on imposing a large number of financial penalties on both corporations and individuals. For example, in 2014 the SEC obtained civil court orders totaling $4.16 billion and it filed 755 enforcement actions.[68] In particular, the SEC imposed civil sanctions on Kohlberg Kravis Roberts & Co,[69] three Credit Rating Agencies[70] and UBS Securities LLC.[71] One of the most notable civil actions successfully pursued by the SEC was against Deutsche Bank, who were fined $55 million for 'filing misstated financial reports

[64] It is important to note that it wasn't until the 1980s that the Securities and Exchange Commission began to tackle insider trading due to the introduction of the Insider Trading Sanctions Act 1984.

[65] However, the effectiveness of these has been questioned. See Colin Maher, 'Crisis not averted: lack of criminal prosecutions leave limited consequences for those responsible for the financial crisis' (2013) 39 *New England Journal on Criminal and Civil Confinement* 463.

[66] Henry Pontell, William Black and Gilbert Geis, 'Too big to fail, too powerful to prosecute? On the absence of criminal prosecutions after the 2009 financial meltdown' (2013) *Crime Law and Society* 3.

[67] Aaron Smith, 'Madoff sentenced to 150 years' CNN, 30 June 2009, available at http://money.cnn.com/2009/06/29/news/economy/madoff_prison_sentence/index.htm.

[68] Securities and Exchange Commission, 'SEC Announces Enforcement Results For FY 2015' 22 October 2015, available at www.sec.gov/news/pressrelease/2015-245.html.

[69] Securities and Exchange Commission, 'SEC Charges KKR With Misallocating Broken Deal Expenses' 29 June 2015, available at www.sec.gov/news/pressrelease/2015-131.html.

[70] Securities and Exchange Commission, 'SEC Announces Charges Against Standard & Poor's for Fraudulent Ratings Misconduct' 21 January 2015, available at www.sec.gov/news/pressrelease/2015-10.html.

[71] Securities and Exchange Commission, 'SEC Charges UBS Subsidiary With Disclosure Violations and Other Regulatory Failures in Operating Dark Pool' 15 January 2015, available at www.sec.gov/news/pressrelease/2015-7.html.

during the height of the financial crisis that failed to take into account a material risk for potential losses estimated to be in the billions of dollars'.[72] Further evidence of the SEC using its civil enforcement powers was illustrated in 2016 when it announced that 'it filed 868 enforcement actions exposing financial reporting-related misconduct by companies and their executives and misconduct by registrants and gatekeepers'.[73] In particular, the SEC has taken enforcement action against 250 corporations and 548 'standalone or independent enforcement actions and obtained judgments and orders totaling more than $4 billion in disgorgement and penalties'.[74] The SEC continued to impose large financial penalties on both corporations and individuals. For example, Merrill Lynch was fined $415 million for breaching consumer protection rules,[75] the SEC imposed a financial penalty of $267 million on JP Morgan for failing to disclose conflicts of interest to clients[76] and there were several other high profile insider trading cases.[77] The SEC stated that 'this has been a strong year for the Enforcement Division, with groundbreaking insider trading and FCPA cases and other important actions across the full spectrum of the securities laws … through their hard work and steadfast dedication to our mission, the Division's committed staff have helped protect investors and made our markets fairer and more reliable'.[78] In 2017, the SEC described its enforcement activities are its most 'successful and impactful year for the Enforcement Division'.[79] In total, the SEC has instigated over 750 different types of enforcement activity, incorporating 446 standalone actions and over $1 billion compensation for investors.[80] In 2018, the SEC brought over 800 enforcement actions, they were able to return approximately $800 million to investors and imposed financial penalties of $3.9 billion. The SEC stated that this included '490 standalone actions', of which 'market manipulation, insider trading, and broker-dealer misconduct, with each comprising approximately 10 percent of the overall number of standalone actions'.[81] Therefore, the SEC has continued to use its extensive array of civil enforcement powers against both corporations and individuals

[72] Securities and Exchange Commission, 'SEC Charges Deutsche Bank With Misstating Financial Reports During Financial Crisis' 26 May 2015, available at www.sec.gov/news/pressrelease/2015-99.html.

[73] Securities and Exchange Commission, 'SEC Announces Enforcement Results for FY 2016' 11 October 2016, available at www.sec.gov/news/pressrelease/2016-212.html.

[74] ibid.

[75] Securities and Exchange Commission, 'Merrill Lynch to Pay $415 Million for Misusing Customer Cash and Putting Customer Securities at Risk' 23 June 2016, available at www.sec.gov/news/pressrelease/2016-128.html.

[76] Securities and Exchange Commission, 'J.P. Morgan to Pay $267 Million for Disclosure Failures' 18 December 2015, available at www.sec.gov/news/pressrelease/2015-283.html.

[77] Securities and Exchange Commission, 'SEC Charges Hedge Fund Manager Leon Cooperman With Insider Trading' 21 September 2016, available at www.sec.gov/news/pressrelease/2016-189.html.

[78] Securities and Exchange Commission (n 76).

[79] Securities and Exchange Commission, 'SEC Enforcement Division Issues Report on Priorities and FY 2017 Results' 15 November 2017, available at www.sec.gov/news/press-release/2017-210.

[80] ibid.

[81] Securities and Exchange Commission (n 79).

who have been involved in market manipulation and insider trading. The enforcement stance of the SEC is very similar to that adopted in the UK by the FCA, and its predecessor the Financial Services Authority. However, there is one noteworthy exception – the frequency and level of fines imposed on individuals. As a result of comparing the level of financial penalties imposed in both the US and UK, it is clear and as noted in chapter three, that the level of fines imposed in the US are significantly higher than those imposed in the UK. Nonetheless, the enforcement activities of the SEC can be contrasted with the aggressive stance adopted by the DoJ, which this chapter now turns to.

VI. The Department of Justice

The DoJ has played an important role in tackling white collar crime associated with the financial crisis. The Attorney General Eric Holder JR testified before the Financial Crisis Inquiry Commission and stated:

> The DoJ has a long history of prosecuting financial fraud – and we will continue to do so. Working in concert with our Federal, state, local, tribal and territorial partners, the Justice Department is using every tool at our disposal – including new resources, advanced technologies and communications capabilities, and the very best talent we have – to prevent, prosecute and punish these crimes. And by taking dramatic action, our goal is not just to hold accountable those whose conduct may have contributed to the last meltdown, but to deter such future conduct as well.[82]

The DoJ claim to have 'investigated and held accountable those responsible for financial fraud' during the financial crisis.[83] For example, it has 'prosecuted some of the most significant financial crimes … bringing to justice … numerous individuals across the country who perpetrated investment, securities and other fraud schemes'.[84] This view is supported by Henning, but he noted that 'the cases are local in nature and do not involve large financial institutions'.[85] One of the first measures introduced by the DoJ was the Financial Fraud Enforcement Task Force, which is one of several similar task forces established by the DoJ to tackle white collar crime. Other examples include the Corporate Fraud Task Force,[86] the Enron Task Force and the National Procurement Fraud Task Force. The Financial Fraud

[82] Department of Justice, 'Attorney General Eric Holder Testifies Before the Financial Crisis Inquiry Commission' 14 January 2010, available at www.justice.gov/ag/testimony/2010/ag-testimony-100114.html.

[83] Department of Justice, 'Accomplishments under the leadership of Attorney General Eric Holder' n/d, available at www.justice.gov/accomplishments/accomplishments.pdf.

[84] ibid.

[85] J Henning, 'Making sure the buck stops here: barring executives for corporate violations' (2012) *University of Chicago Legal Forum* 95.

[86] The Corporate Fraud Task Force was established by Executive Order 13271 of 9 July 2002.

Enforcement Task Force replaced the Corporate Fraud Task Force.[87] The aim of the Corporate Fraud Task Force was to 'provide direction for the investigation and prosecution of cases of securities fraud, accounting fraud, mail and wire fraud, money laundering … and other related financial crimes committed by commercial entities'.[88] Arogeti argued that the Corporate Fraud Task Force was created to 'restore market confidence and cut down on corporate fraud'.[89] The Corporate Fraud Task Force secured over 1,200 fraud related prosecutions which included numerous company chief executive officers, chief executives and chief financial officers.[90] President Barak Obama stated that the Financial Fraud Enforcement Task Force would assist the DoJ to 'investigate and prosecute significant financial crimes and other violations relating to the current financial crisis and economic recovery efforts'.[91] In essence, this Task Force specifically focused on white collar crime emanating from the financial crisis including mortgage and securities fraud.[92]

The Task Force contains representatives of a wide range of federal government departments, regulatory agencies and law enforcement agencies. For example, this included inter alia, the Department of the Treasury, the Department of Commerce, the SEC, Department of Homeland Security, Futures Trading Commission, the Federal Trade Commission, the Federal Deposit Insurance Corporation, the Board of Governors of the Federal Reserve System, the FBI, the US Secret Services and the Financial Crimes Enforcement Network. Presidential Executive Order 13,519 provides that the objectives of the Financial Fraud Enforcement Task Force are to:

> provide advice … for the investigation and prosecution of [significant] cases of bank, mortgage, loan, and lending fraud; securities and commodities fraud; retirement plan fraud; mail and wire fraud; tax crimes; money laundering; False Claims Act violations; unfair competition; discrimination; and other financial crimes and violations.[93]

Furthermore, this Task Force has five objectives. First, it investigates and where possible prosecutes white collar crime and other illegal activities that have caused

[87] Ellen Podgor, 'Introduction: examining white collar crime with trifocals' (2011) 39 *Fordham Urban Law Journal* 301.

[88] Exec Order No 13,271, 67 Fed Reg 46,091 (9 July 2002).

[89] Jofy Arogeti, 'How much cooperation between government agencies is too much? Reconciling United States v Scrushy, the corporate fraud task force, and the nature of parallel proceedings' (2006) 23 *Georgia State University Law Review* 430.

[90] See Carrie Johnson, 'U.S. Promotes Its Record on Corporate Crime' 18 July 2007, available at www.washingtonpost.com/wp-dyn/content/article/2007/07/17/AR2007071701767.html.

[91] Exec Order No 13519, 74 FR 60123, 2009 WL 3848641 (Pres).

[92] Tom Arnold, 'It's déjà vu all over again using bounty hunters to leverage gatekeepers duties' (2010) 45 *Tulsa Law Review* 450.

[93] Exec Order No 13,519, 74 FR 60123, 2009 WL 3848641 (Pres).

or arisen from the financial crisis. Secondly, the Task Force will seek to recover the proceeds for such crimes and violations. Thirdly, it attempts to address discrimination in the lending and financial markets. Fourthly, it aims to improve the levels of coordination and cooperation between local, state and federal investigative and prosecutorial agencies. Finally, the Task Force will seek to improve the level of interaction with a wide range of partners including financial institutions and consumers in order to improve the prevention and detection of fraud.[94] In order to achieve these objectives, the Task Force has purposely targeted and prioritised fraud that is directly associated with the financial crisis. For example, this includes mortgage fraud, securities and commodities fraud, the distribution of government funds via the American Recovery and Revinvestment Act and TARP.[95] However, the structure of the Financial Fraud Enforcement Task Force is very similar to that adopted by the Corporate Fraud Task Force, the latter of which consisted of the DoJ, the SEC, the Commodities Future Trading Commission and the Federal Energy Regulatory Commission.[96] Nonetheless, Corporate Fraud Task Force did result in the DoJ and SEC forming a closer working relationship towards tackling white collar crime. The DoJ would use its criminal enforcement powers while the SEC would complement these by using its wide reaching civil powers.[97] The Financial Fraud Enforcement Task Force is an attempt by President Barak Obama to improve the response towards white collar crime by adopting a coordinated response.

One of the highest profile actions of the Task Force has been its 'Distressed Homeowner Initiative', which was launched in 2011.[98] The aim of this measure is to concentrate on fraud that targets homeowners who have fallen into arrears on their mortgage repayments. In such cases, the fraudster will approach the homeowner and promise them that they will be able to prevent the repossession or foreclosure of their property for a large fee. The fraudster promises that investors will purchase the homeowner's mortgage or in some cases will ask them to transfer the home ownership to the fraudulent investors.[99] Eric Holder Jr stated that these 'comprehensive efforts represent an historic, government-wide commitment to eradicating mortgage fraud and related offenses … the success of the Distressed Homeowner Initiative underscore our determination to pursue these and other financial fraud criminals around the country'.[100] At first instance, the actions

[94] Financial Fraud Enforcement Task Force, *First year report – Financial Fraud Enforcement Task Force* (Washington DC, Financial Fraud Enforcement Task Force, 2010) 2.3.

[95] ibid, at 2.4.

[96] Arogeti (n 89) 427.

[97] ibid, at 428–29.

[98] Federal Bureau of Investigation, 'Inside the FBI – Podcast' 11 October 2012, available at www.fbi.gov/news/podcasts/inside/distressed-homeowner-mortgage-fraud.mp3/view.

[99] United States Department of Justice, 'Financial Fraud Enforcement Task Force Members Reveal Results of Distressed Homeowner Initiative' 9 October 2012, available at www.justice.gov/opa/pr/2012/October/12-ag-1216.html.

[100] ibid.

and results of the Distressed Homeowner Initiative appear to be very impressive. However, the figures were questioned by a Bloomberg report that suggested that the statistics incorporated investigations and actions two years prior to Barak Obama being elected President.[101] As a result of the investigation by Bloomberg, the statistics were corrected and restated by the FBI.[102] The report also suggested that the publication of the results was politicially motivated as they were published a month before the 2012 presidential elections.

Another important measure that was utilised by the Task Force was 'Operation Broken Dreams', which was launched in October 2010. The purpose of this initiative was to 'target mortgage fraudsters throughout the country and was the largest collective enforcement effort ever brought to bear in confronting mortgage fraud'.[103] It has been described as the 'government's largest mortgage fraud takedown to date'.[104] By June 2010, Operation Broken Dreams identified 1,215 defendants, 486 arrests had been made, there were 673 indictments, there had been 135 complaints, 336 convictions, estimated losses of $2.3 billion and over $10 million had been seized.[105] Additionally, civil cases had been instigated against 400 defendants and the total number of civil enforcement actions was 191. After announcing these results, the Attorney General stated that that 'mortgage fraud ruins lives, destroys families and devastates whole communities, so attacking the problem from every possible direction is vital ... we will use every tool available to investigate, prosecute and prevent mortgage fraud, and we will not rest until anyone preying on vulnerable American homeowners is brought to justice'.[106]

It has been claimed that the creation of the Financial Fraud Enforcement Task Force clearly illustrates that the 'the investigation and prosecution of financial and investment fraud is a primary concern [for the Obama Administration]'.[107] In relation to the manipulation of LIBOR the DoJ reached an agreement with Barclays Bank that it would pay $160 million penalty for its actions. The DoJ stated that:

> LIBOR and EURIBOR are critically important benchmark interest rates ... because mortgages, student loans, financial derivatives, and other financial products rely on LIBOR and EURIBOR as reference rates, the manipulation of submissions used to calculate those rates can have significant negative effects on consumers and financial

[101] Phil Mattingly and Tom Schoenberg, 'U.S. Mortgage Fraud Initiative Included Bush-Era Case' 11 October 2012, available at www.bloomberg.com/news/2012-10-10/u-s-mortgage-fraud-initiative-data-included-older-cases.html.

[102] ibid.

[103] United States Department of Justice, 'Coinciding with One-Year Anniversary of "Operation Stolen Dreams", Three Loan Officers and a Title Agent Charged in $2.5 Million Reverse Mortgage and Loan Modification Scheme' 6 July 2011, available at www.justice.gov/opa/pr/2011/July/11-civ-884.html.

[104] Federal Bureau of Investigation, 'Operation Stolen Dreams Hundreds Arrested in Mortgage Fraud Sweep' 17 June 2010, available at www.fbi.gov/news/stories/2010/june/mortgage-fraud-sweep.

[105] ibid.

[106] Department of Justice, 'Financial Fraud Enforcement Task Force Announces Results of Broadest Mortgage Fraud Sweep in History' 17 June 2010, available at www.justice.gov/opa/pr/2010/June/10-opa-708.html.

[107] Caitlin Saladrigas, 'Corporate criminal liability: lessons from the Rothstein debacle' (2012) 66 *University of Miami Law Review* 464.

> markets worldwide. For years, traders at Barclays encouraged the manipulation of LIBOR and EURIBOR submissions in order to benefit their financial positions; and, in the midst of the financial crisis, Barclays management directed that U.S. Dollar LIBOR submissions be artificially lowered. For this illegal conduct, Barclays is paying a significant price. To the bank's credit, Barclays also took a significant step toward accepting responsibility for its conduct by being the first institution to provide extensive and meaningful cooperation to the government. Its efforts have substantially assisted the Criminal Division in our ongoing investigation of individuals and other financial institutions in this matter.[108]

Additionally, the DoJ has also attempted to use various civil enforcement mechanisms including filing a $1 billion civil law suit agsinst the Bank of America Corporation,[109] it played a key role in obtaining the largest settlement ($25 billion) for robo-signing,[110] it also acquired the largest fair lending settlement ($335 million) with Countrywide Financial Corporation[111] and the second largest fair lending settlement ($125 million) against Wells Fargo Bank.[112] For example, in relation to the manipulation of LIBOR the DoJ reached an agreement with Barclays Bank that it would pay $160 million penalty for its actions. The DoJ stated that:

> LIBOR and EURIBOR are critically important benchmark interest rates … because mortgages, student loans, financial derivatives, and other financial products rely on LIBOR and EURIBOR as reference rates, the manipulation of submissions used to calculate those rates can have significant negative effects on consumers and financial markets worldwide. For years, traders at Barclays encouraged the manipulation of LIBOR and EURIBOR submissions in order to benefit their financial positions; and, in the midst of the financial crisis, Barclays management directed that U.S. Dollar LIBOR submissions be artificially lowered. For this illegal conduct, Barclays is paying a significant price. To the bank's credit, Barclays also took a significant step toward accepting responsibility for its conduct by being the first institution to provide extensive and meaningful cooperation to the government. Its efforts have substantially assisted the Criminal Division in our ongoing investigation of individuals and other financial institutions in this matter.[113]

[108] Department of Justice, 'Barclays Bank PLC Admits Misconduct Related to Submissions for the London Interbank Offered Rate and the Euro Interbank Offered Rate and Agrees to Pay $160 Million Penalty' 27 June 2012, available at www.justice.gov/opa/pr/2012/June/12-crm-815.html.

[109] Department of Justice, 'Department of Justice Sues Bank of America for Defrauding Investors in Connection with Sale of Over $850 Million of Residential Mortgage-Backed Securities' 6 August 2013, available at www.justice.gov/opa/pr/2013/August/13-ag-886.html.

[110] Department of Justice, '$25 Billion Mortgage Servicing Agreement Filed in Federal Court' 12 March 2012, available at www.justice.gov/opa/pr/2012/March/12-asg-306.html.

[111] Department of Justice, 'Justice Department Reaches $335 Million Settlement to Resolve Allegations of Lending Discrimination by Countrywide Financial Corporation' 21 December 2012, available at www.justice.gov/opa/pr/2011/December/11-ag-1694.html.

[112] Department of Justice, 'Manhattan U.S. Attorney Files Mortgage Fraud Lawsuit Against Wells Fargo Bank, N.A. Seeking Hundreds Of Millions Of Dollars In Damages For Fraudulently Certified Loans' 9 October 2012, available at www.justice.gov/archive/usao/nys/pressreleases/October12/WellsFargoLawsuitPR.html.

[113] Department of Justice, 'Barclays Bank PLC Admits Misconduct Related to Submissions for the London Interbank Offered Rate and the Euro Interbank Offered Rate and Agrees to Pay $160 Million Penalty' 27 June 2012, available at www.justice.gov/opa/pr/2012/June/12-crm-815.html.

In December 2012, the DoJ announced that UBS Securities Japan, a subsidiary of UBS, pleaded guilty to wire fraud and its role in manipulating LIBOR.[114] The company had entered into an agreement with the DoJ which required them to pay a $100 million fine. Additionally, its parent company UBS AG, entered into a non-prosecution agreement which resulted in the payment of a further $400 million fine.[115] The Attorney General stated:

> By causing UBS and other financial institutions to spread false and misleading information about LIBOR, the alleged conspirators we've charged – along with others at UBS – manipulated the benchmark interest rate upon which many transactions and consumer financial products are based. They defrauded the company's counterparties of millions of dollars. And they did so primarily to reap increased profits, and secure bigger bonuses, for themselves … today's announcement – and $1.5 billion global resolution – underscores the Justice Department's firm commitment to investigating and prosecuting such conduct, and to holding the perpetrators of these crimes accountable for their actions.[116]

Additionally, in February 2013 the DoJ announced that RBS Securities Japan Limited, a subsidiary of RBS, had pleaded guilty to wire fraud and manipulation (as part of the Japanese Yen LIBOR) as part of a deferred prosecution agreement.[117] The Assistant Attorney General stated:

> As we have done with Barclays and UBS, we are today holding RBS accountable for a stunning abuse of trust … The bank has admitted to manipulating one of the cornerstone benchmark interest rates in our global financial system, and its Japanese subsidiary has agreed to plead guilty to felony wire fraud. The department's ongoing investigation has now yielded two guilty pleas by significant financial institutions. These are extraordinary results, and our investigation is far from finished. Our message is clear: no financial institution is above the law.[118]

The enforcement stance of the DoJ towards financial crime originating from the 2007/08 financial crisis has tended to concentrate on the imposition of a large number of administrative sanctions. However, it is important to note that these financial penalties and civil fraud actions of the DoJ are small when compared to its enforcement stance against the Bank of America in 2014. Here, the DoJ reached a civil settlement with Bank of America Corporation of $16.65bn, the largest imposed in the US. Additionally, Bank of America and several of its

[114] Department of Justice, 'UBS Securities Japan Co. Ltd. to Plead Guilty to Felony Wire Fraud for Long-running Manipulation of LIBOR Benchmark Interest Rates' 19 December 2012, available at www.justice.gov/opa/pr/2012/December/12-ag-1522.html.

[115] ibid.

[116] Department of Justice above (n 114).

[117] Department of Justice, 'RBS Securities Japan Limited Agrees to Plead Guilty in Connection with Long-Running Manipulation of Libor Benchmark Interest Rates' 6 February 2013, available at www.justice.gov/opa/pr/2013/February/13-crm-161.html.

[118] ibid.

subisdiaries agreed to pay a $5 billion penalty under the Financial Institutions Reform, Recovery and Enforcement Act 1989.[119] The DoJ described this as a

> historical revolution – the largest such settlement on record – goes far beyond the cost of doing business … under the terms of this settlement, the bank has agreed to pay $7bn in relief to struggling homeowners, borrowers and communities affected by the bank's conduct … the significance of this settlement lies not just in its size, this agreement is notable because it achieves real accountability for the American people and helps to rectify the harm caused by Bank of America's conduct through a $7 billion consumer relief package that could benefit hundreds of thousands of Americans still struggling to pull themselves out from under the weight of the financial crisis.[120]

It is interesting to note that this one financial penalty, imposed by the DoJ for conduct that occurred during the 2007/08 financial crisis, is more than the total number of fines imposed by the SEC and the UK regulators for market manipulation and insider dealing. This financial penalty should act as a reminder for those within the global financial services sector that market manipulation and insider trading will not be taken lightly by the DoJ. The DoJ has struggled to secure any criminal convictions for traders who were involved in market manipulation before and during the financial crisis. For example, in October 2018 convictions of two former Rabobank Group traders were overturned by the appeal court. Conversely, the DoJ were able to obtain convictions for two former Deutsche Bank traders who were convicted of conspiracy to manipulate the LIBOR rate. Matthew Connolly was convicted on one count of conspiracy and two counts of wire fraud, whilst Gavin Campbell Black was convicted by the jury on one count of conspiracy and one charge of wire fraud.[121] The DoJ stated that both traders 'undermined the integrity of our financial markets by manipulating LIBOR, which is widely considered to be the most important number in the financial world because of its impact on trillions of dollars in financial products'.[122] Therefore, the DoJ has followed a similar enforcement stance towards market manipulation and has imposed a number of large financial sanctions on corporations who were involved in market manipulation. The DoJ, like its counterpart in the UK, the Serious Fraud Office, has found it very difficult to obtain criminal convictions against traders associated with market manipulation. Maher noted that there have been 'zero convictions of executives of the companies responsible for the financial crisis. There are several reasons for the lack of convictions, including the lack of government resources, the difficulty of building a case against a white-collar crime defendant, and a lack

[119] Department of Justice, 'Bank of America to pay $16.65bn in historic Justice Department settlement for financial fraud leading up to and during the financial crisis' 21 August 2014, available at www.justice.gov/opa/pr/bank-america-pay-1665-billion-historic-justice-department-settlement-financial-fraud-leading.

[120] ibid.

[121] Department of Justice, 'Two former Deutsche Bank traders convicted for role in scheme to manipulate a critical global benchmark interest rate' 17 October 2018, available at www.justice.gov/opa/pr/two-former-deutsche-bank-traders-convicted-role-scheme-manipulate-critical-global-benchmark.

[122] ibid.

of aggression by the Department of Justice'.[123] The next section of the penultimate chapter examines the role of the CFTC and examines its enforcement role in relation to market manipulation during the 2007/08 financial crisis.

VII. Commodities Futures Trading Commission

The CFTC has been heavily involved in tackling market manipulation and in particular the LIBOR scandal. The CFTC was created in 1974 following the enactment of the Commodity Futures Trading Commission Act and its purpose is to promote market integrity. The CFTC has adopted a comparable enforcement strategy to that of the SEC, imposing a series of financial penalties on offending financial institutions for market manipulation. For example, in June 2012 the CFTC fined Barclays $200 million for its attempted manipulation and false reporting of LIBOR and EURIBOR.[124] The CFTC's Director of Enforcement David Meister took the view that:

> The American public and our markets rely upon the integrity of benchmark interest rates like LIBOR and Euribor because they form the basis for hundreds of trillions of dollars of transactions and affect nearly every corner of the global economy … banks that contribute information to those benchmarks must do so honestly. When a bank acts in its own self-interest by attempting to manipulate these rates for profit, or by submitting false reports that result from senior management orders to lower submissions to guard the bank's reputation, the integrity of benchmark interest rates is undermined. The CFTC launched this investigation to protect the markets and the public from such illegal conduct, and today's action demonstrates that we will bring the full force of our authority to bear as we carry out that mission.[125]

Furthermore, CFTC fined UBS $700 million for its attempted manipulation and false reporting of LIBOR and EURIBOR.[126] David Meister stated that:

> As our action today makes clear, when a major bank brazenly games some of the world's most important financial benchmarks, the CFTC will respond with the full force of its authority … the American public, as well as people and companies around the globe, rely on interest rate benchmarks every day for mortgages, loans and other transactions, trusting that the underlying benchmark rates are honest. Market integrity is seriously compromised where, as here, a bank spins its rate submissions to boost trading profits,

[123] See Maher (n 65).

[124] Commodities Futures Trading Commission, 'FTC Orders Barclays to pay $200 Million Penalty for Attempted Manipulation of and False Reporting concerning LIBOR and Euribor Benchmark Interest Rates' 27 June 2012, available at www.cftc.gov/PressRoom/PressReleases/pr6289-12.

[125] ibid.

[126] Commodities Futures Trading Commission, 'CFTC Orders UBS to Pay $700 Million Penalty to Settle Charges of Manipulation, Attempted Manipulation and False Reporting of LIBOR and Other Benchmark Interest Rates' 19 December 2012, available at www.cftc.gov/PressRoom/PressReleases/pr6472-12.

> pays off a network of brokers to disseminate false rate information, or makes false submissions to protect its reputation.[127]

In February 2013, the CFTC fined RBS $325 million for its manipulation, attempted manipulation and false reporting of Yen and Swiss Franc LIBOR.[128] David Meister stated that 'the integrity of LIBOR depends on truthful information provided by a select group of some of the world's most important banks. The public is deprived of an honest benchmark interest rate when a group of traders sits around a desk for years falsely spinning their bank's LIBOR submissions, trying to manufacture winning trades. That's what happened at RBS'.[129] In September 2013, the CFTC fined ICAP Europe Limited $65 million civil monetary penalty for 'manipulation, attempted manipulation, false reporting, and aiding and abetting derivatives traders' manipulation and attempted manipulation' of LIBOR.[130] The Chairman of the CFTC, Gary Gensler stated that the 'Order against ICAP once again shows how LIBOR, a critical benchmark interest rate not anchored in sufficient transactions, has been readily rigged. Unfortunately, this is yet another reminder of why we have to coordinate internationally to transition to an alternative to LIBOR to best restore the integrity to markets. Today's Order also highlights the importance of Congress' reforms through the Dodd-Frank Act to bring oversight to swaps trading platforms. Required registration of swap execution facilities becomes a reality next week, finally closing exemptions that had allowed for unregistered, multilateral swaps trading platforms'.[131] Michael Spencer, the ICAP Chief Executive Officer stated:

> We deeply regret and strongly condemn the inexcusable actions of the brokers who sought to assist certain bank traders in their efforts to manipulate YEN Libor. Their conduct contravenes all that ICAP stands for. As soon as their actions came to light, we provided assistance to regulators in the US and UK to understand what had happened. None of the three individuals at the center of the activity remains with the firm. Others are either no longer with the company or are being disciplined. There were no findings that any senior management were involved in this matter nor that the firm engaged in deliberate misconduct.[132]

[127] ibid.

[128] Commodities Futures Trading Commission, 'CFTC Orders The Royal Bank of Scotland plc and RBS Securities Japan Limited to Pay $325 Million Penalty to Settle Charges of Manipulation, Attempted Manipulation, and False Reporting of Yen and Swiss Franc LIBOR' 6 February 2013, available at www.cftc.gov/PressRoom/PressReleases/pr6510-13.

[129] ibid.

[130] Commodities Futures Trading Commission, 'CFTC Charges ICAP Europe Limited, a Subsidiary of ICAP plc, with Manipulation and Attempted Manipulation of Yen Libor' 25 September 2013, available at www.cftc.gov/PressRoom/PressReleases/pr6708-13.

[131] Commodities Futures Trading Commission, 'Statement of chairman Gary Gensler on settlement order against ICAP' 25 September 2013, available at www.cftc.gov/PressRoom/SpeechesTestimony/genslerstatement092513.

[132] ICAP, 'ICAP Europe Ltd Reaches Settlements with FCA and CFTC' 25 September 2013, available at www.icap.com/news-events/in-the-news/news/2013/130925-icap-europe-ltd-reaches-settlements-with-fca-and-cftc.aspx.

In April 2015, the CFTC imposed its largest financial penalty, $800 million, on Deutsche Bank for the attempted manipulation of the LIBOR and EURIBOR interest rate benchmarks.[133] In May 2015, Barclays agreed to pay a fine of $400 million for attempted market manipulation and false reporting.[134] In May 2016, Citibank paid a financial penalty of $250 million for attempted market manipulation and false reporting of the US dollar ISDAFIX benchmark.[135] In 2018, the CFTC imposed a financial penalty of $475 million on Société Générale for numerous instances of attempted manipulation of both LIBOR and EURIBOR between 2006 and 2012.[136] The CFTC described this financial penalty as an example of its

> continued commitment to ensuring the integrity of global benchmarks that impact the U.S. markets. During the course of these Libor investigations, we have seen some market participants knowingly make false reports in an effort to increase their trading profits or misrepresent their financial health. But we also have seen the Commission and its staff work tirelessly to identify this misconduct, root out the bad actors, and to ensure those responsible are held accountable.

The enforcement actions of the CFTC for market manipulation are not limited to LIBOR or EURIBOR. For example, in 2007 the CFTC fined BP Products North America Inc $303 million for attempted manipulation in the propane market.[137] Furthermore, in January 2018, Deutsche Bank was subjected to a $30 million fine for manipulating the precious metal market.[138] Therefore, the enforcement activities of the CFTC are identical to those adopted by the SEC – the imposition of a series of administrative penalties. It is questionable if the financial penalties imposed by the CFTC will be any deterrent to the future misconduct of financial institutions.

[133] Commodities Futures Trading Commission, 'Deutsche Bank to Pay $800 Million Penalty to Settle CFTC Charges of Manipulation, Attempted Manipulation, and False Reporting of LIBOR and Euribor' 23 April 2015, available at www.cftc.gov/PressRoom/PressReleases/7159-15.

[134] Commodities Futures Trading Commission, 'Barclays to Pay $400 Million Penalty to Settle CFTC Charges of Attempted Manipulation and False Reporting of Foreign Exchange Benchmark Rates' 20 May 2015, available at www.cftc.gov/PressRoom/PressReleases/7181-15.

[135] Commodities Futures Trading Commission, 'CFTC Orders Citibank to Pay $250 Million for Attempted Manipulation and False Reporting of U.S. Dollar ISDAFIX Benchmark Swap Rates' 25 May 2016, available at www.cftc.gov/PressRoom/PressReleases/7371-16.

[136] Commodities and Futures Trading Commission, 'CFTC Orders Société Générale S.A. to Pay $475 Million Penalty to Resolve Charges of Manipulation, Attempted Manipulation, and False Reporting of LIBOR and Euribor' 4 June 2018, available at www.cftc.gov/PressRoom/PressReleases/7736-18.

[137] Commodities and Futures Trading Commission, 'BP Agrees to Pay a Total of $303 Million in Sanctions to Settle Charges of Manipulation and Attempted Manipulation in the Propane Market' 25 October 2007, available at www.cftc.gov/PressRoom/PressReleases/pr5405-07.

[138] Commodities and Futures Trading Commission, 'CFTC Orders Deutsche Bank to Pay $30 Million Penalty for Manipulation, Attempted Manipulation, and Spoofing In the Precious Metals Futures Markets' 29 January 2018, available at www.cftc.gov/PressRoom/PressReleases/pr7682-18.

VIII. Conclusion

The primary aim of this chapter was to illustrate the different approaches adopted by financial regulatory agencies in the US, to those adopted in the EU and UK towards tackling market abuse. This chapter has revealed a number of important similarities between the enforcement approaches adopted in each of the case studies. For example, the most commonly used enforcement strategy in the EU, the UK and US has been the imposition of financial penalties. The US is generally regarded as a 'role model' or 'world leader' in its efforts to tackle white-collar crime. However, the chapter has presented evidence that the US approach towards market manipulation is flawed. For example, the effectiveness of the SEC is limited by the inability to commence criminal proceedings – and this is heavily reliant on its working relationship with the DoJ. However, efforts by the DoJ towards white-collar crime tended to concentrate on prosecuting employees and, only in some instances, prosecuting corporations. However, since the reversal of the conviction by the Supreme Court of Arthur Andersen, the DoJ has abandoned this approach and is favouring Deferred Prosecution Agreements, which often include hefty financial penalties. Therefore, the SEC and DoJ have adopted identical approaches towards tackling market abuse.

7

Conclusion

I. Introduction

In this book we have sought to address the question as to how and why market manipulation and insider trading is banned, referred to as market abuse, with particular focus on the EU, UK and the US regime. The starting point of the book was the empirical claim that there is an increasing focus by legislators on the need to fight market abuse as one of the major causes of the financial crisis. Despite the elapse of time since the financial crisis of 2007/08, many questions remain unanswered and the shadows emanating from this crisis still shape the regulatory system for how to counter market abuse today. The book sets out to examine why this is the case and how the regulation of market abuse has had a wider impact on the area of financial crimes legislation more broadly and thereby has given rise to a range of questions. Our aim then has been to examine regulatory responses to the financial crisis through the lens of financial crimes in a transatlantic context. The specific aim of the book has been to investigate the different manifestations of market abuse in the EU, UK and the US context in the wake of the financial crisis. We have sought to demonstrate how the law on market abuse needs to be placed in context of the broader approach to fight white collar crime. The book has embarked on a study as to why this is the case.

As is examined in this book, the underlying theme of the EU's involvement has to a large extent been the fight against financial crime in order to boost investor confidence and thereby contribute to the establishment of the internal market. As explained in chapter two the rationale for the Market Abuse Directive which is to be read in conjunction with the Market Abuse Regulation[1] is to ensure market integrity and enhance public confidence in the market. As examined in chapter two, the EU market abuse instruments adopt both administrative and criminal law sanctions to increase the effectiveness of the system.

However, the EU's fight against market abuse raises many interesting regulatory questions within the EU's internal policy and highlights the delicate competence divide between the Area of Freedom, Security and Justice and that of the

[1] Regulation (EU) No 596/2014 on market abuse (market abuse regulation) and repealing Directive 2003/6/EC of the European Parliament and of the Council and Commission Directives 2003/124/EC, 2003/125/EC and 2004/72/EC, OJ L 173, 12.6.2014, pp 1–61.

EU internal market. It also raises some intriguing questions about the proportionality of the system as well as the increasingly important question of the reach of the so-called reporting obligations of suspicious activity related to market abuse as well as the question as to what harm market abuse causes. This book also tracks the EU history of the use of sanctions and how the Market Abuse instruments have served as good test cases for the increasing use by the EU of both administrative and criminal law sanctions in this area. This double approach is difficult to reconcile with the proportionality principle. Thereafter, the chapter highlighted the often complex relationship between the principle of subsidiarity and that of effective EU action. In addition, the chapter discussed some of the current issues with the evolving regulation of data protection as part of the EU fundamental rights *acquis* and how it can be upheld while fighting crime effectively.

This book also investigates the extended powers granted to EU Agencies as it asks difficult questions about democratic oversight of the EU 'Area of Freedom Security and Justice'. The book stresses the political dimension of the area as Brexit and other national sentiments across Europe predict a difficult future ahead of the operation of, for example, the European Public Prosecutor's Office (EPPO), despite the urgency of its proper functioning. It remains to be seen whether EPPO in future will have the authority to prosecute EU market abuse that is not directly related to the EU budget but has an impact on consumer confidence in the EU market. The book also discusses the question of proportionality and fundamental rights protection and the delicate question of data protection with regard to the risk-based approach to the EU's fight against financial crimes. Indeed, a central task of this book is to link the law on market abuse to the wider fight against financial crime, inter alia EU anti-money laundering and anti-fraud policies.

We then set out to look at the particular cases of the UK and the US.

In the UK context, the efforts to tackle market manipulation have been largely associated with the enforcement actions of the 'City Regulator', the Financial Services Authority and now the Financial Conduct Authority (FCA). The legislative efforts to tackle market manipulation are contained in the Financial Services and Markets Act 2000 (FSMA 2000) and the Criminal Justice Act 1993 (CJA 1993). The enforcement response to the market manipulation associated with the 2007/08 financial crisis has focused on the use of administrative penalties on financial institutions and individuals who have breached the related legislation. The highest fines imposed by the FCA are associated with the LIBOR scandal. The use of such administrative penalties has attracted a great deal of criticism and this research has presented evidence that the effectiveness of these penalties must be questioned. However, this must be placed within the context of how difficult it is for the FCA or other law enforcement agencies to impose criminal law standards on corporations in the UK. This part of the book concludes that the use of administrative penalties has not had the desired effect of preventing future misconduct by financial institutions. The financial penalties imposed in the UK have had a limited impact on preventing the future misconduct of financial institutions. The fines only represent a small proportion of the annual profits made by these financial institutions and therefore have had a limited impact. This could be contrasted with the administrative penalties imposed in the UK on individuals who in some cases have also been banned from working within the City of London.

Traditionally, the US is perceived as adopting a robust enforcement response towards financial crime and it has attempted to tackle market manipulation and in particular insider trading since the introduction of the Securities and Exchange Act 1934. These legislative measures were initially enforced by the Securities and Exchange Commission (SEC) who were able to instigate a wide range of administrative penalties. However, the SEC are unable to instigate criminal proceedings and they were forced to liaise with the US Department of Justice (DoJ), who would only investigate one in ten cases. The enforcement stance of the SEC and DoJ was hindered by the uncertainty of the criminalisation of insider trading and the US judiciary assisted in the evolution of this criminal offence. However, this book has presented evidence that US financial and law enforcement agencies have concentrated on imposing large administrative penalties for market manipulation associated with the 2007/2008 financial crisis.

II. Final Remarks

As this book has shown, the financial penalties imposed in the US are larger than those imposed in the UK and the EU systems. This is largely due to different legal cultures and political choices. The EU system is very focused on market integrity and increasing confidence in the market and thereby transparency and market disclosure is essential to the EU model. The picture looks slightly different in the US and the UK. For instance, the UK has adopted a very tough legislative stance towards insider dealing and it has been heavily influenced by the Insider Dealing Directive and the eagerness of US authorities to criminalise insider dealing activities in Europe. Despite the laudable intentions of the early insider dealing legislative provisions, their ineffectiveness was illustrated by the small number of successful prosecutions brought during the 1980s. It was hoped that the civil enforcement provisions that were initially introduced by the Financial Services Act 1986 would be an effective weapon against insider dealing. However, these provisions were heavily underused by the Securities and Investment Board and that subsequently influenced the then Labour government in 1997 to announce the creation of the Financial Services Authority, which became the financial regulatory agency to tackle insider dealing. The criminalisation of insider dealing in the UK is largely seen as a failure as a result of the high burden of proof required in such difficult evidentiary cases. The attempt to address this perceived failure has come in the form of a civil regime enacted as part of FSMA 2000. The Financial Services Authority and the FCA have adopted an aggressive enforcement policy, at least in respect of market abuse. However, the Financial Services Authority and FCA have resorted to the enforcement stance towards market abuse that was first introduced by the Financial Services Act 1986, thus representing the continuation of a weak and failing strategy.

The enforcement stance towards market abuse in the US was initially reliant on the criminalisation of insider trading following a series of judicial decisions. However, the SEC has adopted a proactive and innovative stance towards tackling insider trading. Therefore, the US has adopted a very tough stance towards insider trading, which was criminalised in 1934. The enforcement powers of the SEC were broadened during the 1980s which resulted in the SEC pursuing more civil penalties against those who breached the insider trading provisions. The SEC, due to the inadequacies of the international insider trading legislative measures, has taken the initiative and has influenced several other countries to criminalise such activities. Other law enforcement and financial regulatory agencies in the US such as the DoJ and CFTC have continued to seek to impose financial penalties on offending corporations. The significant difference between the approach in the US to the UK is the level of financial penalties, which are significantly higher

The EU in turn is mainly focused on ensuring confidence in the EU market throughout the EU market place and where the principle of proportionality needs to be applied when considering the severity of any sanctions imposed.

BIBLIOGRAPHY

Alistair Alcock, 'Market abuse-the new witchcraft' (2001) 151 *New Law Journal* 1398.

Alistair Alcock, 'Market abuse' (2002) 23(5) *Company Lawyer* 142.

Kern Alexander, *Insider dealing and market abuse: The Financial Services and Markets Act 2000* ESRC Centre for Business Research, University of Cambridge, Working Paper No 222 (Cambridge, University of Cambridge, 2001).

Richard Alexander, *Insider Dealing and Money Laundering in the EU: Law and Regulation* (London, Routledge, 2007).

Ahmad Alkhamees, 'Private action as a remedy against market manipulation in the USA' (2012) 20(1) *Journal of Financial Regulation and Compliance* 41.

Tom Arnold, 'It's déjà vu all over again' using bounty hunters to leverage gatekeepers duties' (2010) 45 *Tulsa Law Review* 450.

Jofy Arogeti, 'How much cooperation between government agencies is too much? Reconciling United States v Scrushy, the corporate fraud task force, and the nature of parallel proceedings' (2006) 23 *Georgia State University Law Review* 430.

Estella Baker, 'Taking European Criminal Law Seriously' (1998) *Criminal Law Review* 361.

Stephen Bainbridge, 'The insider trading prohibition: a legal and economic enigma' (1986) *University of Florida Law Review* 38.

Paul Barnes, 'Insider dealing and market abuse: The UK's record on enforcement' (2011) 39 *International Journal of Law, Crime and Justice* 174.

Maria Bergström, 'The Many Uses of Anti-Money Laundering Regulation – Over Time and into the Future' (2018) *German Law Journal* 1149.

Richard Bosworth-Davies, 'Investigating financial crime: the continuing evolution of the public fraud investigation role – a personal perspective' (2009) 30(7) *Company Lawyer* 195.

Victor Brudney, 'Insiders, Outsiders, and Informational Advantages Under the Federal Securities Law' (1979) 93 *Harvard Law Review* 322.

Madalina Busuioc, Deirdre Curtin and Martijn Groenleer, 'Agency Growth Between Autonomy and Accountability: The European Police Office as a "Living Institution' (2011) 18(6) *Journal of European Public Policy* 848.

Helena Carrapiço and Florian Trauner, 'Europol and its Influence on EU Policy-making on Organized Crime' (2013) *Perspectives on European Politics and Society* 357.

Wayne Carrol, 'Market manipulation: an international comparison' (2002) 9(4) *Journal of Financial Crime* 300.

P Cheston, 'Former Belgo chief spared prison for insider trading deal' *London Evening Standard* (London, 2 March 2009) available at: https://www.standard.co.uk/news/former-belgo-chief-is-spared-prison-for-insider-trading-deal-6821785.html.

Victoria Cllagaghan and Zia Ullah, 'The LIBOR scandal – the UK's legislative response' (2013) 28(4) *Journal of International Banking Law and Regulation* 160.

Sussanah Cogman, 'The devil is in the detail: The Fourth Money Laundering Directive in practice' (2014) 29(5) *Journal of International Banking and Financial Law* 308.

Vicky Comino, 'The GFC and beyond – how do we deal with corporate misconduct?' (2018) 1 *Journal of Business Law* 15.

Carlos Conceicao, 'The FSA's approach to taking action against market abuse' (2007) 29(2) *Company Lawyer* 43.

Gerard Conway, 'Holding to Account A Possible European Public Prosecutor: Supranational Governance and Accountability Across Diverse Legal Traditions' (2013) *Criminal Law Forum* 24.

Gerard Conway, 'The Future of a European Public Prosecutor' in Maria Fletcher, Herlin-Ester Karnell and Claudio Matera (eds), *The European Union as an Area of Freedom, Security and Justice*, (London, Routledge, 2016).

Andras Csuri, 'The Proposed European Public Prosecutor's Office – from a Trojan Horse to a White Elephant?' (2016) *Cambridge Yearbook of European Legal Studies* 1.

Jack Davies, 'From gentlemanly expectations to regulatory principles: a history of insider dealing in the UK: Part 1' (2015) 36(5) *The Company Lawyer* 132.

Jack Davies, 'From gentlemanly expectations to regulatory principles: a history of insider dealing in the UK (Pt.2)' (2015) 36(6) *The Company Lawyer* 163.

Els De Busser, 'EU-US Digital Data Exchange to Combat Financial Crime: Fast is the New Slow' (2018) 19 *German Law Journal* 1251.

Janice De Grazia, *Review of the Serious Fraud Office – Final Report* (Serious Fraud Office, 2008).

Marielle Delmas-Marty and John Vervaele, *The Implementation of the Corpus Juris in the Member States* (Intersentia Publishers, 2000).

Avihay Dorfman and Alon Harel, 'Against Privatization as Such' (2016) 36(2) *Oxford Journal of Legal Studies* 400–27.

Editorial, 'Insiders beware!' (1993) 14(11) *Company Lawyer* 202.

Vanessa Edwards, 'The Insider Dealing Directive and its implementation in the United Kingdom' (1996) 3(3) *Maastricht Journal of European and Comparative Law* 287.

Lindsay Farmer, *Making the Modern Criminal Law* (Oxford, Oxford University Press, 2016).

Guido Ferrarini, 'The European Market Abuse Directive' (2004) 41(3) *Common Market Law Review* 711.

Michael Filby, 'The enforcement of insider dealing under the Financial Services and Markets Act 2000' (2003) 24(11) *The Company Lawyer* 334.

Michael Filby, 'Part VIII Financial Services and Markets Act: filling insider dealing's regulatory gaps' (2004) 23(12) *Company Lawyer* 363.

Maria Fletcher, Robin Loof and Bill Glimore, *EU Criminal Law and Justice* (Cheltenham, Edward Edgar, 2009).

Michael Frese, *Sanctions in EU Competition Law* (Oxford, Hart Publishing, 2014).

Carlos Gómez–Jare Díez, *European Federal Criminal Law* (Cambridge, Intersentia, 2015).

Carlos Gómez-Jara Díez, and Ester Herlin-Karnell, 'Prosecuting EU Financial Crimes: The European Public Prosecutor's Office in Comparison to the US Federal Regime' (2018) 19 *German Law Journal* 1191.

Julian Harris, 'Getting over Madoff: how the SEC must restore its credibility' (2010) 31(2) *Company Lawyer* 33.

Jesper Lau Hansen, 'MAD in a hurry: the swift and promising adoption of the EU Market Abuse Directive' (2007) 15(2) *European Business Law Review* 183.

Andrew Haynes, 'Market abuse, fraud and misleading communications' (2012) 19(3) *Journal of Financial Crime* 234.

Carol Harlow and Richard Rawlings, *Process and Procedure in EU Administration* (London, Hart Publishing, 2014).

Janne Hayrynen, 'The precise definition of inside information?' (2008) 23(2) *Journal of International Banking Law and Regulation* 64.

Peter J Henning, 'Making sure the buck stops here: barring executives for corporate violations' (2012) *University of Chicago Legal Forum* 95.

Daniel Huynh, 'Pre-emption v. punishment: a comparative study of white-collar crime prosecution in the United States and the United Kingdom', (2010) 9 *Journal of International Business and Law* 108.

Alistair Hudson, *The law of finance* (London, Sweet and Maxwell, 2009).

Ester Herlin-Karnell, 'White-Collar Crime and European Financial Crises: Getting Tough on EU Market Abuse' (2012) 37 *European Law Review* 487.

Ester Herlin-Karnell, 'Is Administrative Law still relevant? How the battle of sanctions has shaped EU Criminal law' in Valsamis Mitsilegas, Maria Bergstrom and Theodore Konstadinides (eds), *Research Handbook on EU Criminal Law* (Cheltenham, Edward Elgar, 2015).

Ester Herlin-Karnell, 'The Challenges of EU Enforcement and Elements of Criminal Law Theory: On Sanctions and Value in Contemporary "Freedom, Security and Justice" Law' (2016) *Yearbook of European Law* 1.

Ester Herlin-Karnell, *The Constitutional Dimension of European Criminal Law* (Oxford, Hart Publishing, 2012).

Ester Herlin-Karnell, 'The Establishment of a European Public Prosecutor's Office: Between "Better Regulation" and Subsidiarity Concerns' in Lennart Erkelens, Pim Geelhoed and Arjan Meij (eds). *The Establishment of the European Public Prosecutor's Office (EPPO): 'State of Play and Perspectives'* (The Hague, Springer, 2018).

Kris Hinterseer, *Criminal Finance, The Political Economy of Money Laundering in a Comparative Legal Context* (The Hague, Kluwer Law International, 2002).

Neha Jain, 'Significance of mens rea in insider dealing' (2004) 25(5) *Company Lawyer* 132.

Thomas Joo, 'Legislation and legitimation: Congress and insider trading in the 1980s' (2007) 82 *Indiana Law Journal* 578.

Andre Klip, *European Criminal Law: An Intergrative Approach* (Intersentia, 2012).

Mike Levi, 'The Roskill Fraud Commission revisited: an assessment' (2003) 11(1) *Journal of Financial Crime* 38.

Katalin Ligeti, *Toward a Prosecutor for the European Union Volume 1* (Oxford, Hart Publishing, 2012).

Lisa Linklater, 'The market abuse regime: setting standards in the twenty-first century' (2001) 22(9) *Company Lawyer* 267.

Alexander Loke, 'From the fiduciary theory to information abuse: the changing fabric of insider trading law in the UK, Australia and Singapore' (2006) 54(1) *The American Journal of Comparative Law* 123.

Alexander Loke, 'From the fiduciary theory to information abuse: the changing fabric of insider trading law in the UK, Australia and Singapore' (2006) 54(1) *The American Journal of Comparative Law* 123.

Eva Lomnicka, 'Preventing and controlling the manipulation of financial markets: towards a definition of market manipulation' (2001) 8(4) *Journal of Financial Crime* 297–304.

John Masters, 'Fraud and money laundering: the evolving criminalisation of corporate non-compliance' (2008) 11(2) *Journal of Money Laundering Control* 103.

Colin Maher, 'Crisis not averted: lack of criminal prosecutions leave limited consequences for those responsible for the financial crisis' (2013) 39 *New England Journal on Criminal and Civil Confinement* 463.

Claudio Matera, 'The Influence of International Organisations on the EU's Area of Freedom, Security and Justice: A First Inquiry' in Steven Blockmans and Ramses Wessel (eds), *Between autonomy and dependence: the EU legal order under the influence of international organisations* (London, Springer, 2013).

Michael McKee, 'The proposed E.U. Market Abuse Directive' (2001) 3(4) *Journal of International Fiancial Markets* 137.

Valsamis Mitsilegas, *EU Criminal Law* (Oxford, Hart Publishing, 2009).

Niamh Moloney, *EU Securities and Financial Markets Regulation*, 3rd edn (Oxford, Oxford University Press, 2015).

Jürg Monar, 'Experimentalist Governance in Justice and Home Affairs, in Experimentalist Governance in the European Union' in Jonathan Zeitlin and Charles Sabel (eds), *Experimental Governance in the European Union* (Oxford, Oxford University Press, 2010).

John Naylor, 'The use of criminal sanctions by UK and US authorities for insider trading: how can the two systems learn from each other? Part 2' (1990) 11(5) *The Company Lawyer* 83, 84.

Thomas Newkirk, 'Conflicts between public accountability and individual privacy in SEC enforcement actions' (2001) 8(4) *Journal of Financial Crime* 319.

Jacob Öberg, Limits to Eu Powers: A Case Study of EU Regulatory Criminal Law (London, Hart Publishing, 2017).

Marleen O'Connor, 'Toward a more efficient deterrence of insider trading: the repeal of section 16(b)' (1989) 58 *Fordham Law Review* 309.

Steve Peers, *EU Justice and Home Affairs Law* (Oxford, Oxford University Press, 2011).

Henry Pontell, William Black and Gilbert Geis, 'Too big to fail, too powerful to prosecute? On the absence of criminal prosecutions after the 2009 financial meltdown' (2013) *Crime Law and Society* 3.

Ellen Podgor, 'Introduction: examining white collar crime with trifocals' (2011) 39 *Fordham Urban Law Journal* 301.

Jed Rakoff and Joanne Easton, 'How effective is US enforcement in deterring insider trading?' (1996) 6(3) *Journal of Financial Crime* 283.

Barry Rider, 'An abominable fraud?' (2010) 31(7) *Company Lawyer* 197.

Nicholas Ryder, *Money laundering – an endless cycle? A comparative analysis of the anti-money laundering policies in the United States of America, the United Kingdom, Australia and Canada* (London, Routledge, 2012).

Nicholas Ryder, *Financial Crime in the 21st Century Law and Policy* (Cheltenham, Edward Elgar, 2011).

Charles Sabel and Johathan Zeitlin, 'Learning from Difference: The New Architecture of Experimentalist Governance in the European Union' (2008) 14(3) *European Law Journal* 271.

Pierre Schammo, 'EU day-to-day supervision or intervention-based supervision: Which way forward for the European system of financial supervision?' (2012) 32 *Oxford Journal of Legal Studies* 771.

Pierre Schammo, 'The European Union Securities and Market Authority: Lifting the Veil on the Allocation of Powers' (2011) *Common Market Law Review* 1887.

Saleem Sheikh, S, 'FSMA market abuse regime: a review of the sunset clauses' (2008) 19(7) *Company and Commercial Law Review* 234.

Kim Scheppele, '"It's Just Not Right": The Ethics of Insider Trading' (1993) 56 *Law and Contemporary Problems* 12.

Joel Seligman, 'The Reformulation of Federal Securities Law Concerning Non-public Information' (1985) 73 *The Reformulation of Federal Securities Law Concerning Nonpublic Information* 1083.

Andrew Simester and Andreas Von Hirsch, *Crimes, Harms and Wrongs* (Oxford, Hart Publishing, 2011).

Marta Simoncini, 'Legal Boundaries of European Supervisory Authorities in the Financial Markets Tensions in the Development of True Regulatory Agencies' (2015) *Yearbook of European Law* 1–32.

Edward Swan, 'Derivatives market manipulation by "wash sales" in violation of the US Commodity Exchange Act' (1995) 3(1) *Journal of Financial Crime* 53–56.

Edward Swan, 'Market abuse: A new duty of fairness' (2004) 25(3) *Company Lawyer* 67.

Annabel Sykes, 'Market abuse: a civil revolution' (1999) 1(2) *Journal of International Financial Markets* 59.

Takis Tridimas, *The General Principles of EU Law*, 2nd edn (Oxford, Oxford University Press, 2006).

Marianne Wade, 'A European Public Prosecutor: Potential and Pitfalls' (2013) 59 *Crime, Law & Social Change* 439.

Stephen Weatherill, (ed), *Better Regulation* (London, Hart Publishing, 2007).

Anne Weyembergh and Ines Armada 'The Principle of ne bis in idem in Europe's Area of Freedom, Security and Justice' in Maria Bergström, Valsamis Mitsilegas and Theodore Konstadinides (eds), *Research Handbook on EU Criminal Law* (Cheltenham, Edward Elgar Publishing, 2016) ch 9.

Sope Williams, 'The Mandatory Exclusions for Corruption in the New EC Procurement Directives' (2006) 31 *European Law Review* 711.

Rosalind Wright, 'Market abuse and market manipulation: the criminal, civil and regulatory interface' (2001) 3(1) *Journal of International Financial Markets* 19.

Other Sources

Attorney General's Office, *Protocol between the Attorney General and the Prosecuting Departments* (Attorney General's Office, 2009).

European Commission, 'Corruption' available from https://ec.europa.eu/home-affairs/what-we-do/policies/organized-crime-and-human-trafficking/corruption_en, accessed 30 November 2018.

European Securities and Markets Authority, 'Enforcement Actions' available from https://www.esma.europa.eu/supervision/enforcement/enforcement-actions 29 May 2017.

Action Fraud, 'Market manipulation' available from www.actionfraud.police.uk/fraud-az-market-manipulation accessed 28 May 2012.

EU Communication, COM (2010) 716, final, Reinforcing sanctioning regimes in the financial services sector.

Commodities Futures Trading Commission, 'FTC Orders Barclays to pay $200 Million Penalty for Attempted Manipulation of and False Reporting concerning LIBOR and Euribor Benchmark Interest Rates' 27 June 2012, available at www.cftc.gov/PressRoom/PressReleases/pr6289-12.

Commodities Futures Trading Commission, 'CFTC Orders UBS to Pay $700 Million Penalty to Settle Charges of Manipulation, Attempted Manipulation and False Reporting of LIBOR and Other Benchmark Interest Rates' 19 December 2012, available at www.cftc.gov/PressRoom/PressReleases/pr6472-12.

Commodities Futures Trading Commission, 'CFTC Orders The Royal Bank of Scotland plc and RBS Securities Japan Limited to Pay $325 Million Penalty to Settle Charges of Manipulation, Attempted Manipulation, and False Reporting of Yen and Swiss Franc LIBOR' 6 February 2013, available at www.cftc.gov/PressRoom/PressReleases/pr6510-13.

Commodities Futures Trading Commission, 'CFTC Charges ICAP Europe Limited, a Subsidiary of ICAP plc, with Manipulation and Attempted Manipulation of Yen Libor' 25 September 2013, available at www.cftc.gov/PressRoom/PressReleases/pr6708-13.

Commodities Futures Trading Commission, 'Statement of chairman Gary Gensler on settlement order against ICAP' 25 September 2013, available at www.cftc.gov/PressRoom/SpeechesTestimony/genslerstatement092513.

ICAP, 'ICAP Europe Ltd Reaches Settlements with FCA and CFTC' 25 September 2013, available at https://newsroom.nex.com/news/25092013/icap-europe-ltd-reaches-settlements-with-fca-and-cftc.

Commodities Futures Trading Commission, 'Deutsche Bank to Pay $800 Million Penalty to Settle CFTC Charges of Manipulation, Attempted Manipulation, and False Reporting of LIBOR and Euribor' 23 April 2015, available at www.cftc.gov/PressRoom/PressReleases/7159-15.

Commodities Futures Trading Commission, 'Barclays to Pay $400 Million Penalty to Settle CFTC Charges of Attempted Manipulation and False Reporting of Foreign Exchange Benchmark Rates' 20 May 2015, available at www.cftc.gov/PressRoom/PressReleases/7181-15.

Commodities Futures Trading Commission, 'CFTC Orders Citibank to Pay $250 Million for Attempted Manipulation and False Reporting of U.S. Dollar ISDAFIX Benchmark Swap Rates' 25 May 2016, available at https://www.cftc.gov/PressRoom/PressReleases/7371-16.

Commodities and Futures Trading Commission, 'CFTC Orders Société Générale S.A. to Pay $475 Million Penalty to Resolve Charges of Manipulation, Attempted Manipulation, and False Reporting of LIBOR and Euribor' 4 June 2018, available at www.cftc.gov/PressRoom/PressReleases/7736-18.

Commodities and Futures Trading Commission, 'BP Agrees to Pay a Total of $303 Million in Sanctions to Settle Charges of Manipulation and Attempted Manipulation in the Propane Market' 25 October 2007, available at www.cftc.gov/PressRoom/PressReleases/pr5405-07.

Commodities and Futures Trading Commission, 'CFTC Orders Deutsche Bank to Pay $30 Million Penalty for Manipulation, Attempted Manipulation, and Spoofing In the Precious Metals Futures Markets' 29 January 2018, available at www.cftc.gov/PressRoom/PressReleases/pr7682-18.

Department of Justice, 'Barclays Bank PLC Admits Misconduct Related to Submissions for the London Interbank Offered Rate and the Euro Interbank Offered Rate and Agrees to Pay $160 Million Penalty' 27 June 2012, available at www.justice.gov/opa/pr/2012/June/12-crm-815.html.

Department of Justice, 'Department of Justice Sues Bank of America for Defrauding Investors in Connection with Sale of Over $850 Million of Residential Mortgage-Backed Securities' 6 August 2013, available at www.justice.gov/opa/pr/2013/August/13-ag-886.html.

Department of Justice, '$25 Billion Mortgage Servicing Agreement Filed in Federal Court' 12 March 2012, available at www.justice.gov/opa/pr/2012/March/12-asg-306.html.

Department of Justice, 'Justice Department Reaches $335 Million Settlement to Resolve Allegations of Lending Discrimination by Countrywide Financial Corporation' 21 December 2012, available at www.justice.gov/opa/pr/2011/December/11-ag-1694.html.

Department of Justice, 'Manhattan U.S. Attorney Files Mortgage Fraud Lawsuit Against Wells Fargo Bank, N.A. Seeking Hundreds Of Millions Of Dollars In Damages For Fraudulently Certified Loans' 9 October 2012, available at https://www.justice.gov/archive/usao/nys/pressreleases/October12/WellsFargoLawsuitPR.html.

Department of Justice, 'Barclays Bank PLC Admits Misconduct Related to Submissions for the London Interbank Offered Rate and the Euro Interbank Offered Rate and Agrees to Pay $160 Million Penalty' 27 June 2012, available at www.justice.gov/opa/pr/2012/June/12-crm-815.html.

Department of Justice, 'UBS Securities Japan Co. Ltd. to Plead Guilty to Felony Wire Fraud for Long-running Manipulation of LIBOR Benchmark Interest Rates' 19 December 2012, available at www.justice.gov/opa/pr/2012/December/12-ag-1522.html.

Department of Justice, 'RBS Securities Japan Limited Agrees to Plead Guilty in Connection with Long-Running Manipulation of Libor Benchmark Interest Rates' 6 February 2013, available at www.justice.gov/opa/pr/2013/February/13-crm-161.html.

Department of Justice, 'Bank of America to pay $16.65bn in historic Justice Department settlement for financial fraud leading up to and during the financial crisis' 21 August 2014, available at www.justice.gov/opa/pr/bank-america-pay-1665-billion-historic-justice-department-settlement-financial-fraud-leading.

Department of Justice, 'Two former Deutsche Bank traders convicted for role in scheme to manipulate a critical global benchmark interest rate' 17 October 2018, available at https://www.justice.gov/opa/pr/two-former-deutsche-bank-traders-convicted-role-scheme-manipulate-critical-global-benchmark.

HM Crown Prosecution Service, *Inspectorate Review of the Fraud Prosecution Service* (London, HM Crown Prosecution Service Inspectorate, 2008) 5.

HM Treasury, 'Criminal Sanctions Directive on market abuse written ministerial statement' (London, HM Treasury, 20 February 2012) available from www.hm-treasury.gov.uk/d/wms_fst_200212.pdf, accessed 1 June 2012.

Securities and Exchange Commission, 'SEC Announces Enforcement Results For FY 2015' 22 October 2015, available at www.sec.gov/news/pressrelease/2015-245.html.

Securities and Exchange Commission, 'SEC Charges KKR With Misallocating Broken Deal Expenses' 29 June 2015, available at www.sec.gov/news/pressrelease/2015-131.html.

Securities and Exchange Commission, 'SEC Announces Charges Against Standard & Poor's for Fraudulent Ratings Misconduct' 21 January 2015, available at www.sec.gov/news/pressrelease/2015-10.html.

Securities and Exchange Commission, 'SEC Charges UBS Subsidiary With Disclosure Violations and Other Regulatory Failures in Operating Dark Pool' 15 Januar5 2015, available at www.sec.gov/news/pressrelease/2015-7.html.

Securities and Exchange Commission, 'SEC Charges Deutsche Bank With Misstating Financial Reports During Financial Crisis' 26 May 2015, available at www.sec.gov/news/pressrelease/2015-99.html.

Securities and Exchange Commission, 'SEC Announces Enforcement Results for FY 2016' 11 October 2016, available at www.sec.gov/news/pressrelease/2016-212.html.

Securities and Exchange Commission, 'Merrill Lynch to Pay $415 Million for Misusing Customer Cash and Putting Customer Securities at Risk' 23 June 2016, available at www.sec.gov/news/pressrelease/2016-128.html.

Securities and Exchange Commission, 'J.P. Morgan to Pay $267 Million for Disclosure Failures' 18 December 2015, available at www.sec.gov/news/pressrelease/2015-283.html.

Securities and Exchange Commission, 'SEC Charges Hedge Fund Manager Leon Cooperman With Insider Trading' 21 September 2016, available at www.sec.gov/news/pressrelease/2016-189.html.

Securities and Exchange Commission, 'SEC Enforcement Division Issues Report on Priorities and FY 2017 Results' 15 November 2017, available at www.sec.gov/news/press-release/2017-210.

Securities and Exchange Commission, 'Manipulation' n/d, available at www.sec.gov/fast-answers/answerstmanipulhtm.html.

Securities and Exchange Commission, 'SEC Enforcement addressing misconduct that led or arose from the financial crisis' n/d, available at www.sec.gov/spotlight/enf-actions-fc.shtml#keyStatistics.

Securities and Exchange Commission, 'SEC Charges Goldman Sachs With Fraud in Structuring and Marketing of CDO Tied to Subprime Mortgages' 16 April 2010, available at www.sec.gov/news/press/2010/2010-59.htm.

Securities and Exchange Commission, 'Goldman Sachs to pay record $500 million to Settle SEC Charges Related to Subprime Mortgage CDO' 15 July 2010, available at http://www.sec.gov/news/press/2010/2010-123.htm.

Securities and Exchange Commission, 'J.P. Morgan to Pay $153.6 Million to Settle SEC Charges of Misleading Investors in CDO Tied to U.S. Housing Market' 21 June 2011, available at www.sec.gov/news/press/2011/2011-131.htm.

Securities and Exchange Commission, 'SEC Charges Citigroup and Two Executives for Misleading Investors About Exposure to Subprime Mortgage Assets' 29 July 2010, available at www.sec.gov/news/press/2010/2010-136.htm.

Securities and Exchange Commission, 'SEC Charges Former American Home Mortgage Executives for Misleading Investors About Company's Financial Condition' 28 April 2009, available at www.sec.gov/news/press/2009/2009-92.htm.

Securities and Exchange Commission, 'SEC Charges J.P. Morgan and Credit Suisse With Misleading Investors in RMBS Offerings' 16 November 2012, available at www.sec.gov/news/press/2012/2012-233.htm.

Securities and Exchange Commission, 'Remarks During News Conference Call About Enforcement Actions Against J.P. Morgan and Credit Suisse' 16 November 2012, available at www.sec.gov/news/speech/2012/spch111612rk.htm.

Securities and Exchange Commission, 'SEC Charges Two Former Bear Stearns Hedge Fund Managers With Fraud' 19 June 19 2008, available at www.sec.gov/news/press/2008/2008-115.htm.

Securities and Exchange Commission, 'Court Approves SEC Settlements with Two Former Bear Stearns Hedge Fund Portfolio Managers; SEC Bars Managers from Regulated Industries' 25 June 2012, available from www.sec.gov/litigation/litreleases/2012/lr22398.htm.

Securities and Exchange Commission, 'SEC Charges Schwab Entities and Two Executives With Making Misleading Statements' 11 January 2011, available at www.sec.gov/news/press/2011/2011-7.htm.

Serious Fraud Office, 'About us' n/d, available from www.sfo.gov.uk/about-us/, accessed 14 November 2018.

Serious Fraud Office, 'SFO case acceptance: Statement of Principle' n/d, available from www.sfo.gov.uk/publications/guidance-policy-and-protocols/#statement, accessed 14 November 2018.

Financial Conduct Authority, 'Anti-money laundering and terrorist financing' (3 August 2015) available from www.fca.org.uk/firms/financial-crime/money-laundering-terrorist-financing, accessed 30 November 2018.

Financial Conduct Authority, 'Barclays fined £26m for failings surrounding the London Gold Fixing and former Barclays trader banned and fined for inappropriate conduct' (Press Release, 23 May 2014, available from www.fca.org.uk/news/press-releases/barclays-fined-%C2%A326m-failings-surrounding-london-gold-fixing-and-former-barclays, accessed 13 November 2018.

Financial Conduct Authority, 'Deutsche Bank fined £227 million by Financial Conduct Authority for LIBOR and EURIBOR failings and for misleading the regulator' (Press Release, 23 April 2015) available from www.fca.org.uk/news/press-releases/deutsche-bank-fined-%C2%A3227-million-financial-conduct-authority-libor-and-euribor, accessed 13 November 2018.

Financial Conduct Authority, 'FCA fines and bans former Deutsche Bank trader, Guillaume Adolph' (Press Release, 5 March 2018) available from www.fca.org.uk/news/press-releases/fca-fines-and-bans-former-deutsche-bank-trader-guillaume-adolph, accessed 14 November 2018.

Financial Conduct Authority, 'FCA fines and bans former RBS trader, Neil Danziger' (Press Release 8 January 2018) available from www.fca.org.uk/news/press-releases/fca-fines-and-bans-former-rbs-trader-neil-danziger, accessed 14 November 2018.

Financial Conduct Authority, 'FCA fines Barclays £284,432,000 for forex failings' (Press Release 20 May 2015) available from www.fca.org.uk/news/press-releases/fca-fines-barclays-%C2%A3284432000-forex-failings, accessed 13 November 2018.

Financial Conduct Authority, 'FCA fines five banks £1.1 billion for FX failings and announces industry-wide remediation programme' (Press Release, 12 November 2015) available from www.fca.org.uk/news/press-releases/fca-fines-five-banks-%C2%A311-billion-fx-failings-and-announces-industry-wide, accessed 13 November 2018.

Financial Conduct Authority, *FCA Handbook*, available at www.handbook.fca.org.uk/handbook/DEPP/6/5.html, accessed 26 January 2016.

Financial Conduct Authority, *FCA Handbook*, DEPP 6.5 and 6.5C, available at www.handbook.fca.org.uk/handbook/DEPP/6/5.html and www.handbook.fca.org.uk/handbook/DEPP/6/5C.html#-DES548, accessed 26 January 2016.

Financial Conduct Authority, *FCA Handbook* MAR 2.1.4 (1 August 2016) available at: www.handbook.fca.org.uk/handbook/MAR/2/1.html, accessed 21.1.2015.

Financial Conduct Authority, 'Final notice – Barclays Bank Plc' (23 May 2015) available from www.fca.org.uk/publication/final-notices/barclays-bank-plc.pdf, accessed 13 November 2018.

Financial Conduct Authority, 'Final Notice – Citi Bank NA' (11 November 2015) available from www.fca.org.uk/publication/final-notices/final-notice-citi-bank.pdf, accessed 13 November 2018.

Financial Conduct Authority, 'Final notice – Daniel James Plunkett' (23 May 2014) available from www.fca.org.uk/publication/final-notices/daniel-james-plunkett.pdf, accessed 13 November 2018.

Financial Conduct Authority, 'Final Notice: Da Vinci Invest Ltd' (12 August 2015) available from www.fca.org.uk/news/fca-secures-high-court-judgment-awarding-injunction-and-over-7-million-in-penalties, accessed 13 January 2016.

Financial Conduct Authority, 'Final Notice: Gyorgy Szabolcs Brad' (12 August 2015) available from www.fca.org.uk/news/fca-secures-high-court-judgment-awarding-injunction-and-over-7-million-in-penalties, accessed 13 January 2016.

Financial Conduct Authority, 'Final Notice – HSBC Bank Plc' (11 November 2015) available from www.fca.org.uk/publication/final-notices/final-notice-hsbc.pdf, accessed 13 November 2018.

Financial Conduct Authority, 'Final Notice: Ian Hannam' (22 July 2014) available from 13 www.fca.org.uk/news/fca-publishes-final-notice-for-ian-hannam, accessed 13 January 2016.

Financial Conduct Authority, 'Final Notice – JPMorgan Chase Bank N.A' (11 November 2015) available from www.fca.org.uk/publication/final-notices/final-notice-jpm.pdf, accessed 13 November 2018.

Financial Conduct Authority, 'Final Notice: Kenneth George Carver' (20 March 2015) available from www.fca.org.uk/news/kenneth-carver-fined-for-insider-dealing, accessed 13 January 2016.

Financial Conduct Authority, 'Final notice Lloyds Bank plc and Bank of Scotland plc' (28 July 2014) available from www.fca.org.uk/publication/final-notices/lloyds-bank-of-scotland.pdf, accessed 13 November 2018.

Financial Conduct Authority, 'Final notice Martin Brokers (UK) Ltd (Martins)' (15 May 2014) available from www.fca.org.uk/publication/final-notices/martin-brokers-uk-ltd.pdf, accessed 13 November 2018.

Financial Conduct Authority, 'Final Notice: Michael Coscia' (3 July 2013) available from www.fca.org.uk/your-fca/documents/final-notices/2013/michael-coscia, accessed 13 January 2016.

Financial Conduct Authority, 'Final Notice: Mineworld Ltd' (12 August 2015) available from www.fca.org.uk/news/fca-secures-high-court-judgment-awarding-injunction-and-over-7-million-in-penalties, accessed 13 January 2016.

Financial Conduct Authority, 'Final Notice: Patrick Sejean' (24 January 2013) available from www.fca.org.uk/your-fca/documents/final-notices/2013/fsa-final-notice-2013-stefan-chaligne, accessed 13 January 2016.

Financial Conduct Authority, 'Final Notice: Stefan Chaligne' (21 January 2013) available from www.fca.org.uk/your-fca/documents/final-notices/2013/fsa-final-notice-2013-stefan-chaligne, accessed 13 January 2016.

Financial Conduct Authority, 'Final Notice: Szabolcs Banya' (12 August 2015) available from www.fca.org.uk/news/fca-secures-high-court-judgment-awarding-injunction-and-over-7-million-in-penalties, accessed 13 January 13 2016.

Financial Conduct Authority, 'Final Notice: Tamas Pornye' (12 August 2015) available from www.fca.org.uk/news/fca-secures-high-court-judgment-awarding-injunction-and-over-7-million-in-penalties, accessed 13 January 2016.

Financial Conduct Authority, 'Final Notice – The Royal Bank of Scotland Plc' (11 November 2015) available from www.fca.org.uk/publication/final-notices/final-notice-rbs.pdf, accessed 13 November 2018.

Financial Conduct Authority, 'Final Notice – UBS AG' (11 November 2018) available from www.fca.org.uk/publication/final-notices/final-notice-rbs.pdf, accessed 13 November 2018.

Financial Conduct Authority, 'Final Notice: 7722656 Canada Inc' (24 January 2014) available from www.fca.org.uk/your-fca/documents/final-notices/2014/7722656-canada-inc, accessed 13 January 2016.

Financial Conduct Authority, 'Former senior trader sentenced for insider dealing', (Press Release, 19 March 2015) available at: www.fca.org.uk/news/former-senior-trader-sentenced-for-insider-dealing, accessed 18 November 2015.

Financial Conduct Authority, 'ICAP Europe Limited fined £14 million for significant failings in relation to LIBOR' (Press Release 25 September 2013, available from www.fca.org.uk/news/press-releases/icap-europe-limited-fined-%C2%A314-million-significant-failings-relation-libor, accessed 13 November 2018.

Financial Conduct Authority, 'Kenneth Carver fined £35,212 for insider dealing (Press Release, 30 March 2015) available at: www.fca.org.uk/news/kenneth-carver-fined-for-insider-dealing, accessed 18 November 2015.

Financial Conduct Authority, 'Lloyds Banking Group fined £105m for serious LIBOR and other benchmark failings' (Press Release, 28 July 2015) available from www.fca.org.uk/news/press-releases/lloyds-banking-group-fined-%C2%A3105m-serious-libor-and-other-benchmark-failings, accessed 13 November 2018.

Financial Conduct Authority, 'Market Abuse Regulation (MAR)' (FCA, 6 May 2015) available from www.fca.org.uk/firms/markets/market-abuse/mar, accessed 1 January 2016.

Financial Conduct Authority, 'Martin Brokers (UK) Limited fined £630,000 for significant failings in relation to LIBOR' (Press Release, 15 May 2014, available from www.fca.org.uk/news/press-releases/martin-brokers-uk-limited-fined-%C2%A3630000-significant-failings-relation-libor, accessed 13 November 2018.

Financial Conduct Authority, The Enforcement Guide (London: FCA, 12.7) available at: www.handbook.fca.org.uk/handbook/document/EG_FCRMAML_20110701.pdf, accessed 26 January 2016.

Financial Conduct Authority, 'The FCA fines Rabobank £105 million for serious LIBOR-related misconduct' (Press Release, 29 October 2013, available from www.fca.org.uk/news/press-releases/fca-fines-rabobank-%C2%A3105-million-serious-libor-related-misconduct, accessed 13 November 2018.

Financial Services Authority 'Annual Report 2010/11' (London, FSA, 2011) 60.

Financial Services Authority 'An update from the Financial Crime and Intelligence Division' (2009) 13 *Financial Crime News Letter* 1–7.

Financial Services Authority 'Barclays fined £59.5 million for significant failings in relation to LIBOR and EURIBOR' (Press Release, 27 June 2012) available from www.fca.org.uk/news/press-releases/barclays-fined-%C2%A3595-million-significant-failings-relation-libor-and-euribor, accessed 13 November 2018.

Financial Services Authority 'Corporate Broker intern and his father receive 12 and 24 month prison sentences respectively for insider dealing' (Press Release, 10 December 2010) available at www.fsa.gov.uk/pages/Library/Communication/PR/2009/170.shtml, accessed 6 October 2011.

Financial Services Authority 'Enforcement Notices' (Financial Services Authority, 14 June 2014) available at www.fsa.gov.uk/pages/About/What/financial_crime/market_abuse/library/notices/index.shtml accessed 1 July 2010.

Financial Service Authority 'Feedback statement on responses to Consultation Paper 10: Market Abuse' (March 1999) available at www.fsa.gov.uk/pubs/cp/cp10_response.pdf accessed 5 July 2010.

Financial Services Authority 'Final Notice Barclays Bank Plc' (27 June 2012) available from www.fca.org.uk/publication/final-notices/barclays-jun12.pdf, accessed 13 November 2018.

Financial Service Authority 'Final Notice: David Einhorn' (15 February 2012) available from http://webarchive.nationalarchives.gov.uk/20130301170532/http://www.fsa.gov.uk/static/pubs/final/david-einhorn.pdf, accessed 13 January 2016.

Financial Services Authority 'Former Cazenove broker sentenced to 21 months in prison for insider dealing' (Press Release, 11 March 2010) available at: www.fsa.gov.uk/pages/Library/Communication/PR/2010/043.shtml, accessed 6 October 2011.

Financial Services Authority 'Final Notice: Greenlight Capital Inc,' (15 February 2012) available from http://webarchive.nationalarchives.gov.uk/20130301170532/http://www.fsa.gov.uk/static/pubs/final/greenlight-capital.pdf, accessed 13 January 2016.

Financial Services Authority 'Final notice UBS AG' (19 December 2012) available from http://webarchive.nationalarchives.gov.uk/20130202001303/http://www.fsa.gov.uk/static/pubs/final/ubs.pdf, accessed 13 November 2018.

Financial Services Authority 'FSA fines broker for failing to prevent insider dealing' (Press Release, 2 September 2009) available at: www.fsa.gov.uk/pages/Library/Communication/PR/2009/115.shtml, accessed 6 October 2011.

Financial Services Authority 'FSA fines GLG Partners and Philippe Jabre £750,000 each for market abuse' (Press Release, 1 August 2006) available at: www.fsa.gov.uk/pages/Library/Communication/PR/2006/077.shtml, accessed 6 October 2011.

Financial Service Authority 'Investment banker and two associates charged with insider dealing' (Press Release, 4 August 2011) available at: www.fsa.gov.uk/pages/Library/Communication/PR/2011/069.shtml, accessed 6 October 2011.

Financial Services Authority 'Investment banker, his wife and family friend sentenced for insider dealing' (Press Release, 2 February 2011) available at: www.fsa.gov.uk/pages/Library/Communication/PR/2011/018.shtml, accessed 6 October.

Financial Services Authority 'Market Abuse Directive' available from www.fsa.gov.uk/pages/about/what/international/pdf/mad%20(pl).pdf, accessed 27 May 2012.

Financial Services Authority 'Market Abuse Part 1: Consultation on a draft code of market conduct' (1998) available at www.fsa.gov.uk/pubs/cp/cp10.pdf accessed 5 July 2010.

Financial Service Authority 'Neil Rollins update' (Press Release 30 June 2011) available at: www.fsa.gov.uk/pages/Library/Communication/Statements/2011/neil_rollins.shtml, accessed 6 October 2011.

Financial Services Authority 'Transaction reporting cases' (2011) (Market Abuse Library) available at: www.fsa.gov.uk/pages/About/What/financial_crime/market_abuse/library/index.shtml, accessed 18 October 2011.

Financial Services Authority 'UK Implementation of EU Market Abuse Directive' (June 2004) available from www.fsa.gov.uk/pubs/other/eu_mad.pdf accessed 5 July 2010.

Financial Services Authority 'UBS fined £160 million for significant failings in relation to LIBOR and EURIBOR' (Press Release, 19 December 2012, available from http://webarchive.nationalarchives.gov.uk/20130201230634/http://www.fsa.gov.uk/library/communication/pr/2012/116.shtml, accessed 13 November 2018.

Financial Services Authority 'Why market abuse could cost you money – The revised Code of Market Conduct is here to help protect you' (2008) available at www.fsa.gov.uk/pubs/public/market_abuse.pdf accessed 29 June 2010.

INDEX